HEARTBREAK AND RAGE:
TEN YEARS UNDER SUN MYUNG MOON

A CULT SURVIVOR'S MEMOIR

SECOND EDITION (REVISED AND UPDATED)

K. GORDON NEUFELD

"Heartbreak and Rage: Ten Years Under Sun Myung Moon. A Cult Survivor's Memoir," by K. Gordon Neufeld. ISBN 978-1-949756-55-5

Second Edition (Revised and Updated).

First Edition published 2002; Second Edition published 2019 by Virtualbookworm.com Publishing, PO Box 9949, College Station, TX 77842, US.

This is a true story.

Nevertheless, except for the names of prominent Unification Church leaders, all names have been changed to preserve the anonymity of those involved.

For Mary Jo

TABLE OF CONTENTS

Introduction to the Second Edition

In the years since this book was published, much has changed, but much remains the same.

In deciding to create a second edition, I have chosen to undo many changes that I made in early 2002. These changes relate mostly to the way the text is organized. The section on "Mind Control at the Boonville Farm" has been placed back into the original text in the position where I originally placed it, instead of being moved to the end as an Appendix. The chapters on The Matching, Screaming for God and The Blessing have been put back together and slightly reorganized as "Two Summers" and "Summer's End," the way I originally wrote them in 2001. I have restored the original brief prologue from the 2001 version.

As well, I have added a new Epilogue to cover the many wonderful changes in my life since the original version was published. It is hoped that the new edition will provide a new generation of readers with the insights and information that I originally made available as a paperback only.

K. Gordon Neufeld
September, 2017

INTRODUCTION TO THE FIRST EDITION

There are two stories in this book.

First, there is the story of a young man who was manipulated through mind control into joining a cult whose true nature he was not told about for some time; and when, after four years, the bonds of mind control began to fray and loosen, it nevertheless took another six years before he was ready to leave.

Second, it is the story of a person with desperate emotional needs who believed the religious group he had joined could address his needs; but later, when he concluded it could not, he left.

For those who have never experienced being caught up in a cult, these two narratives may seem contradictory. The public would like to believe that there is one single cause for cultism; that either cults draw their members exclusively from especially vulnerable and needy people; or alternatively, that they entrap their members through mind control, while their former psychological and emotional states played no part in the entrapment.

The truth lies somewhere between these two models of cult involvement. Certainly, emotional neediness may open a person up to cult involvement; it may even lengthen the time or alter the course of that person's involvement; but it cannot account for the incredible persistence a cult member will show in trying to remain with a cult long after it has stopped relieving his emotional neediness, and indeed has begun exacerbating it. And while mind control may be the "clincher" that gets a person thoroughly enmeshed in a cult, it should not be seen as a static condition that lasts for life. Rather, the bonds of mind control begin to rot and fray after only a few years, though they often leave lasting scars that can persist indefinitely unless treated.

In recent years, cult apologists have tried to assert that mind control has been discredited in the psychological community; but in fact, it is still widely accepted, and is even cited in the DSM-IV, the American Psychiatric Association's diagnostic manual, under 300.15, "Dissociative Disorder NOS", a diagnosis that explicitly refers to cults and brainwashing.[1]

That said, it is also true that mind control has often been misrepresented, leading the public to believe its victims become robotic and lose all ability to think independently. The reality is much more subtle: mind control merely erects road blocks in the mind, so that certain thoughts (such as the idea of

---

[1]   Steven Hassan, *Releasing the Bonds: Empowering People to Think for Themselves* (Somerville, MA: Freedom of Mind Press, 2000), p. 169.

leaving the group or going against its principles) become too frightening to be contemplated for long; however, in other respects, the victim of mind control appears normal. Those mental road blocks can be torn down without having to resort to drastic tactics such as deprogramming; nevertheless, when a cult member is forced to tear them down on his own, his recovery is apt to be slow and fraught with the peril that he may return to the group.

Unlike many other accounts written by cult survivors, this memoir recounts the complete arc of one person's cult involvement—my own—uninterrupted by a deprogramming. It describes in detail the entire process from the initial transfixion to the final letting go. It is my hope that this account will be of assistance to other cult survivors who are still struggling to attain a similar resolution of their own cult experiences.

K. Gordon Neufeld
July, 2002

PROLOGUE

The woman I had met only two nights before, whom the Reverend Sun Myung Moon had chosen to be my wife forever, raised the cup of Holy Wine to her lips and drank. As we had been instructed, Eleanor left about half the wine still in the small glass cup and then passed it over to me. I raised the cup of sweet scented wine to my lips, tipped it slightly, and began to drink..

Nearly forty years have passed since that one moment in my life, yet in my mind's eye it remains in eternal suspension, the wine still just at the tip of my lips, the scent of the perfume Moon had mingled with the wine still tingling in my nostrils. Not only are the sensations still present with me, but preserved also is what that moment meant – not what it was supposed to mean, according to Moon's teachings, nor what it has come to mean since – but what my heart told me it meant. I recall it as a moment of ineffable holiness, the one instant in my life when I parted the veil concealing the Holy of Holies, and drank in the sweetness of God's purest love.

If I could, I would reach back across the unbreachable divide of those forty years and knock the cup out of Eleanor's hands. The wine would spray across her dress, leaving a florid stain; perhaps she would cry out, take one step backwards, and knock the entire tray filled with cups of wine from the hands of the man who was carrying them. The tray would strike the floor with a clatter, spraying the couples standing before and behind; there would be the sound of cups shattering, followed by an outcry from all of the 804 couples assembled on the last day of 1980 to consecrate their engagements.

But that, of course, is not what happened. I tilted the cup a little further, and the wine trickled down my tongue. It was the first food or drink to pass my lips that morning; I wanted it that way, since the wine was said to convey God's forgiveness for the Original Sin. In the future, I'd been told, my children would be free from Original Sin and capable of growing to spiritual perfection – provided, that is, I continued to follow Moon without deviation.

After the ceremony, all of the newly-engaged couples streamed out of the Grand Ballroom of the former New Yorker Hotel (which had been converted into a Unification Church building). As we left, we were each given a white handkerchief, folded up and protected by a sandwich bag. The handkerchiefs were stained with the perfumed wine, and we were told to keep them in a safe place until it was time for the relationship to be consummated – which for most of us would not be allowed for several years. Exactly how these "Holy Handkerchiefs" were to be used was not explained.

Looking back, now over those almost forty years, I wonder if, even if it were possible to reach back and dash that cup of wine (made redolent with fraud) from Eleanor's hands, I would have the heart to do so. I remember as if it were yesterday how I felt in that moment, and what it meant to me then. Standing on the brink of a decade of heartbreak and rage, in a room filled with stolen lives and subverted dreams, I could not have seen Sun Myung Moon for who he was: a man intent on controlling my mind. Instead, I pictured him as the smiling, happy "Father," leaning over the gaping mouth of my mineshaft of loneliness, and hauling me to freedom with that single, wine-stained handkerchief.

Part One:

The Quest for Justification

Chapter One

The Knife Inside Me

I have always felt a desperate need to justify my existence. Of course, such a quest is impossible; yet knowing this has not prevented me from making it the driving force of my life. Since my birth in Edmonton, Alberta, Canada in 1953, and throughout my childhood, I have felt that I do not have the right to exist, and that I must make amends to everyone else on Earth for the fact that I nevertheless continue to take up space on the planet.

Yes, I am aware that this is absurd; indeed, I have long sought to free myself from these thoughts. I used to experience the pain of this feeling as if it were a knife inside me, piercing me through the heart; and so I have longed for a way—whether through psychological therapy, or through the love of a woman—to pluck this knife from my heart.

Three feelings are particularly connected to what I have called "the knife inside me". First, there is a sense of worthlessness; secondly, a feeling of alienation from everyone else on Earth; and finally—and inevitably—depression.

It would be handy if I could offer some straight-forward psychological explanation for how I ended up feeling this way. Yet my childhood was a largely uneventful one. I grew up in normal middle-class areas—first, near the small town of New Sarepta, Alberta; then, in a semi-rural area near Edmonton; and finally, for most of my school years, in northwest Calgary— and, during that time, I suffered no major traumas. I can find no psychological explanation in my upbringing that can sufficiently account for the intensity of these feelings.

Whatever the source of the knife inside me, its main effect has been to make me feel separate from everyone else. I was shy about initiating friendships throughout my school years, and the boys that I hung around with in grade school were mainly loners like myself. However, when I was old enough to attend dances or start dating girls, I found I could not attempt this at all. I was overwhelmed with feelings of guilt and shame whenever I even tried to approach girls. The only school dance I ever attended was a "sock hop" in the seventh grade. I felt so awkward and out of place at this dance, and so riddled with inexplicable guilt and shame afterwards, that I resolved never to attend a school dance again. I never did.

The guilt and shame I felt then was connected to the feeling that I did not have the right to exist. If I approached a girl, and she then rejected me, this twisted the knife still further inside me; it reinforced the feeling that I don't deserve to be, which (I felt) I ought to have known long before I dared to approach her.

I tried two different tactics during my school years to overcome my feelings of alienation. For a while, I became a quiet dreamer—reading thriller novels and playing with model railroads and building model ships—so I could escape into my own fantasy world by losing myself in my private obsessions. For a while, I went to the opposite extreme and become the weirdest, most rebellious, and just plain oddball student at the entire school. In high school, I was famous for carrying around up to a dozen ballpoint pens at a time, with which I would do bizarre stunts such as simultaneously inserting them into my nostrils, ears and under my lips. Because of my penchant for wordplay, students would often ask me, "Gordon —what's the joke of the day?" and I would try to make something up on the spot. These foolish tricks certainly got me attention, but not the kind I was hoping for; I became an amusing side show, but I still felt alienated from the others. As this sunk in, I became more and more depressed.

As early as age 13, the idea of suicide entered my thoughts, but fortunately I always pushed it away before it formed into any particular plan. One day in the eleventh grade, while pondering whether I should actually go through with my death wish, I came to a decision that instead I would try to make something of my life, even if I couldn't be everything I wished to be. From that moment on, I took more interest in my studies, and fared better in my grades, while toning down my antics.

Around this time I began to take an interest in environmental issues, since I was so stricken with shame about my own consumption of resources. How could I justify the expenditure of so much wealth on myself, given that I lived in a privileged society, when so many other people lived in poverty? I soon expanded this to a concern about overconsumption in my society generally. The buzz-word in those days for environmental problems was "pollution", so I read many books about air and water pollution and assisted some anti-pollution groups. I was especially struck by an image from Henry David Thoreau's *Walden*, where he ironically describes how the average man staggers down the pathway of life trying to shoulder the burden of his many possessions. I resolved that I would go through life carrying as few possessions as possible. (This is one of those youthful resolutions that proved to be less than realistic later on). As well, I became an admirer of Mohandas Karamchand Gandhi, and for more than a year I read every book I could find on the remarkable Mahatma, whom I told people I intended to emulate.

There was one aspect of Gandhi's life that I did not feel I could imitate, however: his celibacy vow (which he took only at middle age, after marrying and having four children). I had a normal teenager's desires for sex, and did not feel I could go through life entirely lonely. Yet as mentioned previously, I couldn't bring myself to approach any girls, so it was starting to look like I was going to end up emulating the Mahatma anyway. Of course, this greatly added to my depression.

However, at age 20, I finally decided to do something about this problem. I dared to telephone a girl. Sandy was someone I knew from a Geography course we had both attended at the University of Calgary. I had only sat beside her through numerous classes and even walked her home several times. It seemed not altogether impossible that she might go on a date with me.

Fortunately, Sandy agreed. But by daring to ask her out, I had exhausted my bravado; after that, I didn't know what to do with myself. My first date might have perished of awkwardness if Sandy had not taken charge. This was early in the summer of 1973; the famous Calgary Stampede was well underway, featuring rodeo events and a popular midway. Skipping the rodeo, we went straight to the midway, and strolled past barkers hawking chances at stuffed animals and tickets for the "Pot o' Gold". "Do you believe in women's lib?" Sandy asked suddenly. I responded vaguely that I sort of thought that maybe I probably did. "Good," she said, seizing my hand in hers.

Sandy was full of surprises. We went to a dance in the beer garden (located in a hockey arena), and at the end she told me that her parents were away for the weekend, so why not come home with her? This was more than I had ever dreamed of. My first date was supposed to be just "practice", basically just to see if I could even do it. Suddenly, the prospect of having actual sex loomed before me—frightening and compelling.

As it turned out, Sandy, a good Catholic girl, merely had in mind an extended session of upper torso groping. She was not about to "go all the way" on the first date, especially with a man as hesitant and retiring as I was. But I was still amazed by what had happened, and I continued to see Sandy or to correspond with her for several more years.

Soon after this date, I moved to Montreal for one entire winter. Montreal was completely different from Calgary. Most people spoke French, and the city was in Eastern Canada, which I had never visited. I went to Montreal to try to start my career as a writer, which I felt was going nowhere because of university. If I didn't have papers and exams hanging over me, I reasoned, I could get some *real* writing done for once. But the truth turned out to be just the opposite: without deadlines, I couldn't get *anything* done. In the entire time I was in Montreal—some nine months—I only managed to write one depressing poem titled "Lonely Man's Song" and one surrealistic short story named "How to be Forgiven for Existing".

I returned to western Canada the following year to resume undergraduate studies at the University of British Columbia, which offered Creative Writing courses I was eager to take. It turned out that my first girlfriend, Sandy, had chosen to attend the same university, so we rode out to Vancouver on the train together. I saw her frequently for the first few months we were there. Sandy took on a greater load than she could handle, however, and when it became overwhelming, she suddenly withdrew, and returned to her family in Calgary. I did not really understand the seriousness of this until I went home for Christmas. I found Sandy in the hospital following a suicide attempt. One day, she simply decided she'd had enough. She drove her car to the airport and threw her keys into a snow bank. Taking a flight to Vancouver, she checked into a hotel and swallowed an overdose of sleeping pills.

Sandy's doctors doled out anti-depressant drugs and told her to take life "one step at a time". I wasn't impressed with this treatment, even though Sandy recovered somewhat and was able to go home a few weeks later. It seemed to me that they were only propping her up temporarily, so that they could discharge her. No long-term solution for her emotional pain, as far as I could see, was evident. Having just read *The Primal Scream* by Arthur Janov, I was much influenced by Janov's views. In this, his most famous book, Janov dismisses conventional therapeutic approaches as "patch-work solutions" which merely put a bandage over a person's problems, but which fail to cure emotional pain. Janov claims that his own Primal Therapy, on the other hand, actually *cures* neurosis by discovering its source. I found these arguments very persuasive, and after reading Janov's first book, I read all his subsequent books, such as *The Primal Revolution*, becoming more and more convinced. Only Primal Therapy would do, I decided; everything else was a waste of time. It seemed to me that Primal Therapy was not only what Sandy needed, but also what I needed. Primal Therapy, I believed, would allow me to draw the knife from my heart.

The short stories and poems I wrote for my university courses started to be entirely centered on this theme, though I used a variety of symbols to get the idea across. In my story "At the Point of Intersection", the symbolism is at its most transparent. There, the nameless protagonist is walking down a highway that cuts through empty space. He is carrying a knife whose purpose he doesn't remember. Nothing else exists. He cannot even remember who he is or why he is there. When, at last, his path intersects with that of someone else—the attendant at a lone gas station illuminated by a single light—he discovers that due to the Laws of Relativity, the attendant's watch reads a different time from his own. He realizes that he is ultimately alone in the universe. He goes into a phone booth and dials the number for Emergency. The voice that answers advises him that "If you want to know who you are, you must look at the face of the one you have killed." By forcing himself to recollect what he has been trying to forget, he discovers that he has in fact killed himself, and simultaneously discovers that the knife is lodged in his own heart. Letting out a primal scream, he wrenches the knife free and sends it sailing "in elegant spirals, blade over handle, handle over blade, blade over handle into space."

Above all else, this story shows the almost magical relief I hoped to obtain from Primal Therapy. However, the treatment I so desperately desired was prohibitively expensive, and only available at two locations in the United States from its inventor. A few other therapies had sprung up which imitated Janov's ideas, but Janov had copyrighted the term "Primal Therapy", so these other therapies were forced to call themselves by similar terms, such as "primal feeling therapy". Janov claimed that these imitators were actually dangerous, since their therapy did not deliver the original Primal Therapy, but instead a perverted and harmful form. Both Janov's Primal Institute and his imitators placed advertisements in *Psychology Today* magazine, so I jotted down their names and phone numbers—mostly in California—knowing full well that I probably could not afford any of them. Nevertheless, the way I saw it, I had to have Primal Therapy or nothing.

I had taken out student loans to complete my Bachelor of Arts in English and Creative Writing. Therefore, not only did I not have any spare money, but the degree I had received was unlikely to open the doors to any money-making jobs in the near future. The only solution I could think of was to work as a construction laborer in northern Canada, where wages were high for manual labor positions. I decided to seek work in northern Canada after my graduation—perhaps in Fort MacMurray, Alberta, where an oils sands reclamation project was under construction.

However, I never got any further north than Edmonton—which is not very far north in Canadian terms. I found a job on a construction site on the outskirts of that city in late spring, 1976, and lasted about two weeks before an accident knocked me out of construction work permanently. I fell from an open roof beam to a platform 30 feet below and the resulting injury to my spine—a crushed lower vertebra—meant a hospital stay and a lengthy convalescence at my parents' home in Calgary. So much for my plans to work in northern Canada! Still, I was receiving Workers' Compensation payments from the Alberta government, and was under doctor's orders not to work for a few months. It occurred to me that I might as well make use of my free time by heading south to California where I could check out Janov's two Primal Institutes, and also investigate his imitators. In addition, I planned to do some sightseeing, since I had never before visited California.

In early August, 1976, therefore, I traveled by bus to Vancouver, where I stopped over to visit some friends with whom I had once lived (in a shared house we had nicknamed "Asylum ½"). I visited with them for several days, and even exhumed my old beer and wine-making equipment from a dank corner of the basement in order to brew up a batch of apple wine, as I had been so fond of doing when I lived there during my university years. I laid down the must, expecting to return later to rack it off. Then I bought a round-trip ticket on a flight to San Francisco that would supposedly bring me back to Vancouver in two weeks' time.

Two weeks. That's how long I expected to be away. My original ticket was for just two weeks.

CHAPTER TWO

FALLING OFF THE EARTH

The T-shirt I wore proclaimed in bold white letters on a dark green background: "The Earth is Flat!" It was a sunny Sunday afternoon, August 22, 1976—my second full day in San Francisco. I was sight-seeing on Fisherman's Wharf near Ghirardelli Square.

"How do you know it's flat?" a stranger suddenly asked. It was a clean-cut young man, wearing round wire-rimmed spectacles and vaguely shapeless, practical clothing, who was standing beside another young man, who was shorter but dressed similarly.

"Because I fell off it," I shot back sardonically. I then explained that I didn't really believe the Earth was flat, but I liked to joke about it. As they questioned me casually, I explained that I was a visitor from Canada, and that I planned to spend two weeks in California before returning. They told me their names: Flip and Drew, and they invited me to a free dinner at a house on Washington Street, in the tony Nob Hill neighborhood. They claimed they were part of a group of people living communally—"teachers, students, professionals and so on"—who called themselves the "Creative Community Project", and proffered a slip of paper with their address on it. Then they told me that they had their own bus, which they called the "Elephant Bus", which I could, if I wished, take right to the free dinner. I told them it sounded all right, but I would think about it.

The well-groomed appearance of the two—in an era when long hair and scraggly beards were almost mandatory—suggested they were part of a religious community, even though they'd said nothing about any beliefs. I suspected this was a come-on for some kind of religious group, and I was not particularly open to religious ideas. Still, what harm could come from just going for dinner? I had nothing else planned. In any case, I still had an hour before the "Elephant Bus" showed up—time enough to make up my mind.

I had flown into San Francisco on a Friday, so even though my main intention was to check out Primal Therapy, I knew there would be no point in visiting any therapy centers before Monday. I might as well make the rounds of all the tourist traps while I had the opportunity, so on Saturday I proceeded to do just that. The next day, after leaving the youth hostel, I continued my meanderings on foot throughout San Francisco, map firmly in hand. First I rambled down the entire length of Market Street to the Embarcadero, then through Chinatown to Telegraph Hill and the Coit Tower. From the top of the

Tower, I saw the full masted sailing ships – a special interest of mine—near Fisherman's Wharf, and decided to go down for a closer look. Somewhere along the way, I bought a postcard depicting some crab vendors and mailed it to my friends in Vancouver, one of whom kept this card (and the letters that followed) and returned them to me years later. That first card contained nothing but puns. "Dear Asylum ½," I wrote, "I don't want to sound like an old crab nor do I want to appear shellfish, nor indeed do I want to clam up rather than being my usual oysterous self, but I met a suspicious-looking fellow on the wharf who said he was a Mafia lobster and showed me his Mafia identification card with his name on it: "Crust, A. Sean, hit man", so I hit him. Gordon."

After mailing this card, I continued on my way until I found a sunny spot on the grass in front of Ghirardelli Square, where I opened my backpack, and pulled out the novel I was reading—*A Singular Man* by J.P. Donleavy—and started to read. It was probably the backpack that attracted the attention of Flip and Drew: it told them I was a traveler, and therefore likely to accept a free meal. As soon as I finished my reading and stood up, they approached me.

After our brief conversation, I turned around and went to a nearby open-air restaurant, and pondered whether I should go. I couldn't think of one good reason why I shouldn't accept their generous offer of a free dinner, so I headed down to find the Elephant Bus.

A number of members of the Creative Community Project were waiting when I arrived, and they approached me at once. I learned that they liked to call themselves "the Oakland Family". It was hard not to like these people; they were so friendly and wanted to know everything about me. Some of the Family members were attractive young women, and I was delighted when they paid eager attention to me.

The "Elephant Bus" was a converted yellow school bus, painted over with a gray mural that looked something like an elephant. When I climbed on board, still more Family members shook my hand, asked my name, and wanted to know where I was from. As soon as the bus started up, a young man at the front produced a guitar and asked everyone to sing along with him. They sang "If I Had a Hammer" and other folk songs. Not only did they know the words to all these songs; a few of them even made hand gestures to go with the words. I was beginning to think they were all a little too cheerful for their own good, but at the same, I was charmed by them.

The bus climbed up San Francisco's famous hills to a classic three-storey home on Washington Street. The house was meticulously painted, clean and brightly-lit; and as soon as I came through the front door, a pert young sister named Annie, sitting at a desk like a receptionist, pushed forward a guest book for me to sign. A basket for "donations" stood alongside the guest book. Annie inquired who had invited me. It seemed to be important to her that either Flip or Drew should sit beside me throughout the evening, but since neither was available, another "brother" from the Family sat with me instead.

The living room contained almost no furniture. Everyone sat cross-legged on the floor, in little knots of four or five. It was easy to distinguish the guests from the Family members: the guests were mostly travelers from all over the United States and Europe; if they were young men, they usually sported long, stringy hair and beards. If asked—which I was repeatedly—I would launch into my usual spiel: where I was from; what I was doing in San Francisco; and what I did for a living—aspiring writer. I met many nice young "sisters" in the Family, and I was flattered by their unguarded friendliness toward me. (Who knows, I thought: I might at last find a girlfriend among these beaming California girls!)

Abruptly the strumming of a guitar signaled that dinner was served. Everyone stood up and assembled in the dining room, where vegetarian casseroles (made from squash and cucumbers from their own farm) and salads were set out. Once everyone had been arranged in a circle around the serving tables, the master of ceremonies called for a number of rituals to be observed. Newcomers introduced themselves and stated where they were from (and, no matter what they said, it was wildly applauded by the Family members); more singing ensued (with or without hand gestures); and a moment of silence was observed to give thanks to "God or whatever you call your higher power". Afterwards everyone formed a line around the buffet table, but even before I got there, a plate of food was thrust into my hands by a smiling "brother". (The Family members evidently considered this an important act of kindness). I accepted the plate gratefully and went back to the living room and sat down on the floor next to my designated Family member.

After all the guests were again seated on the floor and began to eat their dinners, holding their plates over their laps, the guitar-player stood up again, and announced that he was the emcee for the evening. He led the Family members and guests through another round of songs, introduced a few individual Family members who sang their own songs—invariably about being lost souls who had discovered perfect happiness—and then introduced the speaker, an energetic woman in her late twenties named Terry. I recall almost nothing of what she said. It was as bland and effervescent as mineral water, and as insubstantial as air. The only point that sticks with me is a reference to the isolation of urban people—how men and women on elevators or buses are afraid to talk to each other, and therefore end up staring at the elevator numbers or reading a newspaper instead of speaking. That hit home with me because it reminded me of my own shyness and loneliness.

Terry's talk suggested that the Creative Community Project was the answer. At the end of her speech, she introduced a slide show about their farm in Boonville in Mendecino County, where the Family members gathered every weekend for recreation and games, and she invited the guests to go along with them. It all sounded pretty laid-back: one slide even showed a group of people stretched out and napping on the grass, which Terry called "Activity A", as though this happened often at Boonville.

As soon as the lights went up, the hard sell began: registration forms were produced, and a "workshop fee" of twelve dollars was mentioned. The farm certainly sounded like a relaxing, cheerful place to spend a few days, but I had other plans, so I begged off. The brother who had been appointed to sit with me throughout the meal did not try very hard to dissuade me (since I had told him of my agnostic views), and none of the others who dropped by after the slide show were successful in getting me to say more than "maybe" to their very earnest wish that I should go. In the end, they settled for inviting me back for another free dinner again the next day.

And with that, the evening ended. I walked back through darkened streets to the youth hostel. (I suppose I was too naive to worry about being mugged). Somewhere along the way I passed a Shell service station where the letter "S" had fallen off the sign. This amused me because I thought the owner was disparaging his own business. Later, when I became a committed Unification Church member, I decided that the broken sign had been a message from God telling me that the entire world—apart from the Family—was "hell".

When I went to sleep in my hostel bed that night, I had no intention to go back to the Creative Community Project; after all, I had other plans.

The next morning was a Monday, and that meant that I could get on with my main purpose for visiting California. I caught a bus to South San Francisco, where a branch of The Primal Institute was located. I had no appointment; I decided to just show up and look around. I'm not sure what I expected to learn by doing this. In any event, after consulting my map and walking a fair distance, I located the residential side street the Institute was on. Two little boys spotted me as I walked down the street, and began to emit mock "primal screams" in my direction. They shrieked gleefully to my retreating back until I was well down the block. "Weird," I thought. Then I entered the Primal Institute.

There I found an austere receptionist who listened to my explanation of why I had appeared. No, she could not let me "look around", because patients were being treated inside. When I explained that I was also planning to visit some of the therapy centers of which Arthur Janov did not approve, she coldly handed me a magazine article explaining why only Janov's Primal Institute was capable of administering Primal Therapy properly. (The article was written by Janov). I then explained to her my dilemma—I was a visiting Canadian who couldn't afford the official therapy, which was more expensive than the non-approved versions, but I nevertheless felt that there was no choice, since I believed all other therapies were useless. Upon hearing this, she warmed to me a little, and admitted that she too was Canadian who lived and worked illegally in the United States because it was the only way she could afford the therapy. To oblige her, I sat down in the waiting room and read the article, which eased none of my doubts nor solved my dilemma.

After I got back to the city, I moved on to the next item on my agenda. There was a therapy center that imitated Janov's ideas in the Nob Hill district on Washington Street, not three blocks from the Creative Community Project. I went there at once, and explained that I was simply checking the place out. The people here were much friendlier; they had a few ideas about how my financial problems could be resolved. I felt that this second visit was more promising. Returning to the sunshine, I sat down on the grass in nearby Lafayette Park to plan my next move.

I suspect that many important decisions are made in exactly this way: on the spur of the moment, based on casual coincidence, with nothing particular planned. It was a fine sunny day, and though I intended to take the bus to San Anselmo (north of San Francisco) the next day to visit another of Janov's imitators, there was nothing planned for that particular afternoon. I was free to go sight-seeing again. But I realized that I was also only a few blocks from the Creative Community Project, and hadn't they said I should come by early and help them prepare dinner? Making dinner for more than a hundred people was no easy job. Perhaps—since it was so close anyway—I should go over there and do just that. After all, they were such nice people, and I always enjoyed "doing my bit" to help others.

What I did not know—and only learned much later—was that the Family members urged guests to show up early so they would already be inside when the picketers arrived. During the summer and fall of 1976, picketers from an organization called "Eclipse" stood outside the Washington Street house nearly every day, just before dinnertime, to warn people that the Creative Community Project was actually the Unification Church of Sun Myung Moon. But when I arrived at the house, it was still early in the afternoon, so no picketers were there to warn me.

Annie opened the door with surprise—she hadn't yet taken up her customary position behind the reception desk—and I was shown to the kitchen, where I was asked to chop squash and other vegetables for the casseroles they served every day. A few other sisters were already in the kitchen when I arrived, and as I sliced and diced I did not mind answering all the usual questions. They certainly acted as if my story was utterly fascinating, and I reciprocated by asking for their stories. As usual, they all ended their stories the same way, by having discovered the ultimate "Truth" (and the way they said it, you could practically hear the capital "T").

The dinner program that followed was almost identical to the one I'd attended the previous night. This time, however, when I seated myself on the floor, there was no designated "host" for me. Suddenly, however, a buoyant, black-haired and round-figured sister named Mary-Jane sat down next to me. As usual, we asked each other for an outline of our lives. Mary-Jane grew up in Philadelphia, but eventually landed in California. Before long she started to press me to go up to the Boonville farm for a mid-week workshop they called the "Sheep Barn Experience". I offered the usual objections: my round-trip plane ticket was only for two weeks; I wanted to go to San Anselmo the next day; and though the farm sounded very nice, it didn't fit my schedule. Mary-Jane countered by saying that the workshop was only for three days; I could leave on Tuesday and return on Friday night; and in any case, it would be fun.

It suddenly occurred to me that unless I went, Mary-Jane couldn't go. That surprised me. The previous day during the slide show, Terry made it sound like the Boonville farm was a place where the Family members routinely went for recreation. Couldn't you go up there anyway? I asked her. No, she answered, and then, more hesitantly, well, yes. She looked a bit uncomfortable, so I didn't press the point. If I wanted to please Mary-Jane, I realized, I would have to go to Boonville. I began to consider this idea. I didn't, after all, have a fixed agenda for my stay in California; if necessary, I could delay my flight back to Vancouver (and the way my ticket was set up, there would be no extra cost); and no-one back home would be alarmed if I returned late. Why not check it out? It was only three days. Before long, Mary-Jane had convinced me to postpone my excursion to San Anselmo so I could attend the "Sheep Barn Experience", and I produced twelve dollars in traveler's checks to pay for the workshop. As if to clinch the sale, a freckle-faced sister named Becky pointed out to me that the bus to Boonville happened to pass right through San Anselmo. She was probably hoping that if I got on the "Elephant Bus" for a ride to San Anselmo, they could persuade me to go to Boonville instead. (What she didn't mention was that the Elephant Bus only went to Boonville late at night, long after dinner was over, and that I probably wouldn't want to be dropped off in an unfamiliar town in the middle of the night.) In any case, the extra arm-twisting wasn't needed; I had already decided to go, so senior members of the community put their hands together to devise a plan that would get me there early, before I could change my mind. Instead of waiting for the Elephant Bus, they suggested I go with another guest (and his appointed shadow) in a car up the Pacific Coast Highway—the scenic route. The scenery was the clincher; I readily agreed. (It later occurred to me that they also wanted me to take this route for a more mundane reason—namely, because it does *not* pass through San Anselmo).

Late in the morning on Tuesday, August 25, the four of us set out in a Family car along the road that hugs the Pacific coastline. Mary-Jane and I sat in the back seat, while the front seat was occupied by another Family member—I think her nickname was "Poppy"—and another guest, Andrew, a young accountant from England who, like me, just happened to be passing through San Francisco. As usual, we repeated the stories of our lives as we drove along. It was a fine sunny day and the scenery was as beautiful as promised. I noticed, however, that in spite of the mix of men and women in the car, there was no sexual tension in the atmosphere—mostly because the two "sisters" gave off almost no sexual vibes. Our chatter was light and innocent and the day went by with little to mark it in my memory. Around six o'clock we turned off the coastal highway and proceeded east to the town of Boonville, close to Ukiah. After passing through the town, we came to the gates of the farm. A formidable wooden gate, marked with a "No Trespassing" sign, stood in the way, and a brother who acted as a guard checked us over before he let us through. The property was completely fenced off, I suddenly realized. By this time, I was too committed to back out, though the sight of the gate troubled me. We drove on through, passed some small buildings near an apple orchard and a vegetable garden, and then traveled up a rutted dirt road until we arrived at the sheep barn. There wasn't a sheep in sight.

Chapter Three

Except Ye Become as Little Children

When I inquired about the missing sheep, Mary-Jane explained that the barn had once been used for sheep, but the Family now used it for workshops. The first thing was to assign sleeping quarters: the "brothers" stayed in the barn's loft, while the "sisters" stayed in a little trailer down the road. We had arrived a little early, so nothing was planned for the evening.

This gave me a chance to look around the area. The sheep barn was set among some rolling hills covered with coarse grass and an occasional knot of scrubby trees. (Mendecino County is one of the dryer parts of California). There was stark beauty in this landscape, and as the evening grew longer and the shadows deepened into purple, the place took on a serene feeling. Even though it was late August, the scent of fall was already in the air, making the nights a little cool for outdoor sleeping. By early morning, the hillsides were covered with a heavy dew that quickly evaporated.

Everywhere I went, Mary-Jane followed me around, even though she seemed to be at a loss since no activities were scheduled. Finally, I decided to just ignore her, so I plunked myself down on the hillside, fumbled in my backpack, and pulled out the J.P. Donleavy novel. Mary-Jane sat down nearby, mildly annoyed. Refusing to be deterred, I turned to the page where I had left off and began to read, until I came to a comic incident and laughed. Mary-Jane wondered what was so funny.

I knew this was not going to go over well, but I explained it anyway. George Smith is sleeping in the front room of his country cabin while his secretary is in the bedroom. Suddenly a spider drops down on her bed, and she calls out for George to get rid of it. George, unclothed, charges into the bedroom and proposes that she throw her bedsheet (which was wrapped around her nude body) over the offending creature. "You must. It's our only hope," George explains. This of course sets the scene for the love-making that follows. Mary-Jane gave me a withering look when I finished my summary. I was beginning to understand—without hearing a single lecture—that Family members did not want to hear any references to sex. I decided to put away *A Singular Man* until later, but no opportunity to read it ever arose again.

A little after midnight, the other guests arrived on the Elephant Bus. I was already in my sleeping bag in the barn loft, but scooted over to make room for several new brothers. After a brief flurry of activity, the barn's serenity returned.

It was broken the next morning by the sound of guitars accompanied by the singing of various egregiously cheerful songs such as "When the Red, Red Robin Comes Bob, Bob, Bobbin' Along". The music had hardly begun when all the Family members bolted from their sleeping bags as if they had been shot from a cannon. Meanwhile, the guests sat up, bleary-eyed, wondering what the frenzy was about. From that moment on, we were subjected to a regimented series of activities that only ceased at the end of each night.

First, everyone lined up to use the primitive bathroom facilities. The Family members claimed their appointed guests, and rarely let them out of their sights for the rest of the day. It seemed sometimes that Family members were so anxious to stick with their guests that they would have followed them right into the bathrooms—at least if host and guest were of the same sex. Mary-Jane waited discreetly a short distance away whenever I was in the "brother's bathroom".

Immediately after our ablutions, we were called to form a circle, where the unfailingly chipper guitar-player, Bill, again led everyone in a few songs, then put us through a series of exercises, after which all the participants in the Sheep Barn Experience were divided into four groups, each with an experienced Family member as group leader. Upon the announcement of each group, the Family members cheered, clapped, and jumped up and down excitedly. This habit of applauding almost anything seemed eccentric at first, but it was one of many habits I soon acquired without a thought.

At the end of the announcements, they introduced me to an even more bizarre custom of the Creative Community Project: we all formed into a circle, linked hands, and pumped them up and down frantically, yelling "Choo-choo-choo, choo-choo-choo, choo-choo-choo, yay, yay, pow!" This seemed idiotic at first, but I went along with it out of politeness. Later, the childishness of the "chooch" delighted me and made me laugh every time; I became like a little child, for whom no joke ever grows stale, no matter how many times it is repeated.

Having "chooched", everyone went to join their individual groups. My group leader, it turned out, was Becky—the same woman who had proposed putting me on the midnight bus to San Anselmo. I didn't hold it against her; she was nice enough, a freckle-faced and earnest woman, and in any case Mary-Jane seemed to think she was pretty special. (Mary-Jane admired all the "older" Family members this way). We ate breakfast as a group, and as usual we told our personal stories. Mary-Jane sat next to me, earnestly scrutinizing me as I recounted my life once again. Everyone applauded when I finished, as if my tale was something extraordinary. Once we had all had our fill of granola and yogurt and told our stories, we stood up in a circle, "chooched" once more, and then made our way to the Sheep Barn, where chairs were set up in front of a chalkboard for the first lecture of the day.

And that's how it was for the next three days: no time was left unaccounted for. The group moved from meetings to lectures and back to meetings, then to sports activities, and then to another meeting, and finally to another lecture. Through all these activities, there was a constant unspoken pressure to conform. Guests who did not want to participate in the "chooch" soon encountered the very visible disapproval of Family members evident in their attitudes. If I raised objections to the ideas presented in the lectures (as I often did), those objections were called "questions" and I was assured that the "answers" would be given later. In group meetings, my reservations about the lectures were coolly applauded, which made me feel that I had ruined the cheerful atmosphere of the group by even bringing them up.

The pressure to conform was particularly noticeable during the sports activities. Early in the afternoon, to help the guests work off their physical energies before the late afternoon lecture, everyone was divided up into two teams for dodgeball. This game consists of hurling a soft rubber ball back and forth until everyone on one side or the other had been hit by the ball and thus eliminated. I was familiar with this game from high school, but the way the Family members played it was unlike anything I remembered from "Phys.Ed. 10". Each team was required to come up with a chant which they would repeat throughout the game so loudly it would drown out the opponents' chant. In fact, more emphasis was placed on chanting than on dodging or hurling. No matter how many times I played this game in Boonville, the Family members always selected chants with the same oxymoronic theme: "Crunch with love!" or even "Bomb with love!" If the guests momentarily stopped chanting—even after they were eliminated from the game—the team captain would berate them to get back into it.

Getting the guests to conform at dodgeball was one thing; getting them to give unqualified approval to the lectures was another matter. I was one of the guests who made especially skeptical comments at group meetings after each of the lectures. Even so, all I was hearing was a pale, watered-down version of Reverend Moon's teachings (known as the Divine Principle). The lectures I heard during my first three days at Boonville were from a series known as the "Principles of Education," which only vaguely address most of Moon's most controversial ideas. The Divine Principle assumes the inerrant authority of the Bible, but also offers some unusual scriptural interpretations; the Principles of Education, on the other hand, merely allude to the Bible as one possible authority, while citing other authorities as diverse as Abraham Maslow and Alexis de Tocqueville. While the Divine Principle asserts that Adam and Eve were actual people, the Principles of Education treats them as mythic or merely exemplary figures. One could sit through the entire Principles of Education without realizing it was actually an introduction to the teachings of a fervently religious group whose doctrine is a syncretistic variation on Christianity. Nevertheless, I objected to many of their ideas, because even the Principles of Education seemed to be based on unprovable received ideas.

The Principles of Education lecture series was devised by a missionary who had come to San Francisco in the early 1960s, who wanted to appeal to young Americans who could not relate to the stylized rhetoric of fundamentalist Christianity. The lecture series was designed to get them to stick around until they were ready to hear the undiluted Divine Principle. This certainly worked on me.

The use of these unofficial lectures was just one aspect of what was then a growing schism in the Unification Church. Throughout the 1970's, the Bay Area branch was a maverick offshoot of the church which often ignored the disapproval of the larger body. For example, the Oakland Family had a unique fondness for hand-holding and other forms of discreet touching. Nowhere else in Reverend Moon's movement was it acceptable for unmarried brothers and sisters to hold hands; indeed, this was regarded as the first step toward sexual misconduct. The Oakland Family, however, had no such concerns, because they were able to get members to regress to a child-like, presexual state. Oakland Family members would often hold hands during group meetings, or engage in "group hugs", yet it had an entirely innocent quality about it. In my first few days in Boonville, I had a few fantasies about Mary-Jane, but when I held her hands in a group meeting, it meant nothing more than that we were brother and sister.

When I heard the Principles of Education lecture series for the first time, I believed that the Creative Community Project was operating by itself: a courageous band of idealists hoping to change the world by example. Though I was impressed that they would even attempt this, I did not see why I had to be a part of it, especially since I disagreed with so many of their ideas. It seemed only reasonable, therefore, that they would let me go after the three days were up.

But when Friday rolled around, it suddenly turned out that no vehicle was immediately available, and it would be an inconvenience to get me down to the city that night. Wouldn't I really rather stay for the weekend? It was only two more days, and on the weekend, there were lots of people around, so it was more fun. Mary-Jane was looking forward to the weekend with great anticipation. I hated to disappoint her, and— well, after all—it *was* only two more days. All right, I conceded. Two more days, and then that's it; after that, I had to get on with my plans.

Late that Friday afternoon, everyone from the "Sheep Barn Experience" went down the hill to the main set of buildings on the Boonville farm—a cluster of small trailers and converted outbuildings—where another workshop had been proceeding throughout the week. The brothers were assigned to a low-slung structure with openings beneath the eaves called the "Chicken Palace"—so named because it had once been a chicken coop. The sisters were assigned to a trailer not far away, which also served as the camp kitchen. The group I merged into had been staying there all week, and we joined together in the Friday night activities. Later that night, a new load of guests and members arrived aboard the Elephant Bus, and the new men arranged themselves among the bodies already asleep on the floor of the Chicken Palace. It was clearly going to be a much busier place on Saturday morning.

The weekend workshop turned out to be the Sheep Barn Experience times four. More than a hundred people came to the exercise circle, and many more groups were announced. I was, once again, in Becky's group, with Mary-Jane at my side. I was a little surprised to hear that they had an "Advanced" series of lectures, but my name was not called to be a part of it. I had already heard the basic lectures, so wasn't it logical that I should hear the advanced ones next? But they obviously felt I wasn't "ready", and I was in too obliging a mood to quarrel about it. I went with Mary-Jane to Becky's group meeting, and once again told my personal story, receiving the entire group's applause.

The rest of the weekend turned out to be much the same as the Sheep Barn Experience, except that it was compressed into two days instead of three. I heard, once again, the Principles of Education lecture series, given by a different set of lecturers. Once again, we played dodgeball, and once again, I chanted something like "Bomb with love!" The larger number of people added zest to the workshop, but I was still not convinced. I was becoming a little more favorable to their ideas, but I disagreed on many basic issues. Clearly, it was time for me to leave.

Yet on Sunday evening, I again found myself faced with Mary-Jane's earnest desperation that I should stay. I still wanted to oblige her; I liked her and I wanted to show that I was a good, caring, and open-minded individual. Whenever I disagreed with the Family's teachings, Mary-Jane would say, "You've closed your heart!"—implying that by disagreeing I had become a selfish and cold-hearted person. If I really heard the whole series of lectures, she claimed, I would finally understand the Family's message; the problem was that I didn't "understand". I finally decided, with some uneasiness, that I would stay for the more advanced lectures; I would give the Creative Community Project every chance to prove itself to me. I would stay an extra week, and postpone my flight back to Vancouver.

What I didn't realize is that I had become enmeshed in their strategy of indefinite deferral. The point of this strategy is simply to get people who are not willing to join the movement, but who are not firmly opposed, to hang around Boonville indefinitely, deferring over and over again their decision to leave.

To further this strategy, Family members were always getting the guests to act as if they were already believers. For example, on Saturday night each group was called upon to sing a song or perform a skit before the rest of the Boonville camp. The most common way of fulfilling this duty was to take a well-known melody and write new lyrics that expressed the Family's overall message. By singing these lyrics to the entire camp—even out of mere politeness—the guests would end up acting as if they really believed.

One such Saturday night brainstorming session produced the popular song, "Up on the Hill", which borrowed the melody from "Up on the Roof". This song was frequently sung at the Boonville camp. The first words of the song were:

> *"All my life I've been searching to find*
> *A peaceful way of life for all mankind."*

Later on, the lyrics proclaim:

"Father's ideal world is coming true,
But He can't do a thing without you!"

What I did not know when I agreed to stay for the more advanced
workshop was that I was beginning to act as if I was a believer, though I was
still far from believing. All I knew was that I was going to stay on in Boonville
for another week. And after that, I thought, if I still didn't see things their way,
surely, *then*, I would be allowed to go.

Late on Sunday night, August 29, 1976, the Elephant Bus pulled out of
Boonville, carrying away the guests who had refused to stay (along with their
hosts). All the guests and Family members who were staying for the five-day
workshop were gathered on a hill for a late-night meeting before bedtime.
Songs were sung, and as usual, a moment of silence was observed, in which it
was obvious that the Family members were praying. I wasn't into praying yet,
but I respected these silences. The co-ordinator of the five-day workshop, an
energetic, guitar-playing blonde woman named Jenny, welcomed all the
guests, who were warmly applauded. She explained that there was one rule she
wanted everyone to observe while they were in Boonville: as soon as the
music was played in the morning to rouse the guests and members, everyone
should get up immediately: in fact they should leap right out of their sleeping
bags with a joyful greeting to God. A brother was chosen to demonstrate the
preferred method, which they called "jumping it". The demonstration was
rather comical. He lay down, pretending to sleep on the ground; then someone
sang the first few words from "The Red, Red Robin"; the brother then
exploded from his imaginary sleeping bag, exclaiming, "Good morning,
Heavenly Father!"—then, turning to everyone present and addressing them
with a courtly gesture, he added, "Good morning, brothers and sisters!"

It soon became clear that the Family members took this rule very
seriously. Those of the guests who did not leap to their feet at the first musical
strains of the wake-up call were surrounded by Family members who sang
loudly and played guitar to ensure that sleep was impossible. Later, when the
Monday morning breakfast meeting started, the first question was always,
"Did all the brothers jump it today? Did all the sisters jump it?"

The Monday routine (which soon became familiar to me) was different in
other ways. There was a long breakfast meeting in which everyone at the camp
participated, held in the trailer where the sisters slept. Granola and yogurt were
served, and someone (usually a fairly new recruit) would give an extended
version of his or her life story, which Jenny liked to call "Cereal Drama". I
remember one very tall, red-haired man telling his story like a stand-up
comedian. "I'm from Rhode Island," he cracked, "you know—the parking lot
for New York." As usual, all these stories emphasized that the storyteller had
found the ultimate answer to his or her life's quest by joining the Family.

After breakfast, groups were assigned and a group meeting held, but
instead of beginning the lectures immediately, everyone was divided into
teams to do chores (which they called "actualizing"). Some would be assigned
to harvest squash or fruit; others to sweep and scrub the sleeping quarters; and

on one occasion I was among a group of people who descended on the town of Boonville to clean the streets. But before I was sent off to my assigned task, Jenny came around and asked for money to cover the costs of the workshop. It turned out the price was forty dollars—not unreasonable for a week's room and board—so I paid it from my small cache of traveler's checks.

The day of "actualizing" lasted until around five o'clock, and only then was everyone called together to participate in a vigorous song session followed by the first lecture of the week. The first lecture was a simple lecture on "indemnity", or restitution for wrongdoing. The basic idea of the lecture was that if a person did something wrong, they must compensate; a mere apology might be enough the first time around, but not if the wrongful act was done repeatedly. To illustrate these ideas, parables were told involving Family members stealing cookies or coveting someone else's ice cream. Family members in the audience participated by taking on the roles of ice cream gluttons and penitent cookie thieves. I enjoyed this lecture, because it was so simple and full of childish humor, and I had no objection to its ideas on the face of it. I was always happiest on these Monday evenings in Boonville; I had spent the day "actualizing", so I had done my bit and the Family members were grateful for it; the song-fest was lively and fun; the lecture was light-hearted and hopeful; and the group meetings were warm and supportive. On those evenings, I wondered why I was so resistant to their ideas.

On Tuesday morning, the lecture series began in earnest. From that point on, they were delivered by a slim man with a nasal voice who called himself Zachariah. The lectures used by the Oakland Family for the five-day series were much closer to the lectures that are taught by the rest of the Unification Church, but they still pulled some punches. They still did not specifically name Moon, nor mention the Unification Church's belief that Korea is the chosen nation. However, the pretense they had maintained throughout the Principles of Education—that Family members were allowed to entertain differing concepts about God—was dropped. Clearly, they had a very specific concept of a "Heavenly Father", and they believed that the Bible was authoritative. The more they got into it, the more I resisted their ideas. God might exist, I argued, but how could anyone be sure? And why did they only use the Bible as an authority and not the Bhagavad-Gita, or for that matter the Koran?

But it got worse. The second lecture, on the Fall of Man, left no doubt that they believed Adam and Eve had actually existed, and that an archangel named Lucifer, who had become Satan, was also real. Wait a minute! I wasn't even sure there was a spiritual world yet, never mind angels. It was not that I denied the existence of these things; I simply felt that their existence was unprovable. Mary-Jane was flabbergasted. "Where do you think you go when you dream?" she asked, as if this settled the question. I was acquiring a reputation as the most "skeptical" person in the entire workshop. At every group meeting, I put forward dissenting views.

My growing resistance to their ideas peaked on Thursday night, just when they were at their most triumphant. On Thursday, they ran through a series of lectures which claimed that God has been working through a numerical pattern to establish the Kingdom of Heaven on Earth. First, there had been a series of events leading up to the time of Abraham, Isaac and Jacob; then, a parallel series of events leading up to the time of Jesus; and finally, a further parallel series of events culminating in the present day. The parallels indicated that the present age is a time comparable to that of Jesus, in which the Messiah will again appear so that the "Completed Testament" Age can commence. This idea—that the present age is actually the Biblical Last Days predicted in Revelation—is similar to the views of many evangelical Christians. The difference is that to Unification Church members, there will be no literal return of Jesus; instead, a new person will come to carry out the same mission as Jesus. This new person must be born to a chosen nation, and his mission will be to gather together the believers and convert the entire Earth.

In the lecture on Thursday night, there was considerable discussion about where the new Messiah would come. A nation would have to be "prepared" to receive him. Historical parallels indicated that this nation would probably be in the Far East. However, the new Messiah would also need the support of some major nation who would bring his message to the entire world, paralleling the role that Rome was to have played in the time of Jesus. What nation could do this better than America? From that point on, the lecture argued that the United States of America had a special, providential purpose, and had been chosen by God for this very world-leading role.

Now that *really* frosted my patooties.

Don't get me wrong. I have nothing against the United States of America; but it just so happens that I was raised in Calgary, Alberta, Canada. A picture of Queen Elizabeth II, not of George Washington, adorned the elementary school classrooms where I studied. I simply didn't grow up with the concept that the United States was a nation especially loved and chosen by God; so this belief offended my sense of fairness. Why the United States and not Canada? For that matter, why not Bhutan or Mozambique? It was simply not fair to claim that one particular nation was especially loved by God (even if God existed, which I still doubted).

This was not the reaction the Oakland Family usually got to this lecture. Nearly everyone else in attendance was elated by it. The atmosphere during that final triumphant lecture on Thursday night was ecstatic, almost orgiastic. Some Family members even shed tears of joy. We were in the age of the Messiah! And America would bring the Messiah's teachings to the world! And we were going to be the first to do this! It was an enchantingly optimistic vision, utterly enrapturing in its quixotic sweep. I suppose many young Americans liked this lecture because they had been raised with the idea that America was a special nation that God had set apart from other nations of the world. Then the divisive sixties had shattered this beautiful dream, and the brutality of the war in Vietnam—which had ended in such an inauspicious way—left them broken-hearted, wondering what to make of their country. The Oakland Family's lecture gave them back their pride, and they were delighted.

(And then some dumb Canuck had to go and spoil it all by spouting off at the group meeting after the lecture).

For me, Thursday was a bummer. That does it, I thought, I'm out of here. This American civil religion stuff is bad enough; but anyone could see that those "Parallels of History" were just slapped together to suit their numerical purposes. And what about the entire first leg of the parallels, from Adam to Abraham—weren't those numbers taken entirely from the Bible with no historical records to back them up? Give me a break!

I was a stubborn rationalist; in fact, a short story I had written (which coincidentally was published a few months later in a book titled *Canadian Short Fiction Anthology*) was narrated by a character named "Ernest Reasoner", with whom I identified. That story is no literary classic. However, it is worth mentioning because it sets out clearly what I thought about religion just before I joined the Unification Church. "Parker's Elect" is a transparent allegory, in which a collection of bizarre characters meet together to hold the World's Longest Non-Stop Monopoly Game. Each character believes he alone understands the "will of Parker" (that is, of Parker Brothers, the publishers of "Monopoly"). There is a "Mr. Pope", who rules the game by arbitrary fiat; and there is his supporter, "Roger Givens", who goes along with whatever Mr. Pope decrees. There is a cynic, "Mortimer Snurd", who thinks the game is ultimately futile; and a pure aesthete, "Art Sieker", who is only concerned with the "beauty and symmetry of the game". Finally, there is a fanatical visionary ("Bright Vision") and a coldly rational logician ("Ernest Reasoner"). Gradually everyone is eliminated until only Bright Vision and Ernest Reasoner remain. When Reasoner finally prevails—at gunpoint—over Bright Vision, he takes no comfort in his victory: "My sobs boomed off the walls because the place was empty, a void; I could not feel the closeness of Parker, and I knew that when I returned to the outside, there would be no friend waiting to take His place."

Ernest Reasoner's final remarks reveal how unhappy I was with my own rationalism. Though it seemed correct, it left me cold; there were no friends waiting to take the place of Reason, and Reason gave me no hugs, no consolation. So, in spite of how much I criticized the Family's teachings on rational grounds, I was actually vulnerable. The Oakland Family was offering me a view of reality that was full of irrational ideas; yet its members were friendly, warm, and utterly convinced of their views. I, by contrast, had a well-thought-out, utterly sensible view of life, but no deep friendships, no lover, and only ambivalence to guide my way. The conflict between the two caused me to waiver between these extremes throughout my time in Boonville, especially at the beginning.

I went to bed that first Thursday night (September 2, 1976) in a glum mood, convinced that I had heard enough: I couldn't stay. But when Friday arrived, my mood changed; the Friday lecture was a lecture primarily intent on proving that the Last Days were not going to be heralded by actual trumpets nor result in a literal return of Jesus on the clouds of heaven; but since I didn't expect this anyway, it didn't bother me. In the afternoon, they put everyone back to work doing practical tasks, and this pleased me also, since I could again "do my bit" and be praised for it. Around dinner time, Jenny came around asking the guests for a few dollars to help pay for the ice cream that they dished up every Friday night, just after the ceremonial serving of spaghetti. I gladly gave her a few dollars for this purpose. So on Friday night, after dinner and the great ice cream pig-out, I was in a fairly relaxed mood, and I was not particularly surprised when it turned out that it would again be inconvenient for them to take me to San Francisco that evening—so wouldn't I stay for the weekend workshop, and then go down with everyone else on Sunday? I agreed to this further delay almost with alacrity; I had expected it anyway. Two more days, and then I would be out of there.

The weekend workshop was a near-clone of the one I had attended the previous week. I was again placed in Becky's group along with Mary-Jane, and I was again required to hear the "Principles of Education"—they obviously felt that I was still not ready for the "Advanced" lectures. I accepted this and went along for the ride, feeling certain that on Sunday night—after the customary tofu-burger barbecue—they would finally let me leave Boonville. After all, we didn't see eye to eye. Why keep me around? So, on Sunday evening just before dinner, I packed my knapsack for the trip down to San Francisco.

Mary-Jane called on a more experienced member who called himself Isaiah to get me to see the light. Isaiah took me aside after the final supper meeting, and began to zero in on my most vulnerable point. Wasn't it at least possible that they were right, and if so, wasn't I passing up on a chance to find out for myself? As a rationalist, I had to admit that it was, at the very least, *possible* that they were right. Well, if they were right, how was I going to know unless I tried it? He made it sound like a scientific experiment. If what they said was correct, and I tried it out for a while and it worked, everything was fine. If it didn't work, I could always leave later. So what was the problem?

This argument swayed me a little, but I had been through it all before. I had my own plans as well, and I was already overdue on them. And I'd already been through the five-day workshop once, so what new things could they tell me if I stayed for another week? On the whole, no, I didn't think I should stay.

Isaiah tried his last-ditch strategy. Didn't I realize how desperately Mary-Jane wanted me to stay? "Mary-Jane is wringing her hands!" he told me. That did it. I couldn't bring myself to disappoint sweet, simple Mary-Jane, especially over something about which I felt such profound ambivalence. After a long pause I let out a heavy sigh and vowed, "Okay. I'll stay."

They had me then. From that moment on, it was just a matter of time.

***

Later, when the Elephant bus again left Boonville without me, I felt more defeated than I had felt for a long time. I went through the same Sunday night rituals as the previous week, including the demonstration of "jumping it" on the hillside, but I was profoundly depressed. I had clearly made up my mind to leave, and then at the last minute I had overridden my own decision just to please someone else. And though I didn't understand it at the time, my depression signaled the beginning of the sudden psychological collapse which accompanies exposure to mind control. Once the normal reference points by which a person knows who he is are withdrawn, he enters a limbo-like state of emptiness that is so disturbing that it is impossible to bear for long. In that terrifying moment, the new identity offered by the mind controllers appears as a miraculous salvation; the only hope for sanity in a world suddenly stripped of all its normal referents and meaning. This was the limbo state that I now found myself plunging into.

I went to sleep on that night full of a nameless sadness, and slept badly. In the early morning hours, long before the wake-up call, I awoke, in a panic. I felt, with a terrifying urgency, that I had to get out—at once. But when I thought about what it would take to actually leave Boonville, I knew it was impractical. I had missed the Elephant Bus; now I'd have to hitch-hike. I could not explain to anyone why I had to leave immediately, even though I felt such a strong impetus to go. "What are you afraid of?" the Family members would ask, astonished. And indeed, they were so friendly that there was nothing I could point to as frightening about their behavior. And yet I felt I was being—in some indefinable way—*destroyed* by them. I must get out, I felt; yet it was the middle of the night, and I was far away in unfamiliar countryside. What could I do?

In that peculiar state of mind which accompanies sleeplessness, the solution that presented itself to me then—with the full force of my deep depression—was that I should drown myself in the small creek that ran around the perimeter of the Boonville farm. This was absurd, as I well knew; at that time of year the creek was little more than a trickle. Yet, with a peculiar longing, I pictured myself face down in the creek, drowned, safely escaped from Boonville.

In the end I didn't even move from my sleeping bag on the floor of the Chicken Palace; I drifted back into an uneasy sleep, and awakened the next morning still depressed, but gradually began to adjust to my decision to stay. Very well, I thought; I *will* test out their ideas; I will find out if God exists by trying to meet Him in prayer. I will do what they tell me to do, and see what happens.

My second week in Boonville followed the same schedule as the first, but now my attitude was different. Now I was there because I was "trying out their ideas", like some sort of experiment. My behavior began to change subtly; for example, I stopped wearing my "The Earth is Flat" T-shirt, along with another that extolled the merits of Budweiser beer. But most of all, I set out to discover if God actually existed.

My opportunity to do this came during the one hour of "meditation" that was allowed in the late afternoons. During this hour, a guest was free to go for walks (inside the farm gates), or to write letters, or to nap, but with one limitation: he or she must not at any time speak to anyone, except an experienced Family member. The silence could only be broken when the meditation hour concluded and everyone reassembled for the frenzied song-fest just before the evening lecture. (In this way, guests were prevented from "sharing negativity"—that is, from speaking to each other about what was wrong with Boonville).

During my one-hour "meditation" session I liked to go up the hills to a place by myself to try to pray to God, as if He really existed, hoping that I could actually get an answer to my prayers—hoping, in short, that I mattered to even so great a being as God. I would like to be able to say that I got an answer, and that God appeared on the hilltop to reassure me that He existed; but nothing so dramatic occurred. At first, my prayers were very tentative, and I admitted to God that I wasn't really sure that my prayers were going anywhere. But my attempts at prayer were sincere, and I soon realized that I was going to have to try for a long time with great patience if I truly hoped to meet God.

In this one respect I must admit that I benefited from my sojourn in the Unification Church. Until that time, I had been stymied by the fact that God's existence could not be objectively proven, so I did not attempt to build a relationship with Him. Now, at last, I was reaching out to God anyway, and discovering the sustaining and comforting power of prayer; and though I never did have that mystical meeting with God I prayed for, I have often felt God's response to my prayers in subtle and tender ways that reassure me that I am not just expending my breath into the empty air.

On Tuesday, September 7—only the second day into my earnest quest for God—I went up to the hill overlooking the Boonville camp to pray. I was coming off the high point of the week for me, Monday night, and I was in a positive mood. As I looked down from the hillside at the little buildings in the main part of the camp—the Chicken Palace, the Sister's Trailer, and the buildings next to the gardens and orchards—I suddenly felt that there was no longer any reason to continue resisting them. Why not join? Perhaps here, I could find out if God really existed. Also, they were such good, friendly, enthusiastic people, and though I knew that none of the sisters would ever be my girlfriend, it didn't seem to matter anymore. In the child-like atmosphere of Boonville, I was able to talk to young women easily without the emotional barriers that had prevented me before. Perhaps I could become some sort of internal critic, using my rational mind to correct them when they needed it. All I had to do was say "yes" to Mary-Jane's very urgent wish that I should "move in". With a sense of joy and giddy apprehension—as though I was driving at top speed around a blind corner on a single-lane road—I decided at that moment to join the Creative Community Project.

Later, I called September 7 my "spiritual birthday," but, in fact, it does not fit the definition used by the Unification Church. The spiritual birthday is supposed to be the day on which a new member "accepts Father" as the Messiah; but on that day I knew nothing of Father nor of his world-wide church, so I joined blindly, in pure ignorance. I did not know—nor could I have known—that in making this choice my free will had just been subverted by one of the most sophisticated mind control systems ever devised.

***

Robert J. Lifton, in his famous study of brainwashing in Communist China[2], lists eight criteria needed for a thought reform program to be successful: milieu control; mystical manipulation; the demand for purity; the cult of confession; the "sacred science"; loading the language; doctrine over person; and the dispensing of existence. The Unification Church meets all of these criteria, especially at training camps for new recruits such as Boonville.

Milieu control means control of the environment so that the individual is never allowed any significant contact with the world outside of the thought-reforming environment. This includes denying access to newspapers, radios or telephones, as well as limitations on freedom of movement. In Lifton's study, he talked to prisoners who had been held in the thought reform environment by force. At Boonville there was no overt coercion, but the situation and schedule were arranged to create the same result. Boonville was distant from the nearest city, and surrounded by fences and gates; a guest would have had to be extremely rebellious to leave without waiting for the Elephant Bus, and few did so. Also, each day was jammed with activities to such an extent that there was no time to read newspapers or listen to radios—activities that are often disparaged as "spacing out" in the Unification movement at large. Also, during their first weeks at Boonville the guests were almost never without a Family member tagging along, so they rarely had a chance to escape the mind control regime that was being put in place around them.

Mystical manipulation means that totalist groups claim to be acting from the best of motivations and for the highest purposes, and therefore the organization itself is invested with a mystical aura. Any challenge to the dictates of the organization, no matter how cruel and arbitrary those dictates may be, is seen as a challenge to the higher purpose itself. By extension, those who challenge the organization will be viewed as selfish or regressive, while those who surrender to it may experience a temporary exhilaration at having bonded with the mystical glory of the organization. This kind of thinking was often employed at Boonville: whenever I expressed doubts forcefully, I was made to feel selfish and closed-hearted. Mary-Jane told me so explicitly at one point at a group meeting: "Now Gordon's just one person, by himself, not thinking of the whole purpose, while *we* are a Family." Throughout the Unification Church, but especially in the Oakland Family, there was a near-erasure of individual identities and a mystical merger into the holy collective. In San Francisco while I was there, this was taken so seriously that the word "I" was replaced by "we" in many songs and public prayers.

---

[2]	Robert J. Lifton, *Thought Reform and the Psychology of Totalism* (New York: W.W. Norton & Company, Inc., 1961), pp. 419-437.

The *demand for purity* means the application of moral judgments of good and evil to every facet of life, and the extreme polarization between good and evil. Totalist groups require that their members engage in an unending struggle to purge themselves of evil, a task which by definition can never be completed. The result is what Lifton terms a *guilty milieu* and a *shaming milieu*: members of totalist groups are never free of guilt and can easily be shamed by others in the group. This aspect of thought reform is implicit in the ideas taught at Unification Church training sessions, but generally, it is only put fully into practice when the new member has left the training camp. After I was sent down from Boonville to San Francisco, I heard many lectures warning of the terrible consequences of even thinking impure thoughts (which would attract evil spirits); we were instructed to pray or chant until such thoughts went away. On one occasion I became quite agitated because I had merely *dreamed* of having sex. I was only consoled when a more experienced member reassured me that God would not condemn me for events that occurred in my dreams.

The *cult of confession* refers to the practice in totalist groups of confessing one's wrongdoings repeatedly, often to the point where the confession becomes a performance and loses its original purgative purpose. The subjects of Lifton's study were compelled to write and rewrite their confessions many times over, until the confessions were almost complete fabrications, yet sometimes they would come to believe in them anyway—not necessarily that they were literally true, but that they accurately portrayed their shameful "bourgeois" tendencies. In Boonville, too, both guests and Family members were repeatedly asked to tell their life stories over and over again. Family members would often exaggerate the failings of their previous lives in order to underline how beneficial it had been for them to join. One example: I have a fondness for beer, and during my undergraduate years, I sometimes brewed my own beer and wine. In my later confessions, this fondness became exaggerated into an orgy of drunkenness. After a while, the exaggeration seemed like memory, and it became part of my growing hatred and fear of my former self.

The *sacred science* refers to the claim by totalist groups that their doctrine is not only morally right but is based in science and natural reason. Anyone who challenges the doctrine is, therefore, not only immoral but unscientific. In Boonville, a lot of emphasis was placed on the significance of the historical parallels, which were regarded as airtight in their logic and accuracy. Yet I had easily seen through them during my first week in Boonville when I pointed out that they were largely based on the Bible alone and not on verifiable historical sources. Nevertheless, as much as I resisted this part of the doctrine initially, I eventually came to believe that it was the truth and that it represented the last word on how God is working through "providential" history.

Loading the language refers to the use of standard phrases and jargon over and over again. Certain words and phrases are preferred over more diverse forms of expression because they are taken from the doctrine and therefore have the pseudo-scientific authority of the doctrine. In the Unification Church, loaded language forms a large part of the discourse of new members, who often cannot get through a sentence without employing clichés such as "give-and-take", "form spirits", "Chapter Two problem", and "subjugating Satan". As Lifton notes, the repeated use of loaded language results in a "constriction" of thought; the terms have only two-dimensional meanings intended to provoke standardized responses.

Doctrine over person refers to the tendency of members in totalist groups to continue to believe in the doctrine even if it is contradicted by their own personal experiences. A way is always found to "prove" that any disconfirming experience actually agrees with the doctrine, so long as it is "properly understood". In Boonville, I often challenged the ideas I was taught, but usually I was told that my "questions" would be answered later—I just didn't "understand" yet. As the mind control process took effect, it became less and less important to me to solve these apparent contradictions, and eventually I simply forgot about them altogether. I began to assume that the explanation for any contradiction could always be found in the doctrine somewhere, even if I didn't know it yet.

The *dispensing of existence* refers to the claim made by totalist groups that only its members and supporters truly have the right to exist; everyone else, in effect, is a "non-person". In the Unification Church, non-members are viewed as being "under the dominion of Satan"; likewise, every marriage or love relationship except Moon's "Blessed" marriages are "fallen" or "Satanic". Although the Unification Church does not advocate harming "Satanic" people, this is mainly because everyone is supposedly going to believe in Moon eventually anyway; otherwise, Unificationism has very little sympathy for non-believers. Large losses of life are sometimes seen as a payment of "indemnity" by a nation or people for failing to carry out their responsibility in God's providence; for example, the Holocaust has been cited by Sun Myung Moon as the unfortunate but historically necessary price the Jews had to pay for failing to support Jesus when he was alive.

The subtitle to Lifton's book states that it is a study of brainwashing in China. The term "brainwashing" refers to a coercive process, and is therefore inaccurate when used in connection with cults like the Unification Church. However, similar methods can be employed in a seemingly non-coercive environment (such as Boonville) with results that are even more devastating and long-lasting. The correct term for this non-coercive process is "mind control". It was mind control, then, that caused me to suddenly break on September 7, 1976, when I agreed to join the Oakland Family only two days after I had been set on leaving them.

* * *

In less than two weeks, I had been persuaded, through a combination of peer pressure and intense manipulation amounting to mind control, to abandon my previous very firm intention to seek Primal Therapy. Indeed, I had been persuaded that giving any thought at all to my emotional problems was "selfish" in the light of the far deeper suffering of God. However, the Family members did hold out the hope that my emotional pain would be cured automatically—along with all the Earth's environmental problems—by the coming Kingdom of Heaven on Earth. While not yet entirely persuaded of these ideas, which would have seemed ludicrous only a few weeks before, they now sounded almost plausible. The feelings of alienation, which had always been the most painful aspect of my emotional pain, was in any case very much eased by the effusive friendliness of the Family members, so while I no longer expected any girl friend to emerge from their ranks to soothe my pain—I knew that was off limits—I still found much consolation in the mutual support they offered.

Yet even after my decision to join, I continued to object to many of the ideas they taught me at the various lectures. From then on, however, my objections were from the standpoint of a newcomer trying to grasp a difficult point rather than of a skeptic pouring cold water over everything. I was still very negative at times, especially on Thursday nights when the parallels of history and the American triumphalism soured my mood (Mary-Jane rolled her eyes and gnashed her teeth over "these skeptical Canadians!") but I no longer put up much resistance when the question came up whether I should stay longer. I was committed to living with the Oakland Family to try out their ideas, so I no longer had a good reason to leave. Nevertheless, I continued to believe that they would eventually let me go back to Canada to practice their beliefs on my own.

The older members never said I could not return; they just kept convincing me to postpone the trip. On August 31 I sent this ambivalent postcard to my friends in Vancouver: "Dear Friends, I will be delayed in returning to Vancouver. I will not be back until Sept 9-12 and then I will only be able to stay a few days. You see, I'm staying at a lovely farm in Boonville, California run by a lot of people with some moving religious convictions. I *know* their hearts are in the right place—but I don't know about their heads yet. I'm still trying to decide. Love, Gordon." That postcard was written only one week after I came to Boonville, and yet already my writing style had changed markedly. The punning banter was gone; the emphasizing of the word "know" suggests that I was expecting some resistance to my claim that "their hearts are in the right place" (either that, or I was reaffirming it for my own benefit); and the uncharacteristic "Love, Gordon" at the end—addressed to an entire group of people—showed that the group ethic of the Oakland Family was already rubbing off. Still, the postcard claimed that I was going to go back; and even right through to mid-November, my letters mentioned this idea.

When my third weekend at Boonville rolled around, I was again required to hear the "Principles of Education" (probably because I continued to resist the Thursday lectures). Dutifully, I went through the same motions as I had all the previous times, and stayed on for a third time through the five-day lecture series. It wasn't until September 18, 1976 that I was finally allowed to attend the "Advanced" workshop. On the second day of this workshop I was allowed to hear Sun Myung Moon's name toward the end of the lecture series. The "Advanced" workshop was basically the undiluted Divine Principle as it is taught elsewhere in the church. In the Oakland Family these lectures were not taught until the guest was considered "ready".

According to Moon's teachings, the life and work of Jesus was in many ways a lamentable failure. His sacrifice on the cross was simply a secondary plan that had to be resorted to because his primary plan had failed. If the Jews had supported him like God had intended them to, Jesus could have used Israel as a platform from which to bring the Gospel to the entire world through the agency of the Roman Empire.

The chief culprit for this failure was John the Baptist. John had received a revelation from God that Jesus was the messiah, and had even testified to him, but then went away and did little more about it. What he was *supposed* to do, according to Moon, was to become Jesus' chief disciple, converting all of his followers into followers of Jesus. But John's failure was only the most lamentable among a life of many such desertions. Time after time, people who were supposed to support Jesus failed to do so. Even the three wise men were supposed to do more than merely hand over gold, frankincense and myrrh; God was hoping they would raise Jesus and give him an education, and protect him from Herod. When, finally, even Jesus' own disciples failed him at the Garden of Gethsemane, and could not even stay awake for a single hour to pray, it became necessary for Jesus to be sacrificed on the cross, so that those who believed in him might be saved spiritually. Moon's Divine Principle, thus, agrees with Christianity that spiritual salvation was brought about through Jesus' crucifixion; however, Moon argues that this was only half of what was originally sought; a Messiah is still needed to save people in the physical world.

This particular lecture was delivered at the Advanced workshop on Sunday mornings with great emotion. It was intended to portray the life of Jesus as a painful epic of desertion and heartbreak, and most of the Family members wept freely. Indeed, as Jenny told the group after the lecture ended, these tears were "precious to God" because it helped the Family members to understand how heartbroken God Himself felt over these events. After the lecture on Jesus, the Advanced workshop members were taken to an open field to hear one of Moon's speeches from his book, *Twelve Talks*. It was explained that Moon was the source of many of the ideas being taught at Boonville. This was fine with me; I had never heard of him anyway.

The Advanced workshops wrapped up on a hopeful note, with a more detailed explanation of why the Messiah was almost certainly already walking on the Earth and therefore the Kingdom of Heaven was already at hand, and—since this was God's third attempt to establish the "K of H"—it was definitely going to succeed because "God always succeeds on the third try!" Yet even here, no explicit connection was made between the person of Sun Myung Moon and the claim that the Messiah was already living.

That Sunday evening, Mary-Jane was sent back to the city to find a new convert, and I stayed behind at Boonville for one more week. Finally, on September 26, I was also sent down to the city, to begin my life as an active member of the Oakland Family.

***

The Boonville training camp left a deep impression on me that stuck with me throughout the ten years I followed Sun Myung Moon. My memories of that time are more rich and detailed than of many of the events that followed. Above all else, I remember that in the course of a few weeks in September, all my university education, all my rationalism, all my existential sadness, and all the goals I had once been committed to were cast aside, and I became like a child again. Jesus said, "Except ye convert, and become as little children, ye shall not enter into the kingdom of heaven," (Matthew 18:3); the Oakland Family members took this injunction quite literally. Even the words I chose in the letters I sent home became simple and child-like; I began to live each day without planning or foresight, trying to please God and to be a good boy, as God would have me be. I remember one event that demonstrates this most vividly.

It was during my last week at Boonville. I had been chosen to go with a small group of brothers and sisters to the nearby town of Ukiah to sing in old folks' homes as a token of neighborliness and good will. As usual, I was delighted to "do my bit" in such a charming and simple way. I was also pleased for another reason: Diana, camp cook and guitar-player, would be going with us. During my last two weeks at Boonville, I had developed a crush on Diana, but it was really just "puppy love", since I had already regressed somewhat to a presexual state of innocence. Diana sat in the passenger seat at the front of the van, and an experienced brother was the driver. The rest of us rode in the back of the van on the floor because there were no other seats. I felt happy and excited to be going for a ride. After we had sung our cheerful, simple songs in the old folks' homes, the driver took us over to the Thrifty's drug store, where ice cream cones cost only fifteen cents each. Diana dug into the money she had been given, and bought us each a cone, and it was as if Mom and Dad had taken us to the town for the day; we all licked our ice cream cones happily, and felt that things couldn't be better. And then, as the evening sky was softening into darkness, we climbed back into the van, and Diana told us it would be all right to lie down and take a nap on our way back to Boonville. I stared out the window at the first stars of the evening until my eyes grew heavy with sleep. I thought: I'm safe now. Beautiful Diana is watching over me; all I have to do is close my eyes and just let go, and everything is going to be all right . . .

Chapter Four

Raise or Fold

Late on Sunday night, September 26, 1976, the Elephant Bus left Boonville, taking all the guests who were determined to leave along with the Family members who accompanied them. I got onto the bus, not knowing where they would take me or what they would ask of me when I got there. Though I had agreed to join the Creative Community Project, I still knew next to nothing about the Unification Church, and I did not really think of myself as a member of that group yet. The only certainty was that I liked the people in the Oakland Family and I had agreed to try out their way of life as a sort of "experiment". Therefore, I was prepared to go wherever, and do whatever, they required; but I thought they would likely send me to the house in San Francisco where I had first met them.

When we reached the city, though, I learned that I had been assigned to a smaller house on Ashby Avenue in Berkeley which they referred to as a "half-way house", where new members were expected to adjust to the rigors of "center life". The schedule at Ashby Avenue was less demanding than at the regular centers: members were awakened at 5:30 a.m. rather than 5:00 a.m., and they spent less of their day "actualizing" (recruiting or fund-raising) and more time hearing lectures and attending meetings.

The Ashby house program was the first phase of a carefully-planned maneuver, over the course of several months, aimed at changing newcomers from people who were merely "trying out" life in the Oakland Family into people who would be fanatically committed to the world-wide Unification movement and who would go anywhere and do anything True Father (that is, the Reverend Moon) demanded. Therefore, I was not told—until I was "ready"—about many of the more unusual doctrines and practices of the Unification Church. These were only discussed, one at a time, after I and the other new members had adjusted to all the previous off-putting surprises.

The first unpleasant surprise was, of course, how early I had to get up. I recall clearly on my second or third day at the Ashby house, being awakened at 5:30 a.m.—as usual to the tune of "Red, Red Robin"—and thinking, "These people are nuts! They're just totally, completely, nuts!" I had only dropped off to sleep at 1:00 a.m., so I did not feel like greeting the day cheerily, as I was supposed to do, so soon afterwards. As I stood up and crabbily rolled up my sleeping bag, I reminded myself of everything they had said about "living a sacrificial lifestyle serving others"—which always seemed to involve waking up early and getting little sleep—so I didn't complain openly. Nevertheless, I began to wonder quietly if I should call it quits. By mid-morning, however, they had cajoled me into a more accepting mood, and I concluded that I had been "selfish" to be so upset about loss of sleep, and that perhaps I had offended God by not being grateful to start the day so early. I decided to be more enthusiastic the next time I heard the wake-up call, and to bolt out of my sleeping bag instantly, as expected—indeed, required.

This was only the first of many unpleasant surprises. Ashby house members spent their mornings doing "lecture practice"—usually giving each other the introductory lecture to the Principles of Education—and then were taken to tourist areas to spend the afternoons "witnessing"—that is, recruiting. After we sat through the evening program at Washington Street house, seated next to our own guests or assisting others with theirs, we were driven back to Ashby Avenue to hear lectures on more "advanced" aspects of Divine Principle that had not previously been disclosed to us.

It was at one of these late evening meetings that I first heard about True Father's unique scheme of arranged marriages. Up to that point, I had not given the matter of marriage in the Family much thought; having been instructed to avoid "fallen thinking", I had already begun to edit out sexual thoughts, always repenting in prayer if such thoughts entered my mind. Therefore, I had never really considered how Family members got married, or even if they did. In 1976 there still had not been very many mass weddings in the Unification Church, so nearly all the brothers and sisters in the Oakland Family were single. At the lecture, I learned that only a marriage blessed by Father was acceptable to God, and that Father was the only person capable of choosing the right partner for each individual. I learned that a 1975 mass wedding of 1,800 couples had taken place in Seoul, Korea, and that Sun Myung Moon had chosen the partners in each couple himself, often favoring international and inter-racial marriages.

These ideas might have upset some people, but they did not particularly bother me. It sounded like a far-off event, something that Father probably wouldn't get around to doing anyway until after the "Kingdom of Heaven on Earth" was already established.

At another evening meeting at Ashby house, however, I was troubled by a different doctrine they revealed. I had already reluctantly accepted that the United States of America was God's chosen nation. Now they were teaching that the United States was actually chosen only to act in a supporting role, and that it was really the Republic of Korea (South Korea) that was to lead the world into the Kingdom of Heaven on Earth. According to the Divine Principle, Korea was the "Adam" nation, Japan the "Eve" nation, and the United States was the "Lucifer" nation, whose role was to support and protect Adam. The lecturer stated that the main reason that God had allowed America to have its military might was so that it could protect Korea, and if America ever failed in its mission—for example, by withdrawing its troops from Korea—then God would quickly desert America, leading to its rapid decline.

In fact, from what the lecturer said, Korea was a nation of special virtue, whose people were more Godly than those of other nations.

I put up my hand to object.

Prior to joining the Family, I had followed the news closely and had read reports in *Time* magazine that the Korean dictator, Chung Hee Park, was known for human rights violations, including jailing prisoners in cells so small the summer heat made them unbearable. I spoke up at the meeting and said something like, "Wait a minute! I've heard about this man, Chung Hee Park. He's not a virtuous man." But my challenge was treated the same way as all the doubts I raised at Boonville were treated: they claimed that I would understand later, even if I didn't understand now. They explained that Park's heavy hand of authority was necessary in order to counter the threat of communism, which was Satan's chief weapon against the Messiah. I reluctantly accepted this explanation, but still felt uneasy about it. The Oakland Family leaders noticed my uneasiness and it may have caused them to delay my transfer to Washington Street. (I was often seen as a problem member: they said I was too "heady"—that is, too intellectual for my own good).

At any rate, the main focus of each day was to recruit more new members—always more and more and more. So in the afternoons, the Ashby house members went out in pairs to major tourist areas like Golden Gate Park or Fisherman's Wharf to invite people to the dinner program, in the same way that I had been recruited. We were instructed to be selective about whom we invited: any young person wearing a backpack was especially favored, so some of these people were approached three or four times in a day by different witnessing pairs. We were discouraged from approaching older people, and were instructed to ignore any person who was obviously down and out, as this was "not a quality person". Similarly, we rarely witnessed to African Americans, because the head of the Oakland Family, Onni Durst, had said that it was "not their time yet". So it was mainly young white people who came to the dinner programs, which took place both at the Washington Street house and at another large house on Hearst Street in Berkeley. Because of the emphasis on recruiting travelers, a typical evening program would include guests who hailed from all over Europe, as well as Canada, Australia, New Zealand, and the United States.

Witnessing was difficult for me because of my natural shyness. I could rarely bring myself to speak up first when I saw a likely individual, so I relied on my witnessing "partner" to start the conversation. Usually, I would be paired up with a more experienced Family member. There was no rule in the Oakland Family against pairing a brother with a sister (though this rule was often observed elsewhere) so I especially enjoyed working with a sister, though I was reassigned to working with different partners every day. The child-like camaraderie of the Oakland Family made witnessing bearable, but I felt badly that I was ineffective, and after my first week I still had not met anyone who would even sit through the evening program with me. I wanted to justify my existence by bringing tangible results for the Family; besides, if I found a guest willing to go to Boonville, I would be allowed to go there too, and thus enjoy the more relaxed schedule at the farm. I was disappointed, therefore, that my first weekend in the city (probably October 2nd and 3rd) passed without convincing anyone to go up to Boonville. I continued to witness from the Ashby house through the second week of October, but still with no success.

It was a relief, therefore, when on my second Friday in the city, while all the more successful—or more "righteous"—members were leaving for Boonville with their guests, I was given a chance to work through the weekend for the Oakland Family's carpet cleaning company. The work began immediately that night, but I was happy to give up a night's sleep in order to do something that would earn plenty of praise for my "sacrificial" efforts—and which would, furthermore, bring visible results. As I worked with the "maintenance" brothers vacuuming and steam-cleaning carpets in various offices and restaurants (and even on board a ship), I had the satisfaction of seeing dirt going up the suction hose and being emptied out in dirty water buckets. Each bucket of dirty water meant that I had made a real difference for Father. I did, however, warn the carpet cleaners that, being a Canadian, I was not legally supposed to work. That was no problem, they told me; I was not going to appear on their employment rolls anyway. We had a deal.

After working straight through Friday night and most of Saturday, we returned to Washington Street house in time to attend the Sunday service. This was a more elaborate version of the "morning service" that is held every day in Unification Church centers; the sermon is usually longer, and the members are expected to dress up if possible. I had no good clothes, but I was forgiven since I had worked all night on the carpet-cleaning team. Normally, the sermon was delivered by one of the more experienced members, but on this particular Sunday (probably October 10) the head of the entire Oakland Family, Onni Durst, gave the sermon herself. This was a special occasion indeed; the Oakland Family members revered her almost as highly as Father, and indeed, she borrowed some of his techniques at meetings—for example, she would ask everyone who had never seen her before to put up their hands.

Onni was a Korean, originally named Onni Soo Lim, who had joined the Unification Church in the early 1960's in Japan, and had been sent from there to the United States as a missionary to Oakland, California. She quickly surpassed the work of the established missionary in San Francisco, and eventually absorbed his mission into her own (hence the nickname "Oakland Family", even though the group focused on San Francisco and Berkeley). In the early 1970s Father married her to a divorced American professor, Mose Durst, and she became "Onni Durst", but everyone in the Oakland Family called her "Omma" (a Korean term of affection meaning "mama"). Similarly, Dr. Durst—who usually gave the closing lecture at the Boonville workshops—was known as "Oppa", meaning "papa".

Onni did not seem particularly motherly on this occasion. Her morning service was suddenly interrupted when she angrily shouted out a single name.

"Stepan!"

She glowered at her chauffeur, whose eyelids had drooped even though he was standing up at the back of the room. Stepan gave a start and pulled himself erect, looking ashamed. After a moment, Onni carried on with her talk. But soon afterwards, she broke off again.

"Stepan!" she admonished, even more sharply. It was clear that Stepan was in big trouble for being tired, even though we had all been told repeatedly that God needed us to work to the point of exhaustion, so it was also unacceptable for a member *not* to be tired. The obvious unfairness of Onni's anger made me have second thoughts about the group I was getting into.

I knew that I was going to be formally asked to join the Unification Church after the sermon. For many of us, this was a routine step, since we had already verbally agreed to join the Creative Community Project. But when the form was handed to me to sign in order to join, I refused to sign. I told them I was content to remain just a member of the Creative Community Project—and I was planning to do some hard thinking about that, too. They backed off, uttering soothing words.

One week later—following a more conventional Sunday service—I gave in and signed the form. "Time heals all wounds," Jenny noted as she collected the signed paper from me. I made no reply; I was still feeling indecisive, but I had taken one more step down the road to commitment.

Throughout the entire time of my growing involvement with the Unification Church, I found myself repeatedly put in situations where I was asked to make an even greater commitment to the group before I had fully digested my previous commitments. Yet whenever I contemplated leaving, I was afraid I would lose the spiritual gains I had already made. It was like a poker game: unsure of the merits of my hand but afraid to give up completely, I was repeatedly pressured to "raise or fold", and would always hesitantly decide to raise the stakes again.

A letter I wrote around this time gives some insight into my divided state of my mind. The letter is undated, but it could only have been written in mid-October, 1976, because of what it contains. The letter was addressed to all the residents of the communal house where I had once lived:

"Dear Asylum ½,

I hate to admit it, but I'm sure I alarmed you a bit with my mysterious disappearance. Permit me to explicate.

A few weeks ago I dropped a note saying that I was being "detained" on a ranch in Boonville, California. I said that mostly because I was depressed at the time and felt like I was being penned in, although of course in reality I was free to go whenever I wished. Well, my opinion changed and I stayed on at the ranch and decided to join the community. The change came because I was still caught up in all my old plans and so I found it difficult at first to accept that maybe I really had stumbled onto something worthwhile. But finally I had to admit that I had, because the people here are so sincere and generous to each other that I could see that this was my chance to grow my heart so that I could learn to be open and loving to anybody I encountered, the way they are.

The other reason why I decided to stay on is because the philosophy behind this place makes such a lot of sense. Basically, it is this: If everyone could learn to take responsibility for the whole world instead of just themselves, things would be a lot different. Impossible though it sounds, it is after all better to at least try than to do nothing and complain about it. "It is better to light one candle than to curse the darkness", as Confucius remarked 4,000 years ago.

I expect that I'll be coming through Vancouver briefly in mid-November, so I'll see you all then. I'm sorry that I've had so little time to write, but I'm very busy, and I'd sure appreciate a note from you on what you are doing and who is living there now. How are you, Jan and John? How's the bus?

About the wine—it's a shame that I have left it like this but there may still be a chance to save it. Read up in the wine book and if you wish to expend the effort, you can rack it off into 5 sterile one gallon jars or the equivalent. Otherwise, just dump it out. Sorry about that.

Looking forward to hearing from you and seeing you,
Love, Gordon."

In the earlier portion of the letter, my language is stilted and full of phrases I had picked up at Boonville such as "grow my heart" (an expression that I once would have found nauseating) and I even included a quotation from Confucius, lifted directly from the closing talks at Boonville. The second half of the letter is much more casual in tone, and even discusses my abandoned home-made wine. The second three paragraphs are so markedly different from the first three that it is as if two different people wrote this letter, each in turn.

In fact, two different people *did* write that letter. The whole point of a mind control program (such as the one I had been through at the Boonville farm) is to superimpose a new identity over top of the old one. While the original identity is derided as "selfish", the new identity is reinforced through peer pressure. Eventually, the new identity takes complete charge and becomes more natural; but during the early stages, the original self shows through occasionally, while the cultic self may seem wooden and forced.

Besides the marked change in tone, the letter also contains a reference to my plans to visit Vancouver on my way back to Calgary. The fact that I still thought I might be allowed to go home shows that I had not yet understood that the Oakland Family had no intention of letting me go anywhere but a place of their own choosing. They never actually told me that I could not practice the Divine Principle on my own; they simply told me that I was "not ready" to do this yet. I imagined that in another month or two, I would be ready, and then they *would* let me go back home. And they certainly were not about to tell me that they intended to get me caught up in activities so intense and indefinite they would *never* be finished.

During my third full week as an active member, I finally found a guest who would go with me up to Boonville. I was delighted at this chance to try to convert a "heavenly kid". He was not a promising convert, however. A taciturn man from Maryland with long, curly hair and wire-frame glasses, he had been on the road for some time and was not particularly interested in religion or ethical issues. He viewed the proceedings at Boonville with amused detachment. I managed to persuade him to stay on for the full week program, but after that he made it clear he wanted to go, and the church leaders did not try very hard to keep him.

I recall one event in particular from that week. On the final Friday before he left Boonville, my guest satirized the song, "Brother Sun, Sister Moon" (which was in the Boonville song book) by crooning, "Brother Sun, Reverend Moon". This gave me a shock, because he was not supposed to even know about Father yet! No-one had mentioned Sun Myung Moon to any of the new guests; this was reserved for the Advanced workshop, when they were supposed to be "ready" to hear about him. By singing those lyrics, he implied that he knew who his hosts really were. Oh no! Our cover was blown! However, the problem quickly ended, since my guest made no other comments about Father. I suspect he did this just to see the expression on my face.

On my return to San Francisco, the church leaders decided that since I had had the opportunity to care for a guest and to be re-immersed in Divine Principle, I was ready for the next step: Washington Street house. After a cheery "graduation" ceremony, I was sent on to the more demanding lifestyle of a regular center, including not only an earlier rising time but a number of other rituals I had not previously seen.

The strangest of these was probably the "chanting condition", which took place soon after the entire house was awakened at 5:00 a.m. We were given a scant twenty minutes to roll up our sleeping bags, greet God, and take a shower (if the facilities were available—which they usually weren't, so I did this late at night) and then we were expected to be downstairs in good clothing for a chanting session, a sort of incantation calling upon God to do certain things. This practice was unique to the Oakland Family; its main purpose seemed to be to get everyone's mind focused right away on the goals of the Unification Church. All the members would form a circle, with the brothers on one side of the room and the sisters on the other, and we were led through a series of chants, all beginning with the phrase, "Glory to Heaven and Peace on Earth," followed by some other supplication, such as "Victory to True Parents" or "All guests move in" or "Restore the Material Foundation"—a reference to the idea that the success of the fund-raising teams "restored" the material world to its rightful owner. We spoke the chants out loud, in unison, while forming our hands into fists and pumping them up and down in time with the words, as if this would add extra force to the chant. The whole ritual lasted about twenty minutes, and although it seemed almost surreal to me, it was not unpleasant. We were encouraged to continue chanting silently in our own minds as we went about our activities.

On Sundays, another remarkable ritual took place, which is practiced everywhere in the Unification Church. We were awakened at 4:30 a.m., and were required to assemble at five o'clock for "Pledge Service". A large room was prepared for this, meticulously cleaned and brightly lit. At the front of the room, a low table covered with white cloth featured a large picture of Reverend and Mrs. Moon, flanked by a floral arrangement or other decoration. The brothers assembled on the left side of the room, facing the picture, while the sisters stood to their right. When the leader of the ceremony announced that it was time to begin, we all got down on our knees and performed a full, formal bow before the picture of True Parents, pressing our foreheads into the backs of our hands, which were crossed and placed on the floor in front of us. The first time I performed this ceremony, I had been given no forewarning about its contents, so I merely followed the example of everyone else. I therefore awkwardly bowed to the picture three times, following the lead of everyone around me. Then we all stood up again and began to read aloud the words to "My Pledge". Small white cards had been handed out to everyone so they could read the words of this extraordinary oath of loyalty. I still have a "Pledge card" in my possession, and these are the exact words printed on it:

1.   As the center of the cosmos, I will fulfill our Father's will [purpose of Creation] and the responsibility give me [for self-perfection]. I will become a dutiful son, and a child of goodness to attend our Father forever in the ideal world of Creation [by] returning joy and glory to Him. This I pledge.

2.   I will take upon myself completely the Will of God to give me the whole Creation as my inheritance. He has given me His Word, His personality, and His heart, and is reviving me who had died, making me one with Him and His true child. To do this, our Father has persevered for 6,000 years the sacrificial way of the cross. This I pledge.

3.   As a true son [or daughter], I will follow our Father's pattern and charge bravely forward into the enemy camp until I have judged them completely with the weapons with which He has been defeating the enemy Satan for me throughout the course of history by sowing sweat for earth, tears for man, and blood for heaven, as a servant but with a father's heart, in order to restore His children and the universe, lost to Satan. This I pledge.

4.   The individual, family, society, nation, world and cosmos who are willing to attend our Father, the source of peace, happiness, freedom, and all ideals, will fulfill the ideal world of one heart in one body by restoring their original nature. To do this, I will become a true son, returning joy and satisfaction to our Father, and as our Father's representative, I will transfer to the Creation peace,

happiness, freedom, and all ideals in the world of the heart. This I pledge.

5.   I am proud of the one Sovereignty, proud of the one people, proud of the one land, proud of the one language and culture centered upon God, proud of becoming the child of the One True Parent, proud of the family who is to inherit one tradition, proud of being a laborer who is working to establish the one world of the heart.

I will fight with my life.

I will be responsible for accomplishing my duty and mission.

This I pledge and swear.
This I pledge and swear.
This I pledge and swear.

The first time I saw these words, I was so taken aback by their desperate intensity that I refused to say them. Instead, I fell silent, and let the others carry on without me. I had agreed to "try out" their lifestyle, but this? This was a pledge of my very life, and I had better mean it if I was going to say it. Once again, I began to wonder what I had gotten myself into, and considered getting out. But once again, as more normal activities followed, I put aside these concerns, thinking perhaps I just didn't understand yet. By the second or third time I attended Pledge Service, I, too, read out the words of "My Pledge".

The main focus of the Washington Street house was on witnessing, but in a more determined way than at the Ashby Street house. The witnessing pairs were sent out by mid-morning; and should they find no guest for dinner, they were frequently sent out in the evening as well. Sometimes, too, there was a call for volunteers for the fund-raising teams (often called "M.F.T." for short, meaning "mobile fundraising teams"). Being a Canadian, I was never asked to join these teams because there was a risk that my foreign citizenship would be found out if I went fund-raising, which was an aggressive activity that involved entering offices, stores and restaurants. For my part, I was relieved to be barred from fund-raising, since I had heard that it was a difficult and demanding activity, in which members were required to sell flowers and candy from early morning to late at night.

Witnessers from Washington Street house often patrolled the full length of Market Street (the road that bisects the heart of San Francisco) as well as all the usual tourist areas. Yet no matter where I went, I relied on my witnessing partner to start conversations, while I acted in a supporting role. On a couple of occasions I was paired up with Mary-Jane, but on one of those days I exasperated her by expressing doubt that there had been an actual Adam and Eve. Later that day we bumped into Isaiah, who was also out witnessing, and Mary-Jane gestured wordlessly at me as if to say, "Would you get a load of this guy?" "What's the problem?" Isaiah demanded. "Adam and Eve!" she answered, rolling her eyes. He looked at me in a way that made me laugh and scolded, "Gordon: you're a case!"

This incident shows that I had still not fully settled into my superimposed identity; this was one of the days when my original identity—rational and skeptical—was reasserting itself. It was now mid-November, 1976, some two months after my Boonville immersion, and yet my original personality still occasionally resurfaced—but it was now much more subdued, as this letter dated November 11, suggests:

Dear Asylum ½,

Hi! I'm still here but my address has changed. Please re-address any mail you may have to this address. I will only be going home for Christmas for a short while so I unfortunately won't be passing through Vancouver in all probability, alas! I hope I didn't leave anything much of value behind. Please drop a card letting me know what's happening at the house and who's living there, also any salacious gossip or whatever you find uplifting and creative.

Life in the Creative Community Project is hectic but great! Having so many open-hearted, helpful people has really improved my whole outlook on life and self-image. I am learning to relate well to people even on the street when I invite people home to dinner—They are less responsive and more suspicious, but deep down inside, they're so glad that for once someone broke the needless silence and actually spoke to them! I hope that one day everyone in the world can relate like this—Hope to hear from you, Love, Gordon."

I vaguely recall writing this letter (I had a rare opportunity to write letters because I'd found no guest, and had not been sent back out witnessing), and I remember that the request for "salacious gossip" was a deliberate attempt on my part to seem like my old self, in order to counter the claims of "brainwashing" in the press—but I was immediately ashamed of this request, so I tried to make up for it by asking instead for "whatever you find uplifting and creative". Again, I hinted that I would be going back to Canada, but this time just for Christmas, and just for a "short while". I still seemed to think I would be allowed to visit my parents in Calgary briefly at Christmas—since they expected this—even though the leaders of the Oakland Family had never given any indication that they would consider it. Later, they talked me out of it, so I told my parents that I had decided to remain in San Francisco over Christmas to "hold down the fort" while other members visited their families. This was practically a lie; I knew of no-one who was planning to go home for Christmas, but I imagined that there would be a few.

Soon after I wrote that letter, I had the opportunity to return to Boonville, this time in the company of two young men from Montreal that I encountered on Market Street. As usual, I singled them out because they were wearing backpacks, and though they agreed to attend the workshop in Boonville, it was obvious from the start that one of them was more receptive than the other. The church leaders devised a strategy to separate the two, and to keep them from communicating with each other throughout the workshop. They were assigned to different groups, and each had a different "shadow". I was assigned to the less receptive man, though I still prayed that he would be converted. We were able to persuade them to stay for the full week, but toward the end of that week, the two of them got together for an unauthorized session of "sharing negativity" late at night, while everyone else was asleep. When I woke up the next morning, I found that both guests had suddenly vanished; this was quietly explained to me by a more experienced member. It seems that the two had been discovered by a Boonville staff member while they were discussing their doubts, and they were immediately told to collect their things and leave. A brother was assigned to drive them a few miles from Boonville and deposit them on the side of the road with instructions to hitch-hike back to the city. Though surprised, I quickly accepted the sudden change.

No sooner did I return to San Francisco than I learned that True Father himself would soon be giving a speech in Los Angeles to the members, and all Oakland Family members who had never seen him before were instructed to attend. At last I was going to meet the living Messiah! I was excited, but I was warned in a preparatory meeting that the other Family members might not understand some of the customs of the Oakland Family, so we were asked to refrain from certain practices. In particular, we should avoid group hand-holding—especially between the sexes—and to minimize the number of boisterous shoutings of "choo-choo-choo, yay, yay, pow!", even though it had become a habit for us to say this (while pumping each other's hands up and down) before—and after—every meeting. This was my first hint of the schism between the Oakland Family and the rest of the Unification Church.

We drove all night in a bus down to Los Angeles, and then up to a fine Spanish-style mansion perched on a hill in Pasadena, overlooking the Rose Bowl. This was Father's western headquarters, where he often stayed when he was on the way to or from the Orient. It was a two-storey mansion, including a swimming pool and a fine garden. Here we met the other Family members, who were friendly but seemed much more formal and correct than we "Oakies" were. We took it in stride, and resolved to "love-bomb" the Los Angeles brothers and sisters, whom we won over rather easily. Eventually, everyone assembled in the main room to hear True Father speak.

The main room was painted white and had two honorific scrolls with Chinese lettering running down the front wall. True Father strolled around the front of the room, a portly Korean man who spoke in an animated way, sometimes joking and gesturing vigorously with his hands. He spoke in Korean, but was translated into English by an interpreter who struggled to keep up with him. True Father's speech lasted more than two hours, but the only thing I remember clearly was that he predicted the future would be a harrowing and dangerous time, and that the only way to make it safely through this time was to stick with him. He compared himself to a parent carrying a child in a pouch on his back through tiger country; we knew he meant that we were each of us his child, and the threatening "tiger" was communism, which we expected would gain even greater power before True Father vanquished it.

After the main part of his speech, True Father spoke directly to some Japanese members at the front of the room, who were now returning to their native country. This part of his talk was not translated, so I just sat quietly until the speech ended. The speech's end was signaled by a custom that was unfamiliar to me, but which later became routine—the shouting of "Aboji, mansei!" (Korean for "Father, eternal victory!") three times.

For my first encounter with the "living Messiah", it had been something of a let-down. I was really too distracted by the sudden change of surroundings, and too tired from a semi-sleepless night on the bus, to be overawed by Moon's physical presence. In fact, I found nothing extraordinary about his personal charisma that would make me feel he was obviously the Messiah. Still, my expectations had been so built up by the other Family members that I continued to believe I had been in the presence of the living Christ, whose every word was spiritual gold. I returned to San Francisco convinced that I had been blessed merely by having been in the same room with him.

By this time, though I still seemed to think I might be allowed to go home before too long, I was acting in every respect as if I was a fully committed member. The Oakland Family certainly saw me as such, though I had not yet understood this fact myself, and they were prepared to let me take my time to realize it. My thoughts were now completely different from those I had brought with me from Canada only a few months previously. I had abandoned my writing career, assuming that I would go back to it eventually "after the coming of the Kingdom of Heaven on Earth." I now believed that my quest to resolve the "knife inside me" through Primal Therapy had been wrong-headed; God had only caused me to get interested in those ideas so he could lure me south where I would discover the "real" answer. To be fair, life in the Family really did offer me a temporary respite from my emotional problems. To my feelings of worthlessness, I now had a belief system that claimed that I was extremely worthy, provided I followed the new Messiah, and did everything he demanded to the best of my abilities. To my feelings of alienation, I now had a large group of brothers and sisters who, though I rarely had time to get to know them deeply, were infallibly cheerful and supportive, even though we all talked the same way and shared a certain sameness of personality through our cult identity. And to my feelings of depression, I now had a lifestyle so relentless that there was simply no time to stop and think about things that might cause me to become depressed—and in any case, I would be sharply exhorted if I let my thoughts stray down this path.

Throughout November and December I continued to witness from the Washington Street house, always hoping to find a "spiritual child". Onni instructed the witnesses to be as brief as possible; we were to offer the dinner invitation quickly before hurrying away. One reason for this was simply that she wanted to get as many new recruits as possible. The other reason was that by hurrying away, we would avoid getting into lengthy discussions, which always ended with the potential recruit deciding not to go. If I was asked directly whether I was a "Moonie", I would dodge the question as much as possible, claiming instead to be part of the "Creative Community Project"; and I would only concede reluctantly, if pressed, that we "studied the ideas of" Reverend Moon along with those of other luminaries. This deceptive practice was considered to be a necessary response to the deceptions of Satan. Biblical authority for this was found in *Genesis* 25 to 30, where Jacob engages in a number of deceptions to gain the inheritance that would normally have gone to his brother Esau. This practice of deceiving others in order to carry out God's will was known in the Oakland Family as "heavenly deception". By late 1976, this term had become notorious in the press, so we were discouraged from using the actual words, but not from practicing it.

Although we never had time to read newspapers or watch television newscasts, Family members were extremely bitter about the many negative news reports concerning the Unification Church. We felt that Satan was manipulating the news media in order to turn people against Father, and that if parents hired deprogrammers to get their sons and daughters out of the Family, it was because their minds had been poisoned by the "lies" published in the newspapers. In one of the special Family meetings that was called to discuss deprogramming, we were told that to leave the Family was more terrible than death, and it was recommended that members who are seized by deprogrammers slash their wrists or otherwise injure themselves in order to be taken to hospital, where Family members could "rescue" them.

Around the start of December a particularly stunning deprogramming occurred to two senior members of the Oakland Family. Yacov, a trusted fund-raising team captain, and Evey, a frequent group leader at Boonville, were taken by deprogrammers to a house in Arizona known as the Freedom of Thought Foundation, where they were persuaded to quit the Unification Church. A typical deprogramming involves giving a cult member a lot of information about the group that he or she had not previously known; this is not easily done since in this situation a cult member normally withdraws into a shell of chanting and meditation for the first few days. Eventually, when it becomes clear that fears of torture or rape are inaccurate, the cult member may open up to the information his or her family, friends and the deprogrammers are trying to provide. That is what happened to Yacov and Evey.

Since I was in Boonville at the time, I was unaware of the shock and dismay that their defection had caused the Oakland Family until I returned to the city. Soon after my return, members of the Oakland Family were called to a meeting at the Hearst Street house in Berkeley. It was a large gathering, packed to the walls in the main meeting room, with Onni and her husband presiding. As usual, the evening began with many songs, and some musical performances, and it quickly became clear that this was an important occasion when bowls of ice cream were passed around. We were in high spirits, yet we sensed the seriousness of the meeting, though most of the newer members like myself did not know what had prompted it. The answer came when Onni called upon Jenny to describe her spying mission, in which she and a team of other members had tracked down the place where Yacov and Evey had been taken for their deprogramming. The spy team had hidden in the bushes outside the Freedom of Thought Foundation, watching every move of the people who came and went from that house. Jenny reported—with infinite disdain—that she smelled marijuana smoke when a couple of the people from the house had walked near her hiding place; her disgust caused us all to conclude that the deprogrammers were indeed people of "low standard", completely "invaded by Satan". I don't remember whether Jenny or anyone else actually managed to speak to Yacov and Evey; in any case, their attempt to get them back didn't work. Yacov and Evey were now "spiritually dead" according to the Divine Principle—a stunning loss for the Oakland Family.

Following the failure of these efforts, Onni herself went to Arizona to try to retrieve the two former members, but only succeeded in creating a scene outside the house until the police came and briefly detained her. This was considered a shocking event—that a person so vital to God's Providence could actually be detained by the Satanic police!

After Jenny's report, Onni began her talk. She talked, as always, of the absolute seriousness of maintaining loyalty to True Father and to the Divine Principle. Yacov's and Evey's departure was viewed by Onni as a personal rebuke—a blow by Satan aimed at her personally. She was desperate to understand how it could have happened, and she seemed to be grasping at straws. Perhaps she hoped that by treating all the members to ice cream and an evening of song, we would be reaffirmed in our commitment to the Oakland Family. Onni ended the evening with a passionate plea for all members to be determined "not to become betrayers!"

Like everyone who attended the meeting, I became even more fearful of deprogramming, yet I knew that my own family in Calgary was unlikely to take this step. The Unification Church was then little known in Canada, so by writing to my family with reassurances, I hoped to preempt the negative publicity that was surely coming. Also, my parents had always respected the sometimes odd choices made by their children, so I thought they would likely respect this choice also. Years later, my mother told me that when negative publicity about the San Francisco church first appeared in Calgary newspapers in 1978, she almost had a nervous breakdown. Yet in the end, my parents resolved to accept my seeming choice, and they took no overt action against me at any time during my ten-year involvement.

Christmas Day found me witnessing down on Fisherman's Wharf as usual. Initially, we were told that Christmas was not going to be treated as a special day, because Father had taken over the mission of Jesus, and therefore Jesus' birth was no longer as significant as it had been in the "New Testament" era. Then, in a surprise move, a van came around to pick us up so that we could be taken to a celebration at Boonville. Someone speculated that Onni had decided to give us a treat after all, perhaps to lift our morale (and to ensure our loyalty) but I remember little about it except that it was a happy, cheerful day full of songs and group events.

One week later, I was again at Boonville to celebrate a holiday that is taken much more seriously by the Unification Church—"God's Day", the first day of the year. As was the custom, many treats were handed out and all members were given the day off to talk with each other or play games. There was, however, one big meeting at the start of the day which was presided over by Dr. Durst. Onni was unavailable, since she had gone to New York to meet with Father to plan the church's strategy for 1977. That left "Oppa", the well-liked father-figure of the Oakland Family, to run the show at Boonville. After giving a talk, he opened the meeting to questions. I put my hand up and asked him why I never got to follow the news any more, even though I had once been an avid reader of newspapers. Durst evaded the question by saying that he received the newspapers every day, so if I wanted to see them, all I needed to do was ask. But this was impractical; Onni and Durst lived in their own house apart from the other members, so if I asked to see their papers—even supposing I had time to read them—I would have been considered a troublemaker. Even so, I accepted his answer, because by then I was too committed to pull out just because I didn't read the papers any more.

Onni soon returned from New York, full of Father's new plans. He had decided to start up four new witnessing teams in different regions of America, which were to be called the "International One World Crusade". After evangelizing for a month or two, each team was to move on to other cities in the same region, spreading the word of the Divine Principle throughout America. Each team was expected to achieve "one, one, one"—which meant one new recruit for each existing member per month. Ten Oakland Family members were assigned to each of these teams. Without advance warning, I learned that I had been posted to the western regional team, which would begin its work in Los Angeles under Reverend Reiner Vincenz. Vincenz, a German man who had led similar campaigns, was described to me enthusiastically as "Father's right-hand man!" This turned out to be an exaggeration, but he was certainly well-respected in the Unification Church, and the members assigned to his team were reassured they would be working with a man of great spiritual power.

Immediately, we were separated out from the other Family members and began to work together as a team. The forty reassigned members were dubbed "Pioneers" and were moved to the Ashby Street house to prepare for departure. We even had a team song honoring us as "Pioneers" (a misnomer, since this term is supposed to be used for church members who evangelize new towns). At any rate, I was now considered a "Pioneer" who would shortly be leaving for Los Angeles to work with "Father's right-hand man". Separating us into close-knit teams certainly helped, since we were all apprehensive about the move. While the Oakland Family emphasized mutual support and caring, we knew that the larger Unification Church was less concerned about these matters. Therefore, we were determined to convert the other Family members to what we believed was the higher "Oakland standard", and we imagined that soon we would have them all behaving like Oakies—even shouting "Choo-choo-choo, yay, yay, pow!", so long as we stuck to our principles and "served" them more. This was a brave but naive plan: each contingent of Oakland Family members would amount to ten in a team of fifty.

One thing was for sure: by being reassigned to Los Angeles, I no longer had any illusions I was going back to Canada. The moment I was reassigned, I knew that once again, I had been asked to raise or fold. The only way I could avoid going to the new team would be to leave the Unification Church altogether; and having been told that unimaginably terrible consequences would befall me if I did this, I once again agreed to increase my commitment. In the process, I finally understood that I had become a full-fledged Unification Church member who was prepared to do anything and go anywhere to fulfill the aims of Sun Myung Moon. And though I was apprehensive about the future, I believed that God required this of me, so I resolved to take it on.

The Pioneers had one last meeting with Onni before we got in our Dodge vans and headed off in four separate directions. Onni was clearly worried about us, and about what would happen when we found ourselves in the company of members who didn't have the "Oakland standard" of mutual service and caring. She told us that we could come back to her, and she would always take us back; rather than quitting completely, we should just go back to Onni. I was consoled by this promise, feeling that only the Oakland Family could have "saved me" the way it did.

This superior attitude was a miniature version of the attitude Unificationists have towards the rest of society generally. In many of his speeches, Father told us that we were the most dedicated, sacrificial, virtuous people on Earth. We desperately wanted to believe him on this point. The result was a feeling of condescension toward "ordinary Christians", who we saw as not having as high a "standard", nor as complete a Truth. By allowing Oakland Family members to develop a similar condescension toward the rest of the Unification Church, Onni had turned the Oakland Family into a cult within a cult. Her leadership style showed that she was following Father only too well—right down to creating a personality cult around herself that rivaled, in the minds of Oakland Family members, the one surrounding Father.

All the Oakland Family members were in awe of Onni; though we were afraid of her prickly nature, we believed that she was a spiritual giant, capable of defeating Satan in cosmic warfare. During my final meeting with her, Onni spoke from a chair, while we sat before her, cross-legged on the floor, as was customary for such meetings. Though she was capable of lashing out suddenly with great heat—for example when she berated Stepan—she was now subdued, and simply worried about our ability to stay loyal during the trials ahead. I suspect she was still smarting from the loss of Yacov and Evey; in any case, I saw her apprehension as a motherly concern for the members. On that occasion, I viewed this formidable woman as, simply, my loving "Omma". Omma, I thought, was my ace-in-the-hole if things became too difficult elsewhere. She was my angel of harsh reproach and strict correction; she was my enchantress whose prayers kept "Satanic" thoughts from my mind. She was—in short—my heavenly deceiver.

End of Part One.

PART TWO:

JUSTIFICATION BY WORKS

CHAPTER FIVE

ONE WORLD CRUSADE

On January 9, 1977, after a full day of driving, the 10 member contingent from the Oakland Family arrived at a set of dingy cottages near the eastern edge of Los Angeles on Huntington Drive, at the point where it divides into two roads leading either to Alhambra or South Pasadena. This inauspicious-looking Unification Church "center" even had a large wooden sign facing the road with no lettering on it. The center looked as if it had once been a motel before the church acquired the property. It was now the home base for the Los Angeles Family fund-raising teams. As soon as we arrived, the fund-raising team moved out, and for about a day we had the place to ourselves, until the ten Los Angeles Family members who had also been assigned to the International One World Crusade joined us. The rest of the team—including our "central figure", Reiner Vincenz—were not expected for several days. Without a central figure to command us, we weren't really allowed to do anything except clean up the center, which certainly needed it. The cottages had taken on the damp, musty odor of casual neglect which is one of the hallmarks of Los Angeles. This was noted with quiet disapproval by the "Oakies", since we were accustomed to the well-maintained mansions of Berkeley and San Francisco. Together with the L.A. Family members, we set about the task of scrubbing and scouring the place, while singing silly Boonville songs (complete with hand gestures) until, by the end of the week, the Huntington Drive center was as gleaming and spotless as an aging motel could hope to be. Since there were as many of us Oakies as there were of them, we had little problem "love-bombing" the L.A. Family members until they—at first grudgingly, but later happily—joined in our silly songs and foolish customs, such as the obligatory "choo-choo-pow!" Yet though our infectious cheerfulness was easily transferable to an equal number of members from the "rest of the Family", our biggest challenge still remained. Could we convert the entire I.O.W.C. team to the "Oakland standard"? At any rate, we were determined to try. About a week after our own arrival, the rest of the I.O.W.C. team, including our much-vaunted "central figure", finally descended on the Huntington Drive center in a flurry of Dodge vans. It was a shock.

In Oakland I had been warned about the entirely different emphasis and feel of the Unification Church outside the Bay Area. Actually experiencing it, however, was disconcerting. Theirs was a culture of "desperation" and "determination"; a culture of relentless individual effort; of fervent prayers and drastic spiritual conditions to bring results. To them, success depended entirely on achieving a "connection" to God through prayer which, if attained, would be like plugging into an electrical socket. Instantly, one's charisma and power would be turned on, and consequently thousands of people (almost without knowing what they were doing) would flock to hear lectures of the Divine Principle, or would donate money to the cause. There was little mention of mutual support between members, unlike the Oakland Family, where this was considered the first duty. The thirty members who arrived that evening struck me as a wretchedly lonely lot, each individually "determined" to achieve Father's will, yet fretful and frustrated in their determination, doubting themselves and unable to support each other in their doubt. As the newly-arrived members assembled in the common area to bolt down their evening meal, Karen, the "team mother" of the Oakland Family contingent, turned to me and whispered, "I can't believe how little they've been given!"

I was particularly struck by a young man from New York named Simon, whom I later befriended and found to be a warm and sensitive man. Simon had a large hooked nose coupled with a slender, bony appearance and a mournful expression he was likely born with; in fact, his slightly odd appearance was the probable reason he was sent away from New York in the first place. Many of the thirty were perceived as "problem" members who had been reassigned to the I.O.W.C. team because somebody wanted to get rid of them. As well, there were quite a few Europeans and Japanese who had taken refuge on the team to avoid deportation because they had overstayed their visas. The ten Japanese members on the team had come to the United States to assist the campaign leading up to Father's speech at Washington Monument on September 18, 1976; but instead of being sent home after the campaign ended, they were reassigned to fund-raising teams and later the I.O.W.C. Few of them spoke English well, though they were all willing and cheerful workers.

This was not the case for a few of the other members. One brother from Idaho insisted on reading adventure novels in his sleeping bag after bed-time. I thought this an impossibly rebellious act: we were expected to devote all our reading time to studying the Divine Principle or Father's speeches, so how dare he read anything else? Worse still, this brother refused to get up for the normal 6:30 a.m. wake-up call, even when he was unceremoniously deposited—sleeping bag and all—on the driveway.

Now that we were outnumbered four to one, the Oakland members knew there was little chance of persuading the entire team to join hands and shout "choo-choo-pow!" Even so, we set about being friendly to them and getting them to tell us their personal stories, and this undoubtedly charmed them and helped to break the ice. But as for turning them all into Oakies, this would have been possible only if Reverend Vincenz himself had come from the Oakland Family; but in fact he was a German who had little use for the Oakland methods. He distrusted Onni and seemed to imply that the Oakland Family was "too horizontal", because it placed too much emphasis on relationships between people, and didn't focus enough on a relationship with

God. As far as Vincenz was concerned, the ten Oakland members represented a disunited faction on the team, as for that matter also were the Los Angeles and Japanese members to a lesser degree, so a way had to be found to blend the team into a homogenous whole. To do this, he resorted to a familiar strategy: he arranged for everyone to go to Camp Mozumdar—the L.A. Family's equivalent of Boonville—to hear yet another round of lectures of the Divine Principle.

In the Unification Church, whenever a member becomes troubled in any way, the solution is always to send that person back to the starting point—to a training session at a church camp. This is viewed as a purgative act that will somehow magically solve the problem. Reverend Vincenz hoped that by sending us to Camp Mozumdar to hear the Divine Principle together, we would, in the course of two days, be completely united, healed and restored.

Soon after, the team left for the camp, which is located in the San Bernardino mountains at the top of a long, twisting road that leads to a magnificent setting overlooking Silverwood Lake and the Mojave desert. The camp was named after an Indian man who once dreamed of creating a place where people of all spiritual traditions could worship together. To support this vision, he had built a stone temple that looks like a miniature Taj Mahal, along with an open air arena encircled by thirteen stone pillars representing Christ and the twelve disciples. Eventually, the camp was taken over by the Y.M.C.A., who used it for many years (or so I was told) until it was acquired by the Unification Church in 1974. We felt that Mozumdar's original vision was being fulfilled by our presence there, since Divine Principle teaches that all the world's religions will eventually unite around the new Messiah.

The workshop, of course, taught me little that was new, and my strongest memory from those two days were the closing prayers, which were led by Reverend Vincenz' assistant, Peter—a young, energetic, cherubic-looking man who had taught many of the lectures. He offered the representative prayer, which was followed by unison prayer, where everyone in the room prayed aloud at once, in a kind of cacophony of pleas and pledges to God. (Many members seemed to believe that if they prayed more loudly or used more forceful hand gestures, it would intensify their prayers). In the representative prayer, Peter prayed that the I.O.W.C. team members would find the many thousands of "prepared people" that God had made ready to "receive the True Parents". He reminded us that God had prepared many thousands of Americans whose hearts were lonely and despairing, and who were just waiting to receive the word of the new Messiah with gladness, if only we approached them in the right way. Indeed, we had been assured that in a few years' time there would be so many Americans demanding to hear Divine Principle that we would have to set up long waiting lists. Certainly by 1981— which was always cited as the turning point—the entire United States of America would give itself over to Father.

Nevertheless, this all depended on our ability to convert at least 30,000 full-time members in the United States to the Unification Church before the end of 1978. If we won America, all the rest of the world would follow soon afterwards, and the Kingdom of Heaven on Earth could quickly be established. Nor would it be difficult to win America: God had prepared thousands of people—in fact (as Peter mentioned in his prayer) three times as many as were needed to fulfill the heavenly quota—so the I.O.W.C. should have no trouble in quickly doubling and redoubling its membership in Los Angeles, before moving on to other cities in the western United States to duplicate the miracle in those cities. The other three I.O.W.C. teams in Texas, New England and the Midwest, would do likewise in their regions. After Peter finished his prayer— a bold pledge to God that we would perform these miracles as He demanded— all the room fell into individual prayers, as each person punched the air and shouted out loud, while screwing his or her face into a mask of fervent "desperation" and "determination", each vowing to achieve these impossible goals.

Of course, we could not allow ourselves to think of our goals as impossible; yet the desperation of our prayers likely had something to do with the fact that we were required to believe in them despite all reason. We were a rag-tag crew of fifty Europeans, Americans and Japanese (and one Canadian), flung together suddenly by Father and handed the mission to overturn a city of many millions with a religious revival that would shake both the barrios of Highland Park and the mansions of Beverly Hills—and we were to do this in three months or less, based solely on prayer and "determination". Like the others, I prayed blindly and resolutely, refusing to believe it was impossible.

When the I.O.W.C. got back to the city, we were organized into witnessing and fund-raising teams. I was assigned to a witnessing team that, for the first few weeks, traveled every day to Hancock Park on Wilshire Boulevard (miles from the I.O.W.C. center) where we attempted to convince people to come to the center for the evening program. Here, for the first time, I encountered the infuriatingly nonchalant attitude of Angelenos toward all manner of religious fanatics. Unlike San Franciscans, who would often question you closely and then dismiss you abruptly if you admitted any connection to Sun Myung Moon, Angelenos were not particularly disturbed to learn that they had been approached by a "Moonie". But they were also not all that motivated to investigate, either; indeed, it was hard to find anything they were particularly motivated to do, especially if it required traveling miles across town for some vaguely-described dinner. In contrast to my own deep desperation, this indifference was infuriating. It seemed to me that Angelenos viewed life as nothing more than a succession of hazily sunny days—bland and insipid—neither urgent nor forlorn.

This, then, was how the month of January ended: no new recruits had been found, despite all our pledges to God. Reiner Vincenz, after returning from his regular monthly meeting with Father in New York, brought the I.O.W.C. to a forest park so we could pray with deep repentance for our failure, and promise to God that we would "restore" our failure in the month of February. Since God had expected us to double our numbers in January (even though we had started in the middle of the month), now we would have to *quadruple* our numbers to meet our heavenly quota for the month of February.

Without hesitation we all prayed with conviction, shouting out loud and assailing the air, that we would do that very thing. Since Father said it was possible, it must be so.

Soon after this, Father had the idea that since people weren't coming to the centers to hear the Divine Principle, the Divine Principle should be brought to the people. A multitude of portable cassette players were purchased, and cassette tapes of the entire Divine Principle lecture series were prepared, and these were all delivered by express courier to the four I.O.W.C. teams, and to many other American centers as well. Everyone on the team was issued one of these cassette players, along with a complete set of Divine Principle tapes to spring on willing passers-by. That initiative lasted maybe two weeks altogether. My team had now moved to the beach town of Santa Monica (which was even further from the I.O.W.C. center), where we hoped to meet tourists who might have time to attend a lecture. I remember persuading only one Christian man and his son to listen to one of Moon's new tapes for perhaps ten minutes altogether, while sitting on the front lawn of the Santa Monica post office. That was the extent of my success with the Messiah's latest brainstorm. Soon afterwards, the portable cassette players were retired for good.

Late in February, a trailer was rented to serve as a mobile lecture hall. The trailer was of the simple box-like type often used as a temporary office on construction sites, but in this case it was intended to be a sort of portable conversion chamber. People were to be persuaded to come into the trailer, hear the introductory lecture to Divine Principle, and presto! they would be so transported by the profound Truths they had heard that they would go to Camp Mozumdar to hear the entire series. That, at least, was the theory. Throughout February and March, the trailer was parked in various locations in central Los Angeles and Santa Monica. For an entire week in late February, we parked the trailer on a street across from Santa Monica College. On the very first day of this campaign, before we were even allowed to enter the campus to begin witnessing, Reverend Vincenz ordered the entire team to silently walk the streets surrounding the college in a circle seven times. He compared this tactic to the one employed by the Israelites under Joshua when they stormed the walls of Jericho.

That was typical of how we thought; we were always trying to bring God's help by carrying out "conditions" of this sort. More experienced members would fast for up to seven days, and all the team members tried "cold shower conditions" which were offerings to God during which we stood under a blast of cold water in the shower stall for several minutes. On another occasion, the team began a prayer chain, which meant that some of the team members were expected to be praying at all hours of the day and night, even if it meant rising after only one hour of sleep. One bright spring day I was discovered by an amused security guard as I knelt beside a window on the unoccupied fortieth floor of the United California Bank building, imploring God to help me save Los Angeles.

Still, for all our prayers, cold showers and fasts, the results were distressingly meager. By the end of February we had found only one recruit, a cheerful young woman named Vivian who—being an American, and therefore legally able to do this—was immediately placed on the fund-raising team after she had finished her stint at Camp Mozumdar. Now we *really* needed to repent.

In the Unification Church, any failure to achieve a goal set by the leaders is never seen as the fault of the leaders. Failure can only be due to the laziness or faithlessness of the followers. As we offered our prayers of repentance and redetermination at the start of March, the I.O.W.C. team was faced with the obligation to *octuple* its numbers before the end of the month, in order to stay on the timetable that God and Father demanded. Not only that; each time we failed, we believed there was an additional spiritual price to pay (a "greater condition of indemnity") before any additional success could be gained. So at the start of March, awash in earnest desperation, I pledged to God that I would do my part, and find seven new recruits for Father. In fact, I told my team leader (following the example of Onni Durst, who once vowed to bring all 30,000 members that Father wanted through the Bay Area alone) that I would try to bring all the new recruits for the entire team *by myself*. (Fortunately, my team leader discouraged me from making such a rash promise).

The blame for the failure of the I.O.W.C. teams was also attributed to the general sinfulness of America as a nation. In many of his speeches to members, Father depicted America as a nation on its last legs, ready to be overwhelmed by Communism and moral decadence. Only the Unification Church could save America, Father claimed. In his speech at Washington Monument in 1976, Father praised America as the hope of the world and a bastion of freedom; but in his private speeches to members, he often condemned America for the consequences of that freedom, particularly individualism. He liked to hold up the Japanese members as exemplars for the rest of us, mainly because they were more reflexive in their obedience to his authority; hearing this, many American members tried to imitate the Japanese. My team leader, an American, began to speak with a trace of a Japanese accent (probably unconsciously), and since I was expected to "unite with my central figure", I began to do so also.

When word came in late March that five American Unification Church members in the Bay Area—four sisters and one brother—were battling a court application by their parents for a conservatorship order, this was interpreted by church members as a fight for the soul of America itself. All the I.O.W.C. team began to pray fervently that the conservatorship orders would be denied, and that the parents of these members, who had obviously been "invaded by Satan", would be prevented from stealing their adult children away from True Father. We were all confident that the application would be denied; so it was a terrible shock when, on March 24, Judge S. Lee Vavuris went ahead and granted the conservatorships, effectively placing the "Oakland Faithful Five" in the hands of their parents.

Instantly our team redoubled its prayers, increasing the intensity of the prayer chain as we prayed that the Faithful Five would withstand the horrible assaults of Satan and remain loyal to Father. We prayed that they would shut out all negative influences, and lock themselves safely away in a cocoon of chanting and prayer, inaccessible to the lies of any deprogrammers. It was with even greater dismay, then, that around March 29 we learned that all but one of the "Faithful Five" had quit the Unification Church, the only hold-out being the brother.

In private discussions among the members, this was interpreted in a number of ways. The fact that this had happened to Oakland Family members was seen as proving that Onni's methods, being more "horizontal" and not as "Truth-based", could not produce truly faithful Family members. Furthermore, the fact that only the sisters had defected, while the brother had remained loyal, was often seen as a sign that women were less faithful or "God-centered" than men. Finally, the fact that it had happened to American members was taken as a further indication that Americans were an unreliable, individualistic people. Not only that; but the faithlessness of these four meant that we on the I.O.W.C. teams would now have to work even harder to restore God's confidence in America. Perhaps, in fact, it was actually all our fault in the first place; perhaps we had simply not prayed hard enough, or felt sufficient "desperation".

Given my lifelong struggle to justify my existence, I am especially prone to this sort of thinking. The harder I worked and the more successful I was for Father, the more I would be able to justify my existence. Nevertheless, I now found myself in a situation where no amount of effort was going to make the slightest difference. I was already working at the limits of my abilities; and yet I was failing, along with the entire team. By the end of March, we found ourselves not only having to pay indemnity for the Faithless Four, but also having to compensate God for having failed to octuple our numbers as we believed He demanded. One encouraging development, however, was that we had managed to recruit two fine new members, a pair of Swiss women who had been sightseeing on Venice Beach. Nevertheless, even two bright and capable members like these were still not sufficient to fulfill our heavenly quota. Once again, we had failed, and another "new beginning" was needed.

In early April, after returning from his monthly meeting with Father, Reverend Vincenz decided he had the answer. The portable conversion chamber was returned, and in its place the team rented a second-floor storefront on Olive Street in downtown Los Angeles, in what had once been a fur store. Now, surely, new members would flock in, when they saw this impressive set-up, where Divine Principle could be taught with authority! The two Swiss sisters could not be sent out witnessing, since they might encounter visa problems, so they were given the chore of cleaning the new center and greeting the guests brought in by the other witnessers. While I was impressed with the appearance of the place, I found the new center was really no better than the portable conversion chamber. I could stand on the corner of 6th and Hope or 7th and Hill from dawn to dusk, lunging desperately at passers-by, engaging them in conversations about religion, and urging them to come to lectures, but I still could find hardly anyone who would actually come hear them. I did manage to get one unemployed man to visit the portable conversion chamber, and subsequently to go up to Camp Mozumdar for the weekend; but he disappeared in the middle of our first night there. Presumably, he decided to hitch-hike all the way back to the city rather than sit through another day of lectures. (Peter said he left because he was "afraid of the Truth").

In my anxiety to find someone, *anyone*, who would listen, I began to lower my standards a trifle. I remember roaming through Pershing Square looking for potential converts, but of course I mostly found only winos and lunatics in that littered, sun-blasted urban park. I convinced one man to come back with me to the Olive Street center, and then was taken aback when his conversation became more and more insane, with references to U.F.O.s and assassinations and incomprehensible things. (One of the Swiss sisters gallantly rushed to my rescue on that occasion, and my guest was hustled out the door). On Hill Street near Fifth I spoke to a man who admitted he had done time in prison for murder. I tried to recruit him anyway.

Then I hit on the idea of running in circles for God. I wanted to show God how determined I was. I thought that if I promised God that I would run seven times in a circle from Flower and Fifth down to Grand, right on Grand to Sixth, up Sixth to Flower, and right again back to Fifth, in a circuit of two blocks around the Los Angeles Public Library, then God would be inspired by my dedication to have a person waiting for me when I finally came to a stop. He or she would just be standing there, on the corner of Fifth and Flower, waiting to be told the "Truth" and to become a follower of the "new Messiah". But it was not to be. I ran the circuit, but that person wasn't there. (I had tried this before, when I was witnessing in Santa Monica, but it hadn't worked then either).

Meanwhile, Reverend Vincenz seemed to be operating on the theory that the more he frightened us about the consequences of failure, the more successful we would be. At every opportunity he would remind us of how essential it was that the four I.O.W.C. teams "bring one, one, one", otherwise Father's mission in America might fail. If this happened, we were assured, God would leave America, and the country would be destroyed by moral decadence or overrun by Communists. Failure to find 30,000 converts by the end of 1978 would almost certainly cause Father to turn his attention to another nation such as the United Kingdom or Brazil, abandoning the United States to its miserable fate. If the Communists took over America, we were informed, there would likely be mass executions, with the blood of Unification Church members cascading through the streets. Every day, I labored under the weight of this appalling prospect.

But the pressure didn't end there. Our leader also informed us that Father was on a "21-year course" which had commenced in 1960 with his marriage and which would end in 1981. If by 1981 a large number of Americans had not accepted Moon as the Messiah, and at least one nation—possibly South Korea or Japan—had not turned itself wholly over to his guidance, a second 21-year course, running from 1982 to 2003, would be necessary, which would be much more bitter and dangerous, possibly involving a Third World War. Hence not just millions of Americans, but the lives of people all over the world depended on our efforts.

And—as if that still wasn't enough—Reverend Vincenz also told us that if Father met the same fate as Jesus and was killed before completing his mission, another 16,000 years would pass before God could again send the Messiah to bring the Kingdom of Heaven on Earth. During those countless millennia, the world would be plunged into a darkness and savagery so absolute that human beings would become little more than animals.

And that was not all. I was also told by my team leader that Father had remarked that if he failed his mission, "Heavenly Father might die" of a broken heart. If God were to die, what would be left of the universe, which most Unificationists thought of as God's "Hyung Sang" or outward form? Thus, even the continued existence of the universe was now contingent on my finding recruits for Father.

Experienced members were able to live with this kind of pressure by performing a sort of doublethink; they believed in it intellectually, but they did not allow it to touch them emotionally. However, I was still a relatively new member, and had not yet learned how to deflect this unrelenting pressure. By the middle of April, I was living in constant fear and anguish, scarcely able to sleep, haunted every minute by the magnitude of my failed obligation to God and the amount of indemnity that I would have to pay to restore it. The strain I was under was noticeable to the entire team. I was on the verge of a nervous breakdown.

One incident particularly illustrates the exquisite agony I felt during this brief moment of my life. My team leader had called the team together in the middle of the afternoon for a meeting at the Olive Street center in order to offer encouragement, and in order to pray together, or share an "inspiration" or two. During the meeting, I was only able to think of one thing: if I left the street for as little as ten minutes, the prepared person that God had supposedly been planning to send to me would walk right by, and not be saved! This was unbearable, unthinkable! I couldn't sit still. My hands and voice shook, and when I was offered an orange for refreshment, I couldn't even peel it properly. My thumbs went right through the peel into the fruit's fleshy pulp, and I tore it to scraps, tossing them down my throat distractedly. Viewing this performance, my team leader said that he wished that there was such a thing as a vacation for Family members. I didn't really understand his remark, and as soon as the meeting ended I raced back onto the street again, wild-eyed and desperate.

A way out finally presented itself in the last weeks of April. There was a call for volunteers for the fund-raising team, and I volunteered. Where before, I had always excused myself from fund-raising by pointing out that I was a Canadian and not legally allowed to do it, I now felt much too eager for a change to care about immigration laws (which Unificationists regarded as "Satan's rules" anyway). This decision saved me from psychological collapse.

I quickly took to fund-raising, which involved running tirelessly from person to person selling candy or costume jewelry or flowers, whether in a supermarket parking lot, a residential neighborhood or a commercial district. It is very uncomplicated, and the extra physical effort paid off in ways that didn't occur in witnessing. On the first day, I made more than one hundred dollars, which was unusual for a first-time fundraiser. Soon after, the team went for a fund-raising excursion up the San Bernardino valley, and I continued to do well. At last I began to feel I was justifying my existence, and the pain of the knife inside me subsided.

When we returned to Los Angeles, the team began preparing for a new fund-raising trip to a different area, but in early May Reverend Vincenz brought terrible news. Father had been arrested for trespassing on Bard College in upstate New York, and had even spent several hours in jail in Rhinebeck before he was released.

From a legal standpoint, this was a minor incident, but to Unification Church members, it represented the failure of America to honor and respect the Messiah. As Reverend Vincenz said in his typically heavy-handed way, this was a "very bad condition for America". Now, we would have to pay even more indemnity to restore this latest failure.

Soon afterwards, our fund-raising trip was canceled when Reverend Vincenz brought the surprising news that Father was recalling the I.O.W.C. teams to New York. Instead of evangelizing the four corners of America, the teams would be assigned to the boroughs of New York, so they could focus on converting this one representative city of America. This was a startling shift in strategy, but we quickly accepted the new plans, forgetting at once what we had once believed about the mission of the I.O.W.C.

Personally, I was glad to see the last of Los Angeles, the city where I had known such deep distress. Still, I felt badly that we had been unable to do what we came there to do; we had not converted thousands of people; our faith must have been lacking, and our conditions of indemnity too weak.

For years afterwards, I shuddered whenever I thought about the Los Angeles I.O.W.C. team. Yet as traumatic as that brief experience had been— and it was only four months, though in my memory it seems much longer—I never seriously considered leaving the Unification Church. By then I had been imbued with deep phobias about the serious consequences of leaving. I had been told that members who left were likely to suffer fatal accidents or endure other misfortunes, because Father's protection derived from his great spiritual power; if I left Father's protection, Satan would set out to destroy me. As well, I was afraid to lose my new ideology which had given me a kind of mastery over the knife inside me since, so long as I worked for Father, I need never feel worthless.

The conviction that nothing mattered more than to hold onto Father, and never leave him, had been growing inside me ever since my indoctrination at Boonville, but after surviving the emotional turmoil of the I.O.W.C., it became fixed as an article of faith. I could be tormented, or humiliated, or abandoned, but never, under any circumstances, should I leave Father. No fate—not even death—would excuse me from this divine obligation.

CHAPTER SIX

TURNING NEW YORK ON ITS HEAD

We left Los Angeles in a convoy of white Dodge vans, traveling through New Mexico, Texas and Oklahoma on the first leg of our pilgrimage to New York. I rode in the lead van, along with about 10 other brothers and sisters. In my van there was a CB radio, which was the latest fad. In those days, everybody took to hailing everybody else by radio, calling each other "good buddies" and warning of "Smokeys" ahead. One of the team leaders seized the CB radio and explained to anyone who would listen that we were the "I-O-W-C"—gleefully drawling out the letters with a Southern accent, because for some reason it seems necessary to have a Southern accent on CB radio.

Since there was little for me to do except pray and chant or watch the scenery go by, I began writing a letter to my parents which my mother saved. The letter sounds as if it was my first attempt to explain exactly which group I was with. Dated "May 16, 1976" (the year was clearly an error) and headed "Yukon, Oklahoma", I began:

> Thank you so much for rushing the checque [*sic*] to me & for the beautiful card in which you expressed so much love and concern for me. . . . Now that I'm on a 2½ day van trip to New York I have plenty of time to write letters so I thought I should explain the Unification Church better and why I'm so involved and what my future in the movement will be.

The check mentioned in the first line was an amount of money I had asked my parents to send to me, which I then gave in full to the I.O.W.C., believing this would bring spiritual blessings to my parents. The letter goes on to give the standard account of Reverend Moon's background that I had heard in many church workshops, and then directly addressed the issue that was on everyone's mind since the "Oakland Faithful Five":

> Basically it was due to the simple and scientific logic of this Principle and the way it explains God (and not due to any mental manipulation or brainwashing) that I was able to believe and accept it in spite of my background of anti-religious feelings. Contrary to the rumors in some of the press, it is a Christian teaching; the life of Jesus is an important part of our Principle, although we believe that

Jesus came not just to die on the cross but rather to gather all the Israelites and finally the world together around his example and his teachings but he could not because of the faithlessness of the people.

A later section of the letter, dated "May 17, 1977" and headed "Nashville, Tennessee", gives a summary of my experience on the I.O.W.C.:

After four months, I can't say we succeeded that well, although I can say that we tried hard. So that's why we're going to New York to work under the direct leadership of Reverend Moon. We will be meeting up with three other 50—60 member IOWC teams from around the country and probably several hundred other members as well. Our objective is to turn New York on its head! If we can change New York, we can move the heart of America, and so you can expect to hear a lot about us soon. I mean this seriously.

The letter also adds a brief postscript, hastily scrawled in a different color of ink: "P.S. Please maintain my [Alberta government] health insurance as it will cover me from all injuries, but thanks for your extra trouble."

The I.O.W.C. convoy finished its journey late on the 18th of May. I had my first look at New York as our van emerged from the Holland Tunnel and drove up the West Side Highway. I had never before seen so much angry graffiti spray-painted on nearly every surface, nor such relentless industrial squalor as I saw on my first glimpse of New York. This only served to confirm my impression from Father's speeches that New York was the capital of sin and decadence in a nation plunging into a rapid decline.

By contrast, the aging New Yorker Hotel, which Father acquired in 1975, seemed to me a beacon of spiritual light in the enshrouding gloom. This 40-storey structure was the hub of Unification Church activity in America. Here, members would stay whenever there was a large celebration or a major campaign; the top leaders would stay in the renovated rooms on the upper floors, while the ordinary members would be given the unfurnished and unrenovated rooms below. In many of these rooms, the plumbing worked poorly, if at all. At one point the entire third floor was converted into crude shower facilities for the brothers. Still, the hotel was *ours*, officially reclaimed by Father from the dominion of Satan, and we were proud of it.

Our fate was soon settled in a meeting among the I.O.W.C. leaders and Father. The four I.O.W.C. teams were assigned to each of the outlying boroughs of New York: Queens, The Bronx, Staten Island, or Brooklyn. Our team was assigned to The Bronx. I remembered Ogden Nash's famous comment: "The Bronx? No thonx!" Yet hardly had I been transplanted to the church's brownstone in The Bronx, when I was abruptly told that I had been traded (like a player on a sports team), along with a French brother, to the Manhattan Family—in a sort of equalization draft among the various I.O.W.C. teams.

The Manhattan Family was based in a sprawling seven-storey structure, the former Columbia University Club, on 43rd Street not far from Times Square. The new brothers and sisters that I met at 43rd Street proved to be a talented and diverse lot. It was the home base of the New Hope Singers International, a choir made up of members from around the world, so I now rubbed shoulders in the breakfast line with an even larger number of nations than I had on I.O.W.C. The choir's finest moment had been their performance at the Washington Monument rally in September of 1976; but now, they waited in New York, wondering when they would next be called upon to give a performance. In the meantime, they practiced their harmonies while singing Holy Songs at morning service, or Family songs before dinner. I very much liked this group, and recall the women especially: a lovely black-haired Spaniard; an exquisite French beauty; a warm-hearted red-head from Vermont. (Of course, if I had any improper thoughts about any of them, I would immediately repent for my "fallen nature"; but I couldn't help admiring them). At public gatherings, Father liked to show off these members from different nations because of their apparent diversity; yet in the end, we became homogeneous, having learned to speak the same standardized jargon derived from Divine Principle lectures.

Our new mission was to sell newspapers. At the start of the year, Father had launched a newspaper, the *News World*, into the crowded New York market, predicting that one day it would overtake the *New York Times*. He directed Unification Church members to sell the *News World* on street corners, even though the paper was legally independent of the church. This created an image problem for the *News World*, which never really lived down its nickname as the "Moonie paper". Although it used extensive color photographs in its early days and was priced at only 10 cents per copy, it found few buyers. Father seemed to believe that people would buy his newspaper simply because the people who sold it were so friendly. After a few months of lagging sales, he decided to bring in the I.O.W.C. teams to sell single copies, and later ordered all the members in the New York area to focus on selling one-month trial subscriptions for $4.00 each. Of course, this was an even harder sell; but if Father said it could be done, then it must be possible.

Mr. Sawata, the Japanese leader of the Manhattan Family, decided that some sort of unity exercise was needed before the subscription drive, so he opted for the usual solution of a Divine Principle workshop. This would probably have been just another exercise in repetition had he not arranged to hold the workshop at the Unification Theological Seminary in Barrytown, New York. When Father had acquired this property in 1975, it was used as a venue for the recruiting workshops, but later it was converted into an academic seminary offering courses in Theology and Church History. In those days, the Seminary was envisioned as a training ground for future church leaders, and only those with undergraduate degrees were permitted to attend. Since I had such a degree, I was qualified, but I was warned that I was really too new a member to be admitted to the Seminary. But given that I was there anyway, I went ahead and filled out an application.

The first day of the Divine Principle workshop proceeded much as they all did, with people falling asleep during lectures (which we tried to solve by prodding and massaging each other's backs, or by going to stand at the rear of the lecture hall). However, on the second day, classes were abruptly canceled and we were all told to go fishing in the Hudson River instead—using a method Father had devised.

The Hudson in this area is much affected by tidal ebbs and flows, so Father had reasoned that a better way to fish would be to stretch a net across a portion of the river at high tide. When the water levels dropped, fish would be trapped behind the nets and could be easily caught as they wearily flopped around on the mudflats. An elevated railroad berm which crossed over the river through the mudflats created a convenient barrier that allowed a portion of the river to be enclosed behind nets. Father began training the Seminarians in the art of building and mending nets. Taking up with this fishing hobby was seen as a way to emulate Father (i.e., to learn "Father's standard"), so even though it meant getting up early to lay the nets, and then trudging knee-deep through mud flats to retrieve the fish, we all felt it was important work. Those who hadn't brought rough clothes (meaning most of us) were forced to borrow old clothes and boots from the Seminarians or to simply grope through the mudflats in city shoes. Many of us secured plastic bags over our shoes, which afforded protection for perhaps half a minute at best. In the end, there was no choice but to let the evil-smelling mud leak into our shoes while we groped around for multi-colored (and sometimes diseased looking) carp or for sullen catfish, which we then thrust into green garbage bags. Later, this harvest of bony fish was presented to the Seminary kitchen staff, who managed to turn it into a passable evening meal. Soon afterwards (to the relief of many of the Seminarians) the Manhattan Family departed from Barrytown.

Just before this workshop, I began a letter to my parents explaining my latest change of address and describing my activities. The letter, dated May 21, 1977, begins in pencil and then switches to two different colors of ink, and is split into two sections with a different date heading up the second section:

> Hello! Many changes are happening with me but I know that the above address is correct at least. When I arrived in New York I was transferred from the International One World Crusade under Reverend Reiner Vincenz to the Unification Church—New York Center, under Mr. Sawata. Essentially this makes no difference to what I will be doing except that I will be in Manhattan rather than the Bronx.

> . . . One thing I'd like to talk about in this letter is the way we raise funds and what we do with them. Essentially all our money comes from donations for candy, flowers and other small items we sell, and from various business enterprises we operate like the Il Hwa Ginseng Tea Co. or the Tong-Il Enterprises Fishing fleet. Many people have interpreted this fact that we have a lot of businesses

associated with our church as signifying that Reverend Moon is nothing more than a businessman with a religious cover. This is not true since all funds go to the Unification Church and not to Reverend Moon personally. Therefore when members of our church decided to give him a fine house to live in in upstate New York, it was a voluntary gift of the Church (and not something he bought himself with the hard-earned cash from our members' efforts). Anyway, he hardly ever gets a chance to live there because he keeps himself busier than the members!

May 27, 1977

I am concerned about what you said in your last letter about me being too involved in Church activities to have time to think. Actually, I do a lot of thinking about why I'm in the Unification movement, and the more I ask myself that question, the more I become convinced that this is the place to be. I certainly am exposed every day to the other side of the question—people I sell newspapers to and others often make all the usual complaints about our movement—but I still am proud to be a Unification Church member, not because I love God—I don't really know Him yet— but because I feel loved by God through all the other people in this Church and I know that even hard work is a way of coming to an understanding of God. Also I feel that I am doing something positive for humanity.

. . . I'm writing this on the famous New York subway going from Bronx to Manhattan and it's not as bad as everyone says. Of course, every train has been defaced all over with spray paint and it's noisy and slow compared to Montreal's but it works.

And now I'm writing this in the dining hall at 43rd St. after dinner. We have just returned yesterday from a 3-day workshop in Barrytown, New York, where the Unification Church has a former Catholic seminary where we now teach Comparative Religions and Unification thought. The main theme of the workshop was how to come together as a family even though there are 180 people living here in a 7-story building! It should be no small task. Write me when you have time. Love, Gordon.

Upon my return, I was assigned to an area of East Side Manhattan in the upper 60's and low 70's, ranging from Fifth Avenue to First, under the guidance of Shelley, an experienced sister who had served a tour of duty on the "National M.F.T." (as the teams which fundraised for the church at large were called). Shelley had already been assigned to this area for several months and knew many of the shop owners, doormen and garagemen, so I simply tagged along as she tried to wheedle them into buying the newspaper. One memorable day we even challenged "Satan" by entering the Soviet consulate, which was in our area, to ask them to buy a subscription to *News World*. (They said "No.")

Our area included some of the most expensive apartments in Manhattan, guarded by doormen. I was all for sneaking into these buildings anyway (a tactic that was popular with fundraisers), but Shelley was adamantly opposed. Her experiences on the National M.F.T. had convinced her that these methods were counter-productive, since they produced bad publicity for the church. Still, what were we supposed to do, I wondered, given the relentless pressure to bring results? We were instructed to "love and serve" a neighborhood that was almost completely inaccessible, and yet we were expected to sign up three *News World* subscribers per day anyway, and recruit new members as well.

Finally, we were forced to go back to the old, familiar method of street witnessing that had brought both of us into the church originally. Roaming the streets of our assigned area, we would approach people with the *News World*, or with our witnessing talk, or sometimes using both approaches. Not surprisingly, most of the people we nabbed on street corners turned out not to be from that area at all, but they were still fair game if we could get them to sign up. If they agreed to take the paper, the member who was actually assigned to their area was supposed to deliver it; but given the limited time the members had, such transfers nearly always went awry. (Nevertheless, we reasoned, if Father said it could be done, then it must be possible!)

In early June a call went out for volunteers to go out of state on a fund-raising team for the Manhattan Family. Because New Yorkers had become almost immune to solicitations by "Moonies", it was necessary to go elsewhere to get acceptable fund-raising results. Mr. Sawata had arranged with one of the National M.F.T. Commanders to allow a Manhattan Family team into his Texas territory. I jumped at the chance to get out of witnessing, which still upset me after my experiences on I.O.W.C.; besides, I was eager to visit a part of the United States that was new to me.

Of course, sightseeing was not a priority for the team. Some eight or nine members crowded into one van for the trip south. We were assigned to Austin—a university town—to sell candy and flowers in malls, shopping districts and housing areas. At night, we stayed in a house owned by the Unification Church. The only memorable incident from this time occurred when one of the brothers tried to sell candy to Madalyn Murray O'Hair, the famous atheist. (She gently spun him around and pointed him towards the door.) It was soon clear that Austin was not yielding excellent results for the team, so Mr. Sawata arranged for the loan of Oklahoma City instead. Since there were no church centers in that city, we stayed in a couple of motel rooms while we continued selling candy and cookies for the Manhattan Family. But even Oklahoma City did not prove sufficiently lucrative, so other cities were eyed—the team captain hinted that our next stop would be St. Louis, Missouri. Those plans were set aside, however, when Mr. Sawata decided that a 21-day "condition" was needed to sell *News World* subscriptions. Our team was recalled to New York so we could participate.

I expected that I would return to work with my mentor, Shelley, on the East Side, but Shelley had already recognized the pattern of frenzied activity that was familiar to her from M.F.T. She got another mission elsewhere, and suddenly I was alone on the East Side.

For his part, Mr. Sawata believed he was in competition with the Japanese M.F.T. commanders to bring results and demonstrate faithfulness. He even decided to imitate the fundraisers' methods, despite the fact our missions were substantially different. On the M.F.T., a 21-day or 40-day "condition" would periodically be declared; during these campaigns the fundraisers would stay out for extra hours every night to try to accomplish an unusually elevated monetary goal. If they could not achieve the goal, they were supposed to stay out all night to show their "desperation and determination". Therefore it was decided that the New York members were to follow this example by going after the unrealistically large number of *News World* subscribers that Father demanded, even if it meant staying out all night, and even though ordinary people might think it odd to be approached at three in the morning to sign up for a newspaper.

Not to be outdone, the East Side team leader (also Japanese) decided to imitate his central figure, so after the usual morning service at 43rd Street calling for (as usual) unflinching determination, we would reassemble in a second-storey flat on Lexington Avenue around 73rd Street to be lectured a second time about "desperation and determination." And then we went out as usual—and failed. The East Side leader put us on fasting conditions in order to reinforce our determination, but still New Yorkers failed to recognize the excellence of the *News World*.

A few days prior to the end of the selling condition, on July 13, 1977, I was standing on 69th Street in early evening when a curious thing happened: all the lights went out. Remembering the news stories about the blackout of 1965, I asked a passerby: "Does this happen here often?" All the members returned to the darkened 43rd Street center for the night. Later it was determined that the blackout was due to an unlucky lightning strike, but church members could not help wondering if it was actually due to our own failure to pay sufficient indemnity. God was showing us the dark future which would result if we failed to achieve our goals!

On the night of July 16—the last day of the 21-day condition— Manhattan Family members were required to stay up all night if they could not find three *News World* subscribers during regular hours. That meant all of us. I was assigned an interesting partner for my allnighter: Kathy, who held a Master's degree in either Philosophy or Sociology (I don't remember which). Kathy had also been one of the member of the fund-raising team that had tackled Texas and Oklahoma. Like most Unification Church members, she was both proud and apologetic about her pre-Family accomplishments— apologetic, because Father would often ridicule members who had advanced education in his speeches, claiming they were not as useful to God as someone who was simply hard-working and dedicated. Kathy and I passed the night roving the streets of my assigned area and the surrounding neighborhoods. We even walked down to the East River and strolled through the low 50's in a vain search for *News World* subscribers.

When the campaign ended, I was reassigned to a new area on the East Side, in the mid-80's—a dramatic change from my old area. Here the apartment buildings were humble, even shabby, but at least there was nothing to stop us from getting into them.

Now I had a new mentor: a Japanese sister named Keiko, who once rebuked me while I was sitting beside her on a park bench, merely because I had pointed my knees toward her instead of keeping them pointed straight ahead. "You Americans are too horizontal," she complained. Normally, though, Keiko was pleasant to work with—a bright, cheerful woman that people instantly liked.

Nevertheless, our new area was scarcely more productive than the previous one; the people I met in that area were often eccentric characters, but hardly what church members would call "quality people". Once again, Keiko and I had to resort to street witnessing, by leaving the 43rd Street center in the evenings after dinner to walk in any direction that caught our fancy. One evening, near Carnegie Hall, we met a young man named David. David went to a dinner meeting at 43rd Street and even agreed to attend the weekend workshop in Tarrytown, but he did not end up joining.

The workshops David attended took place in a house in a genteel part of Westchester County where the Unification Church owned 353 acres distributed among Father's estate and eight other parcels. Not far away was a mansion known as "Belvedere" where Father would frequently deliver speeches to the members on Sundays. Yet even Belvedere was not Father's home; he and his family lived nearby on an even more impressive estate called "East Garden". I attended the Belvedere speeches several times—it was considered a great and historical honor to be able to hear the Messiah speak while he was yet alive. In the future, we were told, our descendants would marvel and thank God that their ancestor had been given such a splendid blessing. So of course, on the Sundays when I was able to travel up to Belvedere to hear these talks, I went.

Every Sunday at 5:30 a.m., members who were going to Belvedere would assemble to board a touring bus for the one-hour trip. During the trip, everyone was expected to pray silently and "prepare their hearts" to receive Father's words. Naturally, after a short night's sleep, silent prayer would usually turn into dozing, much to our private shame.

When we arrived at Belvedere, many other vehicles would already be there, disgorging church members from New York, Connecticut, New Jersey and other states, all anxious to get as close to the front row as possible. We seated ourselves cross-legged on the lawn facing a car port which had been converted into a stage. There would follow a long, slow build-up before Father appeared; first we would engage in silent prayer, and then in public prayer and the singing of Holy Songs. Finally, Father would appear, portly and beaming, with an interpreter in tow.

Father had two main interpreters for these meetings: Bo Hi Pak and Sang Kil Han, both of whom were generally referred to by their military ranks: Colonel Pak and Colonel Han. We were told that their military ranks stemmed from their service in the Korean War.

Father normally began his impromptu speeches on a light-hearted note, usually making simple but attention-getting remarks such as "Generally, men like women and women like men." He would develop these more accessible topics for a while, until he was sure that the audience had warmed to him. Occasionally, to add a light-hearted tone, he would gently rap someone in the front row on the head, or he would grab Colonel Pak and shake him. Pak had an excellent grasp of American idiom, and would translate Father's guttural Korean in an unflappable manner, even when he was being shaken or thumped. The warm-up phase of the speech usually lasted about forty minutes.

Next, Father would turn to more serious themes, drawing on the Divine Principle to develop a complicated point about God's original plan or His workings through history. The idea was to show that Father had a detailed understanding of God's original intentions for the world. When Father cited the Bible during this portion of the speech, it was usually a reference to an Old Testament story, such as that of Jacob and Esau.

After this, he would begin to speak of the serious consequences of failure. It was at this point that he might begin to talk about Jesus, detailing the series of errors committed by the people around Jesus that had allowed Satan to "invade" so that he was killed without converting the whole world. At this point, the specter of Communism was usually raised, and it became clear that any failure on our part would leave the door open for Satan to invade through an expansion of Communism—and even, in the worst result, the death of Father.

Finally would come a phase where Father would offer hope, by saying that our members would be the ones to fulfill God's plan, and bring the Heavenly Kingdom on Earth. At some point during this portion, often suddenly, he would ask the audience to confirm they were committed to this goal. He would listen carefully while the entire audience shouted, "Yes!" He was trying to find out if the audience was really focused on what he was saying and if they had put sufficient commitment into their shouted affirmation. Usually he would ask the same question again, with slightly different wording, two or three more times, and by then the whole audience was ready for it and put every effort into the reply. If we failed to convince him of our complete seriousness, Father might re-launch the speech and continue for up to several more hours (as he did on one occasion when he delivered a mind-bending eleven hours of extemporaneous speech). Usually he had already been going on for some three hours before he reached this point. Even though we had been told that every word was pure gold, we were afraid that if he continued speaking much longer, we would all be asleep from exhaustion. So we knew what we had to do: shout that one word, "YES!" with all our strength. If we did this convincingly enough, he would say a few final words of encouragement and then mercifully release us.

After Father's speech, there was a short period of time while the members milled around waiting for their vehicles, during which we could meet other members and engage in stilted conversations. "Hi! What's your mission?" was the usual opening line. One sunny summer day I sat down on a nearby lawn while I waited for my bus. A friendly dog came out and cavorted among the members on the lawn, and a middle-aged Japanese man, who knew the dog's name, got him to settle down while he stroked him affectionately. I realized with awe that the man was Takeru Kamiyama, the leader of the National M.F.T., who was considered one of Father's most important disciples. It was Kamiyama who ensured that money from the church's Japanese operations flowed into America to finance expensive projects like the *News World*. I didn't dare say anything to him. What does one say to a living saint?

I continued my work with Keiko until late August, when Mr. Sawata assembled a number of fund-raising teams to travel out of New York. Although raising money to maintain the aging 43rd Street building was the main motive, there might have been another reason for his sudden urge to send members out of state: the annual Seminary draft was about to take place.

Every year in late August, the Unification Theological Seminary would scour the ranks of the Unification Church looking for qualified members. Naturally, every leader who stood to lose valuable members to the Seminary would try whatever they could to retain them. They would denounce the Seminary as nothing more than a bunch of people theorizing instead of doing useful work. They would insist that their eligible members were too vital to be sent away. They would go to the members privately and persuade them not to reveal their eligibility to the Seminary. And if all else failed, they would simply make them unavailable when the time came for them to go to Barrytown.

Knowing this, Father was emphatic that the members must be sent anyway, and the Seminary would often be forced to appeal directly to him to ensure that qualified members were produced in spite of their leader's ruses. Nevertheless, just when it was close to the time for me to go to the Seminary to be considered as a candidate, I was placed on a fund-raising team to Philadelphia.

In Philadelphia I gave my best effort as usual, but with unimpressive results. The only incident I recall from this one-week trip happened when I was on a street corner somewhere near the Liberty Bell. I approached two older women to buy my product, but they abruptly ordered me to "Go back to your parents!"

"But I'm 24!" I protested.

"Then get married!" they commanded.

My team returned to New York on the evening of Sunday, August 28, just after the Seminary candidates were supposed to have reported to Barrytown. Just to make sure, one of the church leaders set out to convince me that I really wasn't ready for the Seminary anyway. "You're too young," he told me; "You don't have enough experience and haven't paid enough indemnity yet." Of course, I agreed. The Seminary? Forget it. There were plenty of years ahead—after the Heavenly Kingdom was restored—to learn all that theology stuff.

Nevertheless, two days later, the Seminary got its way. Despite my decision not to go, I was ordered to report to the Seminary. I was given a train ticket to Rhinecliff in upstate New York.

I was the last Seminary candidate to arrive, and I appeared in the middle of a seven-day preparatory workshop. At the end of the workshop, on Saturday, September 3, Father himself arrived to make the final decision as to who would spend the next two years at the Seminary.

We were assembled in one of the larger classrooms, and arranged ourselves in a circle around the perimeter so that Father (in the manner of a military inspection) could look at each of us in turn. He entered the room, with the Seminary President, David S.C. Kim, playing the role of Sergeant-Major. Each candidate was eyed briefly, while Kim would offer some explanatory remark. We all looked straight ahead, saying nothing unless spoken to, like soldiers. Finally, Father stood before me. "One year in Principle," David Kim pointed out dismissively. The Messiah looked at me for one more appraising second, then turned to the next candidate. I was convinced that in that one brief moment, he had peered into my ancestral history, discerning all my sins and weaknesses. That evening, when the next Seminary class was announced, I learned that I was not on the list.

I knew what was necessary for me to be accepted into the Seminary: I would have to spend at least a year on the M.F.T. The full-time fund-raising teams were considered the most "sacrificial" of all the missions that a Unification Church member could do. I was willing to do this, but the decision was not mine to make. Even so, I didn't have long to wait.

Less than a week after my return, a National M.F.T. draft was announced throughout the American church. I was on the list. Now I could prove my loyalty to Father! Quickly I was switched to a small team of Manhattan Family members who had all been assigned to the M.F.T., and I proceeded to annoy the others with my conviction that I would only be on the M.F.T. for one year before being called to the Seminary. Most of the others knew that they were likely stuck on the M.F.T. for many years to come. The only question left was: Which M.F.T. "region" would I be assigned to? Around September 10, 1977, I learned my fate: I was assigned to Maryland, Delaware, Washington, D.C. and West Virginia. I was provided enough money for a rail ticket to Washington and I left at once.

CHAPTER SEVEN

PURE DOING

It was late in the evening by the time the train pulled into Washington. The brother who met me brought me to the M.F.T. regional headquarters in Silver Springs, Maryland, where I was assigned to one of the Baltimore fund-raising teams. The two Baltimore teams were based in a rented house in Eldersburg, a bedroom community for Baltimore. There was a "beginner's team", which focused on the inner-city, and a smaller "advanced team" that worked the more lucrative suburban areas. I went to the beginner's team, whose captain was a tall Austrian man with a ski-jump nose named Johann who set about at once to disabuse me of any thought that I might be on M.F.T. for "just a year, until I get called to the Seminary." In a pointed morning sermon, he scoffed that anyone would think themselves worthy of so great an honor as to be allowed to attend the Seminary, and that all good members ought to be grateful just to be collecting money for Father, and should simply content themselves with doing that for the rest of their lives. Rather than disunite with my central figure, I quickly repented and accepted that I deserved to remain on M.F.T. for many years.

A typical day on a fund-raising team began at 6:30 a.m. with a hasty prayer, followed by a scramble to shower, dress, and prepare the fund-raising products for the day's work. As soon as could be managed, the team would climb into the van and everyone would take his or her customary position. The captain would take the driver's seat, while one of the sisters, the "team mother," would get into the passenger seat. The remaining sisters would take the forward bench seat while the brothers would sit on the rear bench seat. As the captain drove out to whatever "area" he had selected (a secret he normally kept to himself) the sisters would hurry to prepare breakfast cereal and sandwiches for the team. At the first drop-off point, the captain would park the van and begin "morning service", which consisted of a reading from either the Bible or "Master Speaks" (which were the transcripts of Father's speeches), followed by a representative prayer from the team mother. The captain would then deliver an off-the-cuff, and often scolding, sermon, which was concluded with unison prayer, in which all the team members shouted out their prayers simultaneously, pledging to "smash Satan" and "bring victory for Father." This cacophony of prayer would come to an abrupt close whenever the team captain began singing a Korean song, "U-ri e so wo nun tong-il," which was both a plea for Korean reunification and for unity among believers. Then the bowls of cereal and sandwiches would be hastily handed out while the team captain passed along announcements from the Commander about church affairs. Each member of the team would declare his or her monetary goals for the day—a target dollar figure—and the team mother would write these down. It was bad form to set a goal of less than one hundred dollars, which was "Father's standard", although a member who was "struggling" might do so. The first person chosen to go to work would be given quick instructions and told a time and place when the team captain would return to look for him or her. He or she would then have to jump out immediately, taking breakfast along, and go around to the back of the van to collect a box of fund-raising product. The van would then leave at once for the next drop-off point. There was no time to waste.

Of all the moments in the day, it was the instant that the team captain turned to me and said, "Gordon, please go here," that I found the most difficult. I was anxious to do well, but so often in a typical fund-raising day I would encounter people who cursed me for being a hated "Moonie"; or I would endure a solid hour of steady rejection, or I would be sent away from my assigned area by police officers or by mall security, and end up with little to show for my work. Not surprisingly, my anxiety would start to build during the long drive out to the area; so when I was finally assigned to an area, I would have a stricken look on my face rather than the enthusiastic demeanor I was expected to have. The team captain was watching for this or any other sign that I was not as instantly and reflexively obedient as I was supposed to be. Some M.F.T. captains would even set out to provoke resentment intentionally, just to see how team members would react—for example, by dropping them off suddenly in a difficult or sparsely populated area.

Usually, however, as I got into my fund-raising day, I would warm to the task. My main duty was simply to never stop working. Johann explained it this way: given our Fallen state, God's only condition to accept us is through our work for Father; and so long as we are actively working for Father, God can protect us; but as soon as we stop working, Satan has a condition to tempt us or harm us. This injunction to "never stop" fit in with my emotional need to justify myself through works, so I was careful to never commit the cardinal sin of "spacing out."

Beyond not stopping, I was expected to run as fast as I could between every sale, and to approach as many people as possible, scouring even the back rooms of stores and factories in search of potential donors. I did this, too; yet despite all my efforts, I often fell short of my monetary goals. This frustrated me greatly. I felt that if I was not bringing in the amount of money Father asked for, then I was good for nothing. Ironically, the more I agonized over my failure, the worse my results became.

Meanwhile, another member on my team, Betty, invariably received several hundred dollars per day. I admired her unabashedly. What a virtuous sister she must be, I thought! How pure must her heart be in the eyes of God! And beyond even Betty's achievement, I had been told about the legendary members who had performed even greater feats, such as a sister from

Baltimore who sometimes earned more than a thousand dollars per day. Above all else, I wanted to be like these M.F.T. champions.

Betty did particularly well on the Friday and Saturday night "blitz runs", when the team members would run into bars and restaurants late at night, approaching as many customers as possible before being sent away. We carried buckets of carnations on these weekend blitzes instead of the usual boxes of peanut brittle or trays of costume jewelry. The flowers usually sold well in the numerous small pubs around Baltimore's core, such as along Eastern Avenue. I was more than a little baffled, then, when one night I overheard Betty confessing to the captain that she was "struggling" with her success. "I'm just using God!" she exclaimed. I didn't know what to make of this, so I put it out of my mind.

Besides the weekend "blitzes", there were four other kinds of fund-raising runs: parking lots (of supermarkets and department stores); "shop to shop" (that is, commercial roads); factories and warehouses; and "house to house" (residential). Many of these places did not allow soliciting, but we didn't let that stop us. In the case of mall parking lots we were expected to keep working until someone with authority came along to stop us. In factory areas, I soon learned to look for back doors and even holes in fences to slip through. Invariably, I would be sent away by an angry foreman or manager, but if I happened to be dropped off in the same area a month later, I wouldn't hesitate to go in again. As far as M.F.T. members were concerned, other people's rules were unimportant next to Father's work.

Finally, at the end of a fund-raising day—as late as 3:00 a.m. on Fridays and Saturdays—the team would drive back to the little bungalow in Eldersburg. On the trip home everyone would have counted up their results to the last penny, and then placed the money in a vinyl bank bag, which was kept on the engine hump at the front. We would then publicly announce our "totals", which the team mother would write on the same piece of paper on which she had written our goals that morning. Once we arrived in the driveway, instead of getting out of the van, we would often have our evening prayer service while still parked.

First, the team captain would make any new announcements he may have learned from the Commander, and sometimes would even launch into another impromptu scolding sermon, which we would struggle to stay awake for, though we were all exhausted. At last we would be released, and the team mother would offer a representative prayer, followed by a unison prayer. Only then were we permitted to go to bed.

Even though I had not yet "broken through" like Betty, my sheer doggedness and sincere efforts eventually won me the right to be placed on the advanced team, which traveled to a number of smaller towns in northern Maryland. These towns were considered better fund-raising area than the hardened urban centers like Baltimore and Washington. I can only remember the names of a few of these places because it was not my responsibility to know where I was. However, I do recall one snowy evening late in 1977 when I sold candles in a parking lot in Elkton, and a peaceful morning when I sold costume jewelry in a pretty coastal town called Havre de Grace. I also recall a brief fund-raising trip to the Eastern Shore of Maryland, when the team passed through resort towns like Salisbury and Crisfield, where the late autumn air was fresh and invigorating with the salt of the sea.

By December, I was back in the Baltimore area, and the M.F.T. had changed products to take advantage of the Christmas buying frenzy. Now we sold wax candles poured into glass brandy snifters, available in a variety of colors. The Christmas season definitely brought better results for the whole team, and I found myself coming much closer to "Father's standard" most days. But the season also reminded me of the promises I had made to my family in Calgary to try to visit them at Christmas—as they expected me to do—so I put in a request to go, though I knew I would likely be refused. Sure enough, the team captain quickly dismissed the idea: our work was much too important for such trivial diversions, he said. On Christmas Day the team was allowed to relax, so we were given a rare chance to attend to housekeeping and then went bowling, followed by a movie—I believe it was "Close Encounters of the Third Kind" (I slept through most of it).

One week later it was God's Day, the biggest holiday in the Unification Church calendar. Throughout all the neighboring states, Unification Church members piled into vans for the drive to New York, where Father presided over the celebrations in the Grand Ballroom of the New Yorker Hotel. Our M.F.T. region was no exception; the Baltimore teams eagerly threw their sleeping bags on top of the fund-raising product in the back of the vans and left for New York in a state of high excitement. God's Day with the Lord of the Second Advent! I looked forward to my first such experience eagerly.

The arriving droves of church members were assigned to the unfurnished rooms in the World Mission Center, where they hastily changed into their best clothes to attend the midnight speech that Father gave on New Year's Eve. While other New Yorkers were raising toasts to the New Year, in the Grand Ballroom, Unification Church members, seated on the floor, waited for Father's midnight speech. In subsequent years I attended a few more of these God's Day celebrations, and the script was always the same. After preparatory songs and prayers, Father would enter, beaming, rotund and energetic, accompanied by an interpreter. The midnight talk was really just a warm-up speech to prepare for the longer talk Father gave the next morning, when he would announce the slogan for the year. That slogan would usually be something vague and grandiose such as "Substantial Realization of the Kingdom of Heaven on Earth," which Father would then daub with black paint in Chinese characters on a white paper banner in front of a cheering audience.

After the keynote speech of the year, the members were permitted a little time to mingle or to rest, and food was available in generous quantities, including Korean *kimchee*, a fiery pickled cabbage. For me, the best part of these Family holidays was the opportunity to meet brothers and sisters I had not seen for a long time, especially former "Oakies" with whom I could reminisce about Boonville and the Oakland Family. For a brief moment, we would still feel that we were part of a superior standard—"Onni's standard"—even though we actually had no remaining connection to Onni's group.

In the evening, a huge celebration was mounted in the concert hall of the adjoining Manhattan Center, which also belonged to the Unification Church. The Little Angels Korean dance troupe, the New Hope Singers International, and other church acts performed to great applause. The greatest cheers were reserved for the "True Children"—Father's young sons and daughters, who came shyly onto the stage to sing songs; and of course for True Father himself, who would always appear at the end, and, pretending to be reluctant, would sing an old Korean song such as "Um Maya" or "Arirang" in his gravelly, tuneless voice. There was something charming about his performance; it made him seem more vulnerable and human, as though in that moment he had suddenly become our own real father, singing off-key but happily for some family event.

The next day it was back to work. The team loaded up the van and headed back to Baltimore, a journey that took most of the day. We expected that we would head back immediately to our home base in Eldersburg, but the team captain had other ideas. He stopped in a housing area and told us we were to go fund-raising for the evening. Our obedience was being tested. I felt that familiar wrenching feeling, as I did at the start of a fund-raising day, but I prayed for forgiveness, and then I went out and worked hard as usual. I passed the test. A few days later, our team was called to the regional M.F.T. headquarters for a meeting with the Commander and the other teams.

After a partial day of fund-raising in the Washington, D.C. area, the Commander brought us together for a fine dinner at a Korean restaurant. Afterwards, at a meeting with all the members in the region, the results of each individual member were reviewed, and those whose results were the highest received rewards of some kind, usually a large color photograph of the "True Parents." Although I was not among the highest earners in the region, I still did well enough to receive a photograph, depicting "Father and Mother" beside one of their small sons on a toy swing. I valued this photo for years afterwards, as a reminder of the dream I shared with many Unification Church members: that one day I would be permitted by the church leaders to settle down and have a family, with "Blessed Children."

These large gatherings usually had a second purpose: they were a handy forum at which to announce the reassignment of Family members. I learned that I had been reassigned to the West Virginia team—an unmistakable promotion, since West Virginia was supposedly the best area in the entire region. However, the West Virginia team was too far south to make it to the regional meeting, so I was going to have to wait a few weeks before I could join that team. In the meantime, I worked with a team in Washington, D.C. Once again, I experienced fund-raising in a hardened urban center, where people were accustomed to "Moonie" fundraisers—and not particularly fond of them. For the next month I canvassed many of the neighborhoods inside the Beltway. My most amusing memory of Washington, D.C. is undoubtedly the time I was dropped off to "blitz" outside a two-storey McDonald's restaurant.

I had never seen a two-storey fast food joint before, and was quite impressed. The restaurant was very busy; it was an inner city sort of place with people coming and going constantly. I soon found that I could stand right next to the door and approach customers without being ejected by management; they were simply too busy holding down the fort inside to worry about a stray fundraiser outside. (At a suburban McDonald's, the ejection would have been immediate.) Still, I felt that I was not doing as well as I should. There were two exits, and I was only able to cover one at a time, unless—and here I hit on an inspiration—I ran right through the restaurant and caught them as they left by the other door! I proceeded to do exactly that, and still the management said nothing. This was a fundraiser's dream—no kick-out! I did very well that night, considering that most of the people had only small change to spare.

After about three weeks of fund-raising inside the Beltway, the West Virginia team arrived and I joined them. There were about eight of us altogether, with brothers outnumbering sisters as usual. I was looking forward to going to my new area because West Virginians were often more generous than the hard-nosed citizens of Baltimore and Washington. Their generosity stemmed from the strong Christianity that flourishes in many parts of that state (since normally we would claim to be raising funds for a Christian cause, and would only admit to being Unification Church members if specifically asked). On the other hand, if West Virginians did find out we were working for "Mr. Moonie" (as they liked to call him), they would react much more angrily. Nevertheless, we were instructed not to lash back when people cursed Father or the church; we were to "turn the other cheek," mutter "God bless you!" and then run on to the next person as quickly as possible.

My new team drove quite a distance before stopping for our first target area, the modest city of Clarksburg, which is in the middle of the northern part of the state. Unlike the Baltimore teams, the West Virginia team had no fixed home base, and simply stayed in a series of motel rooms while it roamed around the state. Usually the sisters would stay in the motel room while the brothers slept outside in the van. Once the sisters were dressed, the brothers would pile into the shower and bathroom facilities, and then the team would take off for another day. The van was our real home. After settling into a motel in Clarksburg the team quickly became a fixture in the town; for example, by appearing at the Kroger's supermarket and at most of the convenience stores. Being a conservative people, West Virginians do not easily welcome strangers, and when word spread that the Moonies were in town there was likely some discussion among town elders about what could be done. Technically, our activity was legal and constitutionally protected, so the police needed some good excuse if they were going to interfere with us. I managed to give them that excuse.

One morning I was assigned to an area that included a modest factory. Following the normal strategy, I ignored all the "No Soliciting" signs and went into one of the factory buildings and approached the workers. A few of them bought candy from me, but they warned me that I should watch out for the foreman. When, as usual, the foreman discovered me, he ordered me to leave, and I agreed to go. But I wasn't ready to leave yet, so (using a well-worn strategy that had worked for me in Maryland) I simply went to a different part of the factory and continued fund-raising. When the foreman found me again, he was much angrier than the weary Maryland managers I was accustomed to meeting had been. "You *deliberately* lied to me!" he roared, and escorted me out the front gate at once. I shrugged this off as "persecution," and continued fund-raising in the nearby residential area. However, this incident likely stiffened the resolve of the local police to do something about these persistent Moonies.

Later that evening, I was put out on a highway strip leading into Clarksburg, along with a young East Indian sister from New York, to do a "blitzing" run. As usual, we barged brazenly into the various bars and fast food joints we found along the strip, continuing until we crossed over the legal boundary into Clarksburg. Unexpectedly, a police cruiser pulled up behind us.

I had encountered many police cruisers in Maryland, and usually what happened is that I would receive a close questioning from the officers in the car, after which I would be allowed to go. The officers might not like what I was doing, but technically I was not doing anything wrong. I expected the same treatment when I approached the West Virginia police cruiser this time.

The officers rose out of the car and asked me to extend my hands. Accustomed to being obedient to authority figures, I raised my hands and was shocked when they handcuffed me, as well as the sister beside me. We were taken to the county jail and locked up for the night. I was too tired to even ask what I was charged with, let alone demand the right to make a phone call.

The guards led me to a large prison cell where a number of prisoners were busy playing cards at a table in the middle of the room. Off to the side were various smaller cells with bunks in them. The prisoners asked me if I wanted to sit in on the card game, but all I could think of was that I needed a place to lie down. When I found a place, I immediately fell asleep. In the early morning hours I awakened and realized that my team captain would be worried about me. I rattled on the cell door until the guard came around, and told him I hadn't been allowed to make a phone call. He led me to a phone, and I called my Commander—collect—in Silver Springs. The next morning the team captain bailed me and the young sister out. I still didn't know what I was charged with, and I wasn't too concerned either. That was the team captain's business. My job was simply to work.

Seeing the hostility of the local police, the team captain changed his mind about Clarksburg. For the next few days we worked the towns and rural areas outside of town until our charges could be heard. When my hearing came up, the judge stood behind a Dutch door-type partition, looking almost like a coat check clerk, and spoke to me for a few minutes. I believe the charge against me (whatever it was) was dismissed. The sister from New York received the same treatment. I wonder what the judge thought of the actions of these police officers. They could have simply told us to stop; I might have ignored a factory foreman, but I would not have ignored a policeman. In any case, the team captain decided to take the team at once downstate, to work the small towns and villages, as well as the roads that wind up through the valleys into the hills (called "hallers"), which are often populated by houses stretched out every quarter mile or more.

One thing the Clarksburg incident illustrates was my tendency to blunder into police officers, mall managers, building owners, and anyone else who had the authority to stop me from fund-raising. Every fundraiser has such encounters, but I seemed to have a particular knack for meeting up with these people; my first team captain called me "Mr. Kickout". I was a bit too reckless and overly aggressive when I barged into places; worse, I didn't use my head to foresee problems that might arise, mostly because no-one had specifically warned me to anticipate these things. As a good M.F.T. member, I was not supposed to think; that was up to the team captain. I was merely supposed to act.

I continued to display my fine talent for getting into trouble as I worked my way downstate. In a small coal-mining town to which I had been assigned for the entire day, the mayor of the town came out for the express purpose of yelling at me. In Parkersburg, after blitzing a commercial strip leading into town, I boldly ordered lunch from a fast food joint after I had just finished soliciting them. Two police officers stopped me in the middle of my hamburger and took me to the police station, where I slept on a bench until the team captain found me. On another occasion, I unwisely entered a combined police station and city hall in a small town to look for buyers. For the rest of the fund-raising period, the local sheriff followed me to every door I knocked on—which certainly put a damper on sales.

In spite of these problems, I began to be more successful as the team looped around the southern portion of the state, through Charleston and Huntington and then back up to Parkersburg. More and more, I was "breaking through", as I had hoped to do in Baltimore; on many days, I earned more than two or three hundred dollars.

When a fundraiser breaks through—as I was beginning to discover—the normal rules of probability no longer seem to apply. Suddenly, people approach him or her on the street, with their hands already on their wallets and a strange smile on their faces, asking, "What are you selling?"—and they will go ahead and buy, without quite knowing why. When a fundraiser breaks through, a housing district which should be devoid of life on a workday morning is suddenly full of people willing to buy or give. People will even line up in a parking lot, waiting so they can each make a purchase in turn. When a fundraiser breaks through, the usually dreaded mention of the name "Unification Church" is no longer a turn-off; people either fail to recognize the name, or they decide to buy anyway, because they like the individual.

Increasingly, I began to experience the magic of this phenomenon. In Huntington, on an unpromising retail strip called Washington Avenue, I earned more than eighty dollars in about two hours, selling painted butterfly pins from Korea for five dollars apiece. I walked into a small bowling lane and nearly everyone bought them. Using the same product in a residential area outside of Parkersburg, I sold everything I had in three hours, even though the houses were spaced well apart. I can think of only one small change in my daily habits which might explain this "breakthrough."

Every night after the rest of the team had gone to bed, I stayed up to offer a special extra prayer. Usually, once evening service has ended, M.F.T. members are expected to go to bed at once. It is actually a sort of disobedience to do what I did—not immediately rolling out my sleeping bag, but instead going for a walk outdoors until I found a private place where I could pray again. These extra prayers were much the same as my other prayers—pledging determination and so on—so it was not the content of the prayers that made the difference. Nor do I believe that God was listening especially hard to these prayers, simply because they were extra. The change likely came about because, by staying up when I didn't have to, I was demonstrating my willingness to put up with the short hours of sleep that were required of M.F.T. members. It was as though I had said, "Oh yeah? You call that short? I'll make it even shorter!" As a result, I overcame my resentment about how little sleep I was getting, and became more relaxed and at peace with what I was doing. It was likely this that caused people to suddenly respond much more favorably to me. I had finally achieved what Father demanded above all else from his followers—I had become total action without reflection—pure doing.

This, in fact, was what Father had in mind when he insisted that Seminarians should first go to the M.F.T. He wanted them to have the experience of totally emptying their minds, and of thinking of nothing except obedience to him. Then, later, when they would find themselves in an intellectual environment like the Seminary, they would never let mere ideas get in the way of unthinking loyalty and obedience.

I probably could have sustained this furious pace for as much as a year or more, but I could not have continued indefinitely. I had heard of some M.F.T. members—even top members whose achievements were legendary—who had "burned out" and become incapable of continuing to achieve high results. That would likely have also been my fate had not something happened to change everything.

Early in April, 1978, the team had worked its way back north again, passing through New Martinsville and Proctor on its way to Wheeling. I was dropped off one day with a brother from Maine named Jim to work a racetrack on the outskirts of Wheeling. We were to approach anyone who worked on the track until the races started, after which we were to work the entire crowd. Jim and I went to different parts of the track, and I even entered some horse stables and approached a few of the stable hands and jockeys before I made my way back to the grandstand to meet up with Jim again. We were conferring as to how to work the crowd which was starting to assemble when a track security guard approached us. He took us to the security chief, who questioned us closely about birthdates, birth places and addresses. Since we were normally compliant to authority figures (unless specifically told to act differently), we answered truthfully, even providing the Silver Springs regional headquarters as our address. Jim revealed that he was from Maine and I said that I was from Alberta. On learning that I was a Canadian, the security chief picked up the phone and called the Immigration and Naturalization Service to report that he had an illegal alien on his hands. He turned the phone over to me and I was told by the I.N.S. official to report to Pittsburgh in two days. Then we were allowed to go, though we could not continue fund-raising at the race track.

When I explained the incident to the team captain, I thought that I would be simply transferred to another M.F.T. region, such as Texas or Oregon, where the I.N.S. would be unable to trace me. But because we had revealed the regional headquarters address—where many illegal aliens were housed, including the Commander himself—it was clear that I would have to report to Pittsburgh in order to prevent the INS from coming around to look for me, which might lead them to the discovery of those other illegal aliens. The team captain took me to the Wheeling bus station and bought me a bus ticket to Pittsburgh, where I was told to stay at the local M.F.T. center.

I had a full day ahead of me before I was supposed to meet the INS officials, and I felt that I couldn't simply take the day off to relax; so I spent my free time rearranging the cluttered basement where the fund-raising team kept its products. When I went to see the I.N.S., they checked my name against their files and discovered an old record indicating that I had entered the U.S. through Vancouver on August 21, 1976. Since Canadians are allowed to stay for only six months, I had overstayed my visa by more than a year. They told me I had the choice of leaving voluntarily, or being deported. I chose voluntary departure, and then called my Commander.

I was expecting him to arrange to transfer me to the Canadian Unification Church in Toronto, but the Commander was mainly just worried about being stuck with the bill for sending me away. Never mind that I had just spent several months raising thousands of dollars for the church; his first concern was to ask if I could get my parents to pay for the trip. Loyal as ever, I called my parents in Calgary to ask them to bring me home, explaining my predicament. They agreed, and the next day I was on the plane from Pittsburgh to Calgary, via Chicago. Even though I had not seen my family for nearly two years, I don't recall that I was anxious about the reception I would get from them when I got back to Calgary. I was simply planning to represent Father to my family and friends faithfully, believing that one day soon they too would accept Father as the Lord of the Second Advent, and then they would be very proud of my work for him. After a brief visit with them, I figured, I would go on my way to work for the Unification Church in Canada. But even if my family turned out to be opposed to my commitment, I was determined that I would never leave Father under any circumstances.

Chapter Eight

Home Church

My family in Calgary received me back with surprise, but when I made it clear that I intended to return to the church as soon as possible, they did not try to stop me. Being still immersed in the M.F.T. mindset, which insisted that there was never a moment to waste, I felt I was only allowed a short stay in which to visit with family and friends. Furthermore, I believed I was in danger of being "invaded by Satan" if I didn't immediately contact a Unification Church central figure, and I knew I would have to phone Toronto to find one. I called them the very next day after my arrival, even offering to immediately go fund-raising in Calgary if they wanted me to. The baffled subordinate leader in Toronto, evidently unfamiliar with the fanatical M.F.T. mindset, gave me a surprising order: he said I should go ahead and take time to visit with my family and friends before returning to the church. Because he said this, I felt free to take a few weeks for this purpose. Without these directions from an authority figure, I would have been wracked with guilt.

With the methodicalness I had learned on M.F.T., then, I began to mentally catalogue all my family and friends, and worked out a plan to visit as many of them as possible. I did not expect to convert anyone; I merely hoped to "represent" Father to them, so that they would be "prepared" to receive him when the time came for everyone to convert. My idea of righteousness was still heavily tied up with observing church routines, so I awakened myself on Sundays at 5:00 a.m. (in my old basement bedroom) and bowed down before a picture of True Father and True Mother, while quietly reciting My Pledge. I also was determined to impress my family with what a good person I had become, so I made a lot of effort to be helpful around the house, even preparing a few meals for them.

I also began methodically calling all my friends from high school and university, including my former girlfriend, Sandy. Sandy and I had once been cycling enthusiasts, so we arranged to cycle together out to a park on the west side of the city, and then back. I was a totally different man from the one who had once been her friend; no longer was I straggly-haired, with a peach-fuzz beard, obsessed with Sartre and Thomas Mann and European novelists. No longer was I the shy, depressive man who dreamed of being a writer, and who had taken six months just to get up the nerve to ask her out. Now, I was a short-haired, close-shaven zealot for an unusual religion, and I talked about little else, showing few signs of my former love for literature. Yet I probably seemed more assured in my new guise—less visibly unhappy—and Sandy was gracious enough to accept this new outlook.

Sandy told me about her apparent recovery from her psychological distress; she seemed to be back on track. There was no sign, that I could see on that sunny spring day as we rode our bicycles out to a Calgary park, that the storm clouds of mental illness were again gathering on the horizons of her soul. I said goodbye, and Sandy rode away from me on her bicycle. I never saw her again.

With Sandy's name checked off my list, I proceeded on to all the other friends from my high school and university days; meeting some in a bar (where I drank only orange juice) and then going out to visit another high school buddy at his park ranger's station in an isolated part of Alberta. I then rode out to Vancouver by train and visited my friends from the days when I had been a student there, so that they, too, could meet (and be puzzled by) my radically transformed self. Two friends from my high school days, who had subsequently married, were also there studying medicine. I visited them, looked at their wedding pictures, and generally gave the appearance of being thoughtful and self-possessed. In short, I represented True Father to the best of my ability.

Having checked everyone that I could off my list, I decided it was time to return to active duty. Using some of the money gained from a final settlement of my Workmen's Compensation claim from the 1976 accident, I flew to Toronto and presented myself on the doorstep of the church center there, a large house in the university district near the heart of the city. As far as I knew, I would now remain a Unification Church member in Toronto indefinitely; I had no plans to return to the United States at all. For the next two months, from the end of April until mid-June, I occupied myself with whatever tasks the relatively tiny Canadian branch of the church asked of me.

They sent me on fund-raising trips to London, Ontario, and Niagara Falls (and I was astounded to discover that, unlike the American M.F.T., Canadian teams actually took time off to have an evening meal together, and did not believe in bar blitzing!) I witnessed to potential recruits on University Avenue. I went to another of those Divine Principle workshops designed to "unify" the Family at the church's farm in Rice Lake, Ontario, and during a tree-planting campaign at the farm managed to contract a case of poison ivy. As well, I went to Italian neighborhoods and, using the few Italian phrases I had been taught, told people about a planned rally for Canadian unity which was to occur on June 24, 1978 in central Toronto. (The rally was staged by the Canadian Unity and Freedom Federation, a Unification Church political front group.)

I never got to participate in the rally, because in mid-June a familiar series of events occurred: first, the Toronto family was contacted by the Seminary and told that I was a candidate and should be sent to Barrytown for consideration. Secondly, Toronto church leaders went to work on me to convince me that I didn't really want to go, and that I was too inexperienced to go to the Seminary yet; to which argument, I readily agreed. Finally, the Seminary overruled this opinion, ordering the Canadian church leader to produce me anyway. So my "indefinite" sojourn in Canada turned out to be some two months in duration.

I was warned before I left Toronto that as a Seminary candidate I was going to be involved in a campaign in London, England, and that I should get my passport ready and purchase an umbrella suitable for English weather. After obtaining both, I was given bus fare to Rhinebeck (a town near Barrytown) via Buffalo, New York. Worrying that I might be turned back at the border, I prepared an alibi: I told the border official I was going to visit "my friend, Joe Klein," who was then president of the Seminary graduating class. It worked. I was allowed to enter the United States without difficulty.

I arrived a few days early, and waited around until the entire potential Seminary class was assembled—perhaps 60 altogether—of which some 15 were women. Unlike the previous year, we would not be assessed immediately; instead we would be tested by going overseas, along with the senior Seminary class and the graduating class, to "fight the good fight" in England. If we survived this test, we were in. Excited by the prospect of travel, the Seminarians staged a celebration night, which included a memorable version of "Over There!" sung by one of the Seminary graduates, a former Las Vegas crooner.

But first there was the little matter of needing money to get us "over there." This we would have to raise ourselves, so as usual everyone was divided up into teams and once again M.F.T. commanders were called and inveigled to loan out fund-raising territory. My team was assigned to Baton Rouge, Louisiana, along with other points in the American South, and within a few days we were off.

Louisiana in late June is scorchingly hot, but with my recent M.F.T. training I was not about to let this deter me, so I carried on with my characteristic doggedness, selling carnations on street corners in the midday sun. One night, our team decided to save money, so the team captain pulled into the back lot of a large Motel 6, well after midnight. We took out our sleeping bags and slept in the hallway of the motel, and left in the morning before we could be discovered. We also spent a short time selling flowers in New Orleans, and on the way back from Louisiana we passed through Huntsville and Atlanta, but we were always intent on selling products and never bothered to take in the scenery. Two weeks after we had set out, we returned to Barrytown, bringing with us our vinyl bank bags filled with cash.

It was now time to send the Seminarians, Seminary graduates and would-be Seminarians off into the great unknown. This was my first excursion overseas, but my thoughts were mostly dominated by the fervent pledges I was making in my prayers to "bring the victory for Father in London!" In 1978 an upstart airline, Laker Airways, offered inexpensive fares from New York to London by accepting passengers much as a bus would, on a first-come, first serve basis. So we all trooped down to the Laker Airways office in Queens to await our turn to fly into Gatwick, whenever the call might come, night or day. Before long we were all on our way and, upon arrival in London, made our way to the Unification Church headquarters at Lancaster Gate, which is in central London near Hyde Park.

"Lancaster Gate", as all the members call it, is a set of three-storey houses all joined together at the end of a cul-de-sac that is entirely lined with such buildings. The neighborhood is expensive and dominated by tourist hotels. In the middle of the cul-de-sac is a large green on which stood a church that had been partially burned by fire. (We were told that the fire had happened because the priest had "set bad conditions" by preaching against Father and the Unification Church). When the waves of Americans arrived, they were dutifully assigned floor space on which to lay their sleeping bags throughout the building, on either the "brothers' floors" or the "sisters' floors". There were also a large meeting room on one of the upper floors, where Father would address us once we were all assembled in London. Rumors were rampant that Father was planning a really radical campaign unlike anything we had seen before. We were all expecting a street witnessing campaign like the one I had experienced in Los Angeles, where the members all lived at one location and simply recruited people off the streets. But word had started going around that Father intended to send us out to do "Home Church", which meant witnessing to people in their homes. Still, most of us equated this with "door-to-door witnessing", where the members still lived together while they canvassed in assigned neighborhoods. But no, we were told by someone who had inside information; Father was actually going to send us out to *live* in the neighborhoods, and we would be barred from staying at the center. Accustomed as we were to living communally in one assigned place, with the support of all the other brothers and sisters around, this was a daunting idea. It was a jump into the void, and I braced myself for it.

Sure enough, when Father assembled us in the main meeting room for his long-awaited speech, the rumors proved correct. We were to leave Lancaster Gate and go out into Greater London to find our own accommodation. We were allowed a grace period of a few days, but at some point we would be required to leave Lancaster Gate. If we could not find a place to stay, Father helpfully suggested, perhaps we should consider just walking around all night, and then sleeping on a park bench the next day.

Once we had found a place to stay, we were to select 360 homes in the neighborhood which we were to doggedly "love and serve" until eventually the residents recognized us to be the incredible people we were, and would then ask us who had taught us to be so wonderful. We could then witness to Father, and teach them Divine Principle, and they would convert in droves. This was the basic theory behind "Home Church," the nickname Father gave to this plan. As for the Seminarians who would be in London for just two months, we were expected to find at least three new converts before we returned to our studies in America.

Father added that he had considered sending us out without any money, since that would be a greater condition of faith, but other church leaders had advised against it (perhaps because it might result in bad publicity). So we were all to be given an amount of money to get us started, which Father would hand to us personally; we were expected to spend it wisely, using as little of it as possible. One sister I later befriended at the Seminary made a vow right then that she would not use one penny of this money, and her faith was rewarded; she was able to get by for two months without spending any of it. I was not of such strong faith. As we lined up to receive the money, we were instructed about the correct Korean way to receive a gift: with both hands, while bowing low to Father. I forget the exact amount we were given; perhaps forty pounds sterling.

With that, I was launched into the complete unknown of London. I puzzled over the subway maps, since the Tube was at least a good starting point; it provided a pattern of connections between the confusion of places. Only a few place names were familiar to me; I had vaguely heard of Chelsea (wasn't there a popular song about "Chelsea Morning"?) so I went there first. Knowing no other way to go about it than the way my M.F.T. training had taught me, I simply picked a row of houses and shops and began knocking on doors, and to the few who answered, I poured out my strange tale of needing a place to live and being willing to do odd jobs to pay for it. But I found little response in Chelsea, a blue-collar area (at least in the part I visited), so I quickly beat a retreat to the Tube station to look at the map again. Further down the same Tube line was another name I recognized: Wimbledon. Off I went, then, to knock on doors near the Mecca of the tennis world (though I knew nothing about tennis).

Wimbledon is on the opposite end of the economic scale from Chelsea. Large detached homes are common, and so I hit on a new strategy: these rich people might need a babysitter! So I rang doorbells and spoke through intercoms to incredulous people who brusquely informed me that "we already have an *au pair* person." One person warned me that his neighbors might get the idea that I was casing their homes for the purpose of robbery. Obviously, Wimbledon wasn't working out either. I returned to Lancaster Gate to ponder my options.

Next morning, it was back to the Tube station to look at the maps. At the far end on another Tube line, paralleling the one that went to Wimbledon, was a line that led to "Morden." H'mm, I thought, sounds like "Gordon", could this be a sign from heaven? I was in need of such a sign at that moment. Off I went, then, to Morden, and there at last I found a congenial neighborhood that lay comfortably between the economic extremes of Chelsea and Wimbledon.

Morden is at the junction of two roads along which shops and other businesses are concentrated. On the one side of the business area lay the "council flats" (what Americans would call "housing projects") for low-income people; on the other side were the middle-class homes, mostly row houses lined up along tidy streets. It was to these last that I repaired, adopting the strategy so familiar to me from M.F.T. I would simply knock on every door until I found someone who would take me in. I would offer to pay for my stay by doing odd jobs, but if money was asked for, I was prepared to pay.

People in England are not as accustomed as Americans to having strangers knock on their doors with odd pitches. I certainly raised many eyebrows as I went methodically from door to door, telling my story. Nevertheless, I knew from experience that sheer persistence would eventually pay off, and it did. After canvassing one complete road and most of another, I found myself on the doorstep of an elderly couple who just happened to have an unoccupied room because their son was away in the foreign service. Considering me carefully (and perhaps showing some bravery since I had no written references), the old woman offered to let me stay in her son's room for a fixed rent. I quickly accepted, though I knew this meant spending some of Father's money, which I hadn't wanted to do. But I needed somewhere to start, and this was my first real break.

I returned to Lancaster Gate to collect my few worldly goods, and brought them to my little upstairs room where I hoped to launch my plan to win the hearts and minds of the entire neighborhood. The very next day, I began knocking on doors again, this time simply offering to do whatever helpful work needed doing.

Over the course of those two summer months in 1978, I managed to do at least a few useful things for my neighbors. I mowed the lawn of an elderly woman who could no longer manage it, and I played board games with another elderly woman who simply needed some companionship. I unplugged the outdoor drain for an Indian family (while the gentleman of the house gave me an earful about the superiority of Hinduism over Christianity). I helped a number of people with yard work, and in fact, this became my main focus. None of this, however, seemed likely to result in mass conversions to the Unification Church.

When I knocked on the door of the rectory behind the small Salvation Army Church, however, I did find my first opening into another area of interest: contacting ministers and priests. The Salvation Army minister, a friendly young man named Allan, was in fact in the process of repainting his church, so I helped him with this project. In the days that followed I began going around to all the churches in the area to offer my services, and ended up mowing the lawns for the Baptist Church, trimming the hedges for the Catholic Church, and clipping around the edges of the moldering gravestones that surrounded the venerable Church of England. This approach to ecumenism through garden work probably amused many people, but it seemed harmless enough; that is, until I began to raise hackles at the Baptist Church.

The problem was that I was not only doing gardening for these churches, I was also attending their services. In the case of the Baptist Church, I even went to some Bible meetings. At one of these meetings it somehow came out that I didn't believe that Jesus Christ is literally God (the Divine Principle rules this out). So I was a heretic as far as the Baptists were concerned, and from that point on, I was unwelcome to attend their services. I should have left it at that, but I was taking Father quite literally when he said that I could eventually win the favor of my enemies through diligent service. I tried to continue to do garden work for the Baptists, even planting a small tree— unasked—near their front doorstep (this too, was Father's idea: in one of his speeches he said that each member should plant three trees in his Home

Church area). Even more strangely, one day I went to the home of the Baptist pastor and started trimming around the edges of his lawn—again unasked. The pastor's puzzled wife came out to put a stop to that.

My ecumenical outreach yielded few fruits, although I did get Allan to come to one dinner meeting at Lancaster Gate. His church was the smallest and the poorest, so perhaps he had fewer inhibitions about talking to the Moonies, although he was certainly not converted. I even planted a tree in his church yard (as usual, unasked) and he seemed not to mind and even posed for a snapshot beside it.

About half way through my summer in London, the elderly couple with whom I had found accommodation announced that I would have to leave, as their son was returning from overseas. I therefore had to hastily scramble for alternatives, and began knocking on doors again. By this time I had a few other contacts in the neighborhood and was able to secure free accommodation for one week with a young couple. I tried to repay their kindness in the usual way—by doing yard work—but this only seemed to annoy them, and I was soon asked to move on. For the remaining two weeks I stayed with another friend, a bemused elder with the Methodist Church (another church I had attended and sought to serve) who tolerated me mostly because my stay would soon be over.

My Home Church experiment had obviously not worked out according to Father's glorious blueprint. Still, though I gained none of the expected results, I had displayed the same dedication that had served me throughout my M.F.T. career. Indeed, I might have ended up not seeing any of the tourist sights of London at all, had not a young friend from the Baptist Church (before my heresy was exposed) offered to take me. Still, I had worked diligently, going out every day, just as Father asked.

At the end of the summer, when I handed over my Home Church area to another church missionary (who quickly saw that I had nothing much to give him) I was at least able to say that I had not given up. This was about as good as most of the Seminarians had done, and it was enough to qualify me to go on to the Seminary, where my heart truly lay: in the world of academics and reflection. All the same, I regretted leaving Morden; I thought that perhaps if I'd stayed longer, the miracles that Father spoke of would finally have happened. But I was just as eager to move on to Barrytown, too. If Father needed me to study, I reasoned, then I was prepared to study with resolute diligence and unyielding faith.

CHAPTER NINE

SEMINARIANS

The Unification Theological Seminary in Barrytown, New York, occupies a substantial brick building that was once owned by the Christian Brothers. The white crosses on the sides of the building were allowed to remain, but statues of saints were removed. Bodies which had been laid to rest in a small graveyard were exhumed and reburied elsewhere by the Christian Brothers at the insistence of the Unification Church. The Seminary boasted a large chapel, two wings with classrooms, a library, a gymnasium, a dining hall, and dormitories filled with two-tier bunk beds. The students believed they were there to study Theology and Philosophy and Scripture, in order to use this knowledge to convert believers of all of the world's religions to the Divine Principle. More practically, the Seminary was intended as a training ground for future Unification Church leaders who, it was envisioned, would meld intellectual sophistication with unrelenting zealotry.

In 1978, though the Seminary was then unaccredited, it offered a two-year course of study which was considered the equivalent of a "Master of Religious Education" program. The students in those days were all culled from the church's ranks and were mostly Americans, though there was a smattering of other nationalities, including a few Japanese, British, Europeans, and Canadians, who had passed the academic requirements by obtaining some kind of secondary education in their homelands.

The Senior class of some fifty students had already passed one year at the Seminary while the Junior class (to which I belonged) was just beginning its studies. The differences between the two classes were obvious. The Seniors were more individualistic, and included a number of people who had stopped being reflexively obedient to the Seminary authorities. Anywhere else in the Unification Church, this would not have been tolerated; yet at the Seminary they were left alone, provided they kept their irreverence within narrow limits. Meanwhile, the Junior class members were mostly fresh off the fund-raising teams, and could not understand the Seniors at all; but since they were our elders, we merely grumbled quietly among ourselves. Ignoring the "lower standards" of the Seniors, we continued to wear conservative dress and continued to dutifully bound out of bed for all the pledge services and morning sermons.

If academic studies were supposedly the purpose for the Seminary, one would have scarcely known it from the whirlwind of activity that awaited the students. Of course, we were indeed required to attend classes in Philosophy, Comparative Religion, Church History, Bible Studies, Psychology and Religious Education, but these always seemed to take second place to whatever big project was currently being promoted at the Seminary. For example, during the first few weeks of September, 1978, the students were repeatedly asked to go out to the fields to harvest potatoes. There was also a host of other extra-curricular duties, such as helping with the routine maintenance of the buildings and grounds; participating in security watches from a guard booth by the road; attending guest lectures; assisting with conferences for visiting theologians; lecturing the Divine Principle for practice; attending the morning service every day; and fund-raising every Christmas, Easter, and summer holiday, as well as on occasional weekends. In addition, a "Home Church" program was introduced which required students to attend a local Christian church and visit a residential area in one of the neighboring towns. On top of this, a martial arts program known as "Won Hwa Do" was introduced in 1978, led by a Korean man named Dr. Seuk. The gymnasium was converted into a do-jong, and we were expected to dress in martial arts uniforms while practicing punches, kicks, and other maneuvers, in the event these skills might be needed to defeat Communism. (Not being physically skilled, I found this requirement especially difficult).

As well, there was no end to the ingenuity of the students themselves in coming up with celebrations and theme nights that required actors, singers, and other volunteers to bring them off. I have many photographs of these celebration nights, but I have only one photograph in which a professor appears—and he is dressed in costume for a "Medieval Night". So while our ostensible purpose for being at the Seminary was to study, in practice this ended up being the thing most students gave only the bare minimum of their time to.

Even so, the Seminary authorities had assembled a diverse faculty of professors: a Jesuit priest, a Methodist minister, a Dutch Reformed minister, a Greek Orthodox scholar, and so on. In 1978, only one of the professors was a Unificationist, and she had been a Swedenborgian prior to her conversion. This eclectic group brought a contentious mix of viewpoints and prejudices to their academic duties, which was a source of some hilarity among the students. Every year without fail, the good rabbi who taught Old Testament studies would stir up a huge argument by disputing the Divine Principle's assertion that Abraham had failed when he did not cut the dove and pigeon at one of his sacrificial offerings (*Genesis* 15). This argument would then continue pointlessly for the remainder of the class, without anything being resolved. Meanwhile, the Greek Orthodox scholar loved to pointedly condemn the Roman church for the actions of the Crusaders a millennium previously, when they had needlessly sacked Constantinople. The Polish Jesuit priest, ignoring these barbs, was famous for being the only professor who would get upset when one of his students fell asleep in class (which, given our schedules, happened a lot). "Please, stay within these four walls!" he would cry out in a plaintive voice we loved to imitate. "Do not go to other world!"

How, then, was I to excel at all the classes—and thus to "justify my existence" as a Seminarian—when I had all these other things to do as well? My solution was to volunteer to be the note-taker for many classes; my notes were copied and memorized by other students who were too tired or too busy to take in the lectures. I was especially valued because I took notes in complete sentences, wherein I tried to summarize what was said.

Many things were different about the way the Seminarians lived compared to other Unification Church members. Seminarians had the time and opportunity to build real friendships that were not strictly focused on "mission" or "duty." They had the luxury of knowing where they would be situated for the next two years, and did not have to carry around the ever-present possibility of a sudden move. Their activities were not strictly monitored, and they were not as likely to be publicly singled out and criticized. Sporadically, they were granted small financial stipends, which they could spend in neighboring towns like Kingston and Poughkeepsie at their discretion. They could arrange to borrow a car to leave the Seminary grounds, and if a car was available, they were allowed to go.

But this relaxation of external controls only gradually changed the way Seminarians thought and behaved. It was usually not until the second year that they would start to become noticeably individualistic and begin to have markedly distinct personalities. In my first year, I was as duty-bound as ever, never deviating from my determination to earn justification by works. If Father wanted me to be the best student, then I would attend all the classes, no matter how tired I was. If he also asked me to be a martial arts expert, well, I would do my best. If on top of this he expected me to bring converts through "Home Church", and to go fishing on the Hudson River, and to pray constantly and attend every morning service, then I bent my efforts to do all of these things—and for the most part I did well at these things.

The degree of my separation from my own feelings can be seen in one incident that happened during my first year. Foreign students were (initially) exempt from fund-raising because of potential visa problems. As an English-speaking Canadian, I was considered only "sort of" foreign by church authorities. But just to be on the safe side, I went into their alternative program anyway, where students were assigned to split wood which was harvested from the Seminary grounds, which could then be sold for firewood. One day while performing this chore, my left middle finger became caught in the wood-splitter. My finger might have been severed if someone had not quickly shut it off. Without a word I then ambled back to the Seminary, bleeding profusely the whole way, and climbed the stairs to the Administration office to ask for the nurse. She took one look at the crushed finger and immediately got a car to take me into Kingston, where a doctor put in several stitches while I stood there silently. "You're a good stoic," he told me.

Yet splitting wood did not, in the end, exempt me from fund-raising. I still went out with the fund-raising teams at Christmas and Easter. During the two-month summer break in 1979, the Seminarians were again expected to go onto M.F.T. teams for the entire summer. An exception was made for "foreigners" like myself: instead of the M.F.T., we were to sell attractive novelties for a company known as "Original World Products" (which channeled its funds, curiously, into the budget of the struggling *News World* newspaper).

The novelties we sold were preserved butterflies perched on small wooden twigs with dried vegetation around them. These beautiful creatures were encased in clear Lucite boxes or in glass domes with wooden bases, and they were quite striking, especially a gorgeous Brazilian butterfly with shimmering metallic blue wings. This was an expensive product for fund-raising, with price tags ranging up to fifty dollars, but many people were impressed by the butterflies, and were willing to pay the higher prices. During the summer of 1979 I traveled with a team that roamed through seven states in the American northeast, beginning in Ohio and passing through New England before finishing in Pennsylvania. By the end of the summer I had finally "broken through", bringing strong results again, as I had done in my M.F.T. days. Immediately afterwards, it was time for me to return to the Seminary.

I commenced my Senior year in much the same manner as my Junior, by trying to keep up with all that was expected of me, even though the work load became more and more unmanageable. I became the assistant editor of a monthly newsletter, the *Cornerstone*, which was intended to give subscribers a glowing account of what a bright, active group the students were. The *Cornerstone*'s editor was a pert, eternally cheerful sister named Fran who was a pleasure to work with, but even so, my assistant editor duties were yet one more thing on my already overburdened list of tasks. I began to wonder how I was ever going to keep up with it all.

Eventually, about half way through my Senior year, I hit on a solution. I decided to "abolish day and night". That is, I decided that from then on, I would sleep only in "catnaps" of one or two hours' duration, but no longer. I would stay up from midnight to four in the morning to study, because that was the only time when I was not likely to get called away to another activity. After two hours of sleep, I could start my day, and would not go back to bed again until late afternoon, when I would take another two-hour catnap before dinner.

This system seemed to work well. I was always tired, but I was finally able to keep up with nearly everything. My grades improved, and I was able to shine in extra-curricular activities such as editing the *Cornerstone*. This productivity did not go unnoticed. When it came time to select twelve candidates for a new third-year program, known as a "Master of Divinity" program, I was among those chosen by Sun Myung Moon himself when he visited the Seminary in early 1980. This was my highest achievement by the standards of the Unification Church—the pinnacle of my efforts to achieve justification by works.

However, I was not even aware of how exhausted I was becoming as I tried to do everything that was demanded of me. If Father and the Seminary authorities said I was expected to do all of these things, then I had to do them, as far as I was concerned—no excuses. Most of the other students had by this time figured out that they were actually only required to do *some* of them well, and as for the rest they were merely supposed to pretend to do them. My need to justify my existence was forcing me into an emotional bind which (as had also occurred on the I.O.W.C.) was bringing me close to a nervous breakdown. However, this time I wasn't even aware I was in trouble.

Around this time, too, a distressing letter arrived from an unexpected source. The father of my former girlfriend, Sandy, who had previously written saying that she was missing and asking if I knew of her whereabouts, wrote to me a second time telling me what had happened. "Sandy is dead", he wrote. In the months leading up to her disappearance, she had once again taken on a heavy load of work and extra-curricular activities, driving herself frenetically. Suddenly, she was gone. Many months later, someone strolling along the brink of an isolated cliff in Newfoundland happened to look down, and noticed a young woman lying on a ledge about half way down. It was Sandy—dead of apparent suicide.

Although I was much saddened by this news, I was still too preoccupied with keeping up with the Seminary's demands to feel deeply about it in a conscious way. The upsetting story, therefore, slipped down into my subconscious, where it added considerably to the anxiety I was feeling. It wasn't until Fran noticed my distress that I finally became aware of how unhappy I actually was.

Around three one morning, as I was lying on the floor of a study room taking an extra catnap because I couldn't keep my eyes open, Fran poked her head through the door. She saw me lying there, and reacted according to her natural kindness; Fran approached me with love.

It was not romantic love she was offering, since that of course was strictly forbidden. Rather, she simply told me that she could see I was having a "hard time," and offered to lend a willing ear if I wanted to talk about my troubles to her. These simple words—intended only as an ordinary kindness— suddenly unlocked the door to my own real feelings. But even more importantly, Fran showed that she was valuing me for myself, and not just for my achievements. Even though she was not offering romantic love, it still felt to me as though it were a sincere offer of true love.

For days afterwards I could think of nothing else. I even wrote a flowery sermon about it, titled "Seeking the Oasis", which I gave first to my Homiletics class, and then to the entire Seminary. Suddenly, my desperation to excel at an impossible list of activities was replaced with one single obsession: to pour out my feelings into Fran's empathic ear. Before I joined the Unification Church, I had dreamed of finding a woman who could, by her love for me, pull out the knife inside me. It now seemed that in some way Fran had become that woman, even though we were not having a romantic relationship. So instead of thinking of it as a love affair with Fran, I viewed it as an intense need to talk—to get at my real feelings—and this was how I described it to myself and to others.

However, this new emphasis meant that I was no longer the loyal, reflexively obedient church member I had been until then. No longer did I make it my top priority to get "results" for Father; instead it was my goal to be a kind and loving person like my new role model, Fran. She was startled by the intensity of my reaction but was pleased to help me, and in turn pointed me to her own mentor in the people-helping business: a student in the Junior class named Nancy. The emotional pain of the knife inside me had been brought to the surface by Fran's kindness, and now I clung to Fran and Nancy with a desperate emotional neediness.

Yet since Nancy was a Junior class member, while Fran and I were Seniors, it was controversial that either of us would defer to her for anything as significant as emotional counseling. Compounding the controversy, Nancy started a group counseling session consisting of a mixed group of brothers and sisters who met in a circle at the back of the chapel after every morning service. Nancy's emphasis in these sessions was on emotional honesty: members were not to try to pretend that they felt fine if they did not. But in the opinion of the Seminary administrators, we were supposed to get all our emotional help from the groups to which we had been assigned—that is, from the brothers groups and sisters' groups. However, the brothers groups that I belonged to served little purpose except to divide up cleaning chores and to go out for ice cream in Red Hook or Kingston. As sources for emotional support, they were meaningless. Still, that a Divinity program candidate like myself would belong to a group like Nancy's definitely raised eyebrows around the Seminary.

Still, this was not my worst crime. Nancy insisted that for me to gain the full benefit of her ideas, I should go to visit *her* mentor, Lee, who worked at a warehouse in Queens owned by the Unification Church. I did this one weekend when I was free from classes. Lee was a petite woman with a friendly manner, and she promised that she could help me get over my emotional pain.

This caused me to transfer my original emotional neediness primarily to Lee, and I became convinced she was the solution to my revived emotional pain. I still wanted to be a "good" member, but I didn't want to go back to simply repressing my feelings, as I was expected to do; I wanted to deal with my feelings first, and then go back to being a good member afterwards. I did not yet understand that this was a complete contradiction of all my church training, whose entire intent had been to get me to suppress all my thoughts and feelings, in order to think only of obedience to Father.

The Seminary authorities were angry with me for going down to New York on a weekend to see Lee, yet they might have let it pass if I had obeyed their instructions never to go see her again. But by this time, such a request was emotionally impossible, and even Nancy was encouraging me to do what once would have been unthinkable for me to do: to disobey a "central figure". As far as I could tell, my psychological state was collapsing rapidly. I *had* to see Lee again. So I went.

When I got back, the predictable explosion occurred. I was ordered by President David Kim, through his assistant, never to go to Lee again, on pain of being kicked out of the Seminary. Furthermore, the informal counseling group started by Nancy was ordered disbanded. Worse, I was not to talk to either Nancy or her closest supporter, Donna, again. But worst of all, I was not to talk to Fran, except about *Cornerstone* business. By this time, I loved these women, especially Fran, with a desperate neediness. Not talk to them? I might as well be dead.

I spent the next few weeks under a dark cloud. I remember climbing a staircase up to the third floor brothers' dormitory and thinking of jumping out the window. Still, I had an overwhelming need to talk, but since I could not talk to the ones I preferred, I poured out my feelings to some other sisters, though I knew they might report my words to the Seminary leaders. I remember sitting on an outdoors bench with one of these sisters on a sunny day, pouring out my grief over Sandy's fatal fall from a cliff thousands of miles from her home. Somehow, though it wasn't realistic to expect this, I hoped that my "counselor" would keep this sad story in confidence.

Two days later, a Seminary administrator threw the story in my face, remarking abruptly that he understood that I once had "a girlfriend who killed herself." He expressed dismay at my obsession with my feelings and said, among other things, that I should simply try to stop thinking about them. He even told me that "intense fund-raising is therapeutic."

Eventually, my emotional storms began to ease, but only slightly. There was, however, still one more blow to endure. Nancy was suddenly expelled from the Seminary and sent to West Africa as a foreign missionary.

By this time it was June of 1980, and my parents had arrived from Canada to visit me. Originally, they had been invited to attend my graduation ceremony, before I learned I was to stay on for an additional year. They came anyway, and I showed them around Barrytown, concealing from them the emotional storm I had just passed through. But it was never far from my thoughts. On a side trip to New York City, while we rode on the tourist-oriented Circle Line ferry, I kept staring across the river at the Queens skyline, searching for the silhouette of the church warehouse, and my heart cried out with desperate neediness, "Lee!" But I knew that the days of Lee, Nancy, Donna and Fran were over. From this point on, I was going to have to make my way without them.

End of Part Two.

PART THREE:

JUSTIFICATION BY LOVE

CHAPTER TEN

THE BOSTON DIARY

For the first time since I joined the Unification Church four years before, I found myself at odds with the church leaders. I now no longer believed that it was my first duty to obey them even if I disagreed with their views. Two years at the Seminary had freed up independent thought sufficiently that I was no longer swayed by the argument that, above all else, a church member must maintain unity. That view had been my credo, as it was for nearly all church members, up until that moment. But now I found the Seminary leaders were urging me to stuff back down all the strong feelings that Fran's kindness and Nancy's emphasis on honesty had brought to the surface. I was supposed to go back to repressing all my feelings in order to focus on doing Father's work, and to think only about how to do Father's work.

While I emphatically did not want to follow this advice, I also felt that it would be unthinkable to go to the opposite extreme, and leave the church entirely. That decision was, as I saw it, tantamount to accepting death. Well then, my internal argument would run, if I wanted to remain a member, wasn't I obligated to do whatever the church leaders demanded, whether I liked it or not? Yet I had come to believe that the church's failure to achieve the incredible results we had all been expecting was precisely *because* the church demanded that its members repress their feelings. It followed, therefore, that if I obeyed the church leaders and went back to suppressing my feelings, I would actually only be helping them to carry on with their counter-productive ways.

Therefore, I began to adopt the previously unthinkable opinion that it might be more useful to Father and God if I defied the church authorities by continuing to express my feelings, and by encouraging other members to do so as well. I began to picture myself in a new role, imitating the kindness of Fran and the honesty of Nancy, by becoming an empathetic listener to other members. In short, I would now seek to justify my existence through love, and not by works.

However, I simply couldn't settle into this new role easily and comfortably, because it was so contrary to normal church practices; and I did, after all, still want to be considered a good church member. My new attitude was certainly not going to earmark me as prime leadership material, and I knew that taking this maverick path would be viewed with suspicion by church leaders and members alike. Furthermore, I wasn't entirely sure of its validity myself. Sometimes I wondered if I was becoming "invaded by Satan" and was going off on the wrong track. But whenever I thought about the pure sweetness of Fran's love, and how deeply it had affected me, I felt certain that this was not an evil path. Even so, I was now at war with myself. My views and feelings kept going back and forth over and over again, with no resolution in sight. As the Seminary school year ended and the summer of 1980 began, I was forced to take my internal war with me to wherever the church chose to send me next.

Meanwhile, a new witnessing campaign was sweeping the Unification Church, this time using the church's campus front organization (known as the Collegiate Association for the Research of Principles, or "C.A.R.P."). All of the Seminarians who had graduated that year, including my beloved friend Fran, were reassigned to C.A.R.P. However, I was still scheduled to return to the Seminary in September for the Master of Divinity equivalency program, so I and the other Divinity students were sent to Boston instead for what was supposed to be a "practicum". This was a program similar to those offered by conventional seminaries, where for one academic term students would go into communities to gain practical experience in some pastoral capacity.

This had never been tried in the Unification Church before, so the exact nature of what we were to do was not clear. We had to figure it out for ourselves, by looking in advertisements for volunteer workers and contacting agencies to find groups that might permit a well-meaning "Moonie" to work with them on a volunteer project.

For a Unification Church member, it was a bizarre assignment, especially since we were staying at the C.A.R.P. center on Beacon Street across from the Boston Common, alongside other members who were being whipped into a frenzy by the recruiting campaign. The leader of C.A.R.P., a charismatic Korean named Reverend Park, came to Boston and lectured the members on what a waste of time it is to go around wanting love. He especially attacked the Oakland Family members, whom he blamed for this trait. He also pounced delightedly on the epithet "Cemetarians"—which had been making the rounds in the church—and used it several times to ridicule the Seminarians who, he said, were too caught up in theory to be of much practical use. In spite of this difficult environment, the Divinity students managed to maintain a separate group identity, and met every day to discuss what had been learned through the volunteer work.

I eventually settled on two volunteer assignments, one as a teacher of cardio-pulmonary resuscitation to teenagers (who received an extra credit from this for their school work), and the other as an assistant to a project whose aim was to write simple grammar lessons for a remedial English course. However, neither of these activities ended up playing a large part in my summer in Boston. Rather, the single most important thing I did that summer was to start a diary, in which I wrote down and debated with myself the growing division between the two warring camps inside me. I still wanted to be a good member who followed Father faithfully, doing everything that he required; but at the same time, I wanted to examine my own feelings deeply, and not repress them, as I was supposed to do. Sometimes I stayed up late at night so I could scribble in my diary while sitting in one of the many Brigham's restaurants near Boston Common.

I still have this diary, the only one of the many diaries I kept during my Unification Church years that I did not later destroy in a fit of self-reforming zeal. This one was special to me because the entries in it are so heart-rending, so full of lacerating pain and desperate questioning, that I could not bring myself to repudiate it. It is a small book with cream-colored pages, covered with brown cloth, in which I wrote in ballpoint pen, my handwriting sometimes scrawling and expansive, sometimes cramped and mechanical, as I vacillated between the two sides of myself. Often it is merely a bland record of events, but then it abruptly tosses out a startling admission. On July 10, 1980, I wrote:

> I felt guilty that I was home and comfortable while the C.A.R.P. members were out on the streets, working hard. But I didn't want, on the other hand, to just go out and work, (as if, by not working, I lose my right to even exist!) I often feel this way: that I have no right to exist, that I deserve to be annihilated.

At several points in the diary, I reported that people have told me to stop thinking so obsessively about my problems, and for a few days in early August, I tried to follow that advice. I resolved that the diary would be nothing more than a report of what I did; and so, for example, on August 1, in handwriting that was suddenly tiny, I reported:

> Arose 5:00 AM for pledge, 7:00 AM arose a second time for breakfast and prayer service in the Green Room. CPR at 9:00 AM after stopping at Brigham's over coffee to write the above entry in this diary.

Inevitably, this lasted only a few pages. The dilemma was too painful for me to leave alone. By August 17, 1980, the last entry in the diary, I was back to recording my feelings in the frankest way possible. I blamed myself relentlessly for not being able to follow Father in a simple way, without all this anguish—and yet I could not, for all of that, refuse to feel it. Here is that entry:

> I arose for pledge service as usual, but I was little able to concentrate on the prayer. My depression of yesterday had settled down over me like a shroud, obsessing me with suicidal fantasies. The only way I could stop my tired mind from playing out these brutal games was to think about [Fran].
>
> The rest of the day was just as lousy. I found little motivation to act. I sat in three different Brigham's restaurants drinking coffee, and took a stroll down the Charles River to the Science Museum where my attention was diverted momentarily by a locomotive and

a geological display. I started reading Kazantzakis' *The Last Temptation of Christ* and I wrote in my journal. I hated myself.

One event that *did* give me some spiritual power was listening to Mrs. Doris Orme as she gave the Sunday Service at the C.A.R.P. center. She testified about her experiences as a pioneer in Rome and told us that the way to experience God is in welcoming persecution and the hatred of the world. She also talked about some of her experiences with Father in London and about his great faith in that time of difficulty.

I admired Mrs. Orme and felt that I would like to command some of her spiritual power. At the same time, I felt utterly worthless, and even telling myself that God loved me had a hollow ring. I went to the prayer room later and asked God why he didn't despise me. I told him how much raw anger I felt and how much I wanted to kill or mutilate myself. I told him I knew that [doing] that wouldn't gain me anything but more suffering, and I reassured him that I wouldn't do it. But I challenged him to "do something" or to abolish me in body and spirit from the face of the earth.

With that, I ran out of pages in the little brown diary. The degree of my distress, running even to suicidal feelings, is a testimony to how torn I was by, on the one hand, my commitment to Father and the church, and on the other, to my conviction that I must not suppress my real feelings, even if it meant defying the church leaders.

Yet defying church leaders had always been considered as one of the worst things a church member could do, likened in many lectures to the act of Cain striking down Abel. I began to feel torn apart by the internal division. I wouldn't retreat and I couldn't advance. Stuck in this dilemma, I began to feel suicidal.

The severe pain I was in is best demonstrated by an event that occurred one evening when the Divinity students met together to discuss their thoughts and feelings. At such meetings snacks were usually served, such as ice cream or fruit. On this occasion a watermelon had been carved up for the group. As the discussion went around the table, I felt only deep depression. Indeed, I felt a feeling of profound worthlessness, as though I deserved to end my life right then and there. While I listened to the others talk, I began to idly finger the blade of the knife that had been used to carve up the watermelon. I wondered what it would be like to plunge the knife into my own heart, since I felt as if it were already lodged inside me anyway. I had no intention of doing it, but I couldn't shake this thought.

Somehow the leader of the Divinity students picked up on what I was feeling, and called me on it before the group. Combined with my other eccentric behavior, such as my late nights sitting in coffee shops, it was becoming clear to everyone that I was locked in obsessive introspection (and was toying with self-destructive thoughts), and of course this was passed on to the Seminary authorities.

What followed next was predictable, but it took me by surprise. At the start of September, the Divinity students returned to Barrytown. Despite my eccentricities, I had many extraordinary plans for my Divinity year. I began to put together ideas plans to write a definitive Unification novel which would capture the world's imagination—and that was just my thesis project! I also began to ponder the idea of starting philosopher's conferences, similar to the theologian's conferences that were already held at the Seminary. Plus, I planned to do all the other duties that the Seminary demanded. But there was a difference to my attitude now, and there was no question that I now put relationships with people first, ahead of achievements.

Predictably, during a meeting of the eleven remaining Divinity students (since one of the original twelve had quit the church during the summer), I felt a tap on my shoulder. Called away to a private meeting, I was told that I was to be sent away from the Seminary. The way they handled it was unusual for the Unification Church; normally, I would have either been sent away to a specific mission such as M.F.T., or they would have given up on me entirely, by sending me home to my family in a broken, humiliated state. But they did neither: they left it up to me where I would go next.

I was astounded that this had happened at all, and felt aggrieved at the sudden loss of so many friends at the Seminary; but after a few days it occurred to me that this could be my opportunity to return to my original plans from four years before. I could seize this chance to return to California to get Primal Therapy, without having to leave the Unification Church to do so. I put this idea to them, and they quickly agreed, even promising financial support, though that support turned out to be limited to just paying for my airfare. (I suppose they mostly just wanted to get me out of there). The Los Angeles Family leader, a former Seminarian, agreed to accept me despite my strange mission. He likely did this solely out of respect for the Seminary President's authority.

CHAPTER ELEVEN

TWO SUMMERS

The Los Angeles Family leader assigned me to the same church center that I had lived in nearly four years before, as a member of the I.O.W.C.: a former motel in East Los Angeles consisting of a cluster of small cabins around a large double driveway. The same massive blank wooden sign still wordlessly beckoned traffic on Huntington Drive. This was the home base of the Los Angeles Family's fund-raising team, and I was to be a member of that team, though (rather unconventionally) I was to be allowed to keep some of my earnings for Primal Therapy. As with all the fund-raising teams I had been on, I was expected to report my entire results each day, but now I was required to turn in only forty percent, while putting the rest in the bank. I was not even obligated to go out with the team every day; my participation was voluntary. I was now my own "central figure," and my mission (to heal myself psychologically) was something that few other members understood and many thought was a waste of time.

Even so, I was proud of my new situation, because I was convinced that I was pioneering something important that would help other members. But even as I set out to save money for therapy, I also tried to assist the Los Angeles church, and occasionally contributed my entire fund-raising results, or participated in other projects they engaged in, such as inviting people to a rally. I wanted to show that even though I had an unusual purpose for being there, I remained committed to the church's main goals.

The fund-raising team leader, Jack (also a Canadian), was patient with me in spite of the strangeness of my situation. Jack had the habit of boasting about how evil his pre-church past had been, including having supposedly associated with known criminals. However, he was an efficient fund-raising captain, and would ferry a team of eight to ten people daily around the greater Los Angeles region, while also striving to please the church leader, who lived in comfort at the church mansion in Pasadena.

The fund-raising team would usually sell costume jewelry pinned to black velvet display boards, but would return to Huntington Drive around 5:00 p.m. on Fridays and Saturdays to collect roses and floral bouquets wrapped in plastic to sell in the evening. The rose runs were the highlight of the week. We would go to all the dating hot spots in town: Chinatown, Hollywood Boulevard, Westwood and Marina Del Ray. The roses were easy sellers at $3 each or two for $5. I was often assigned to Hollywood Boulevard, a famed but seedy strip that included Mann's Chinese Theater and other tourist traps. Many Saturday nights I would find myself selling roses on one corner of the Boulevard while the Hare Krishna would be leaping up and down and pounding tambourines on another, and a Christian evangelical group would be passing out tracts on a third.

My position on the team was a bit awkward, because of the fact that I did not turn in my entire result, as everyone else did. I tried to make up for this by being the most caring team member. Many times Jack would put me out with an inexperienced member and I would try to help him or her by simply being friendly and listening to that person. One day I took a young, inexperienced African American sister on a tour of a shop that was full of rare, exotic parrots that we happened to stumble across in our fund-raising area.

Everywhere I went, though, I took my daily journal with me. I still felt that I had to fill out my daily record of thoughts and activities, and would even sometimes take time away from fund-raising to sit in coffee shops to write, or would go out at the end of the day to a 24-hour donut shop to record my thoughts. I continued to try to balance my desire to be a "good" member with my new-found concern with exploring the depths of my own feelings, and being sensitive to the feelings of other members.

Gradually, I accumulated the money needed to go to Primal Therapy, but it was clear that I would need far more than I was earning with my somewhat unfocused fund-raising methods. Early on during my time in Los Angeles, I wrote to the Primal Institute, which was located in an industrial area in West Los Angeles, and learned that I would need several thousand dollars (I forget how much) just to get started. At the rate I was going, it would take years to save that much. Even so, I believed that God supported my plan to get this treatment, so I kept hoping that some miracle would make the money available to me suddenly.

I was not, however, behaving in a single-minded fashion to get the money. I did not always go out with the fund-raising team, and I spent too much of my earnings in coffee shops as I recorded my thoughts and feelings in my many journals. In November, I even got involved with trying to recruit two young women that I met while fund-raising, which meant that I spent several weekends with guests at Camp Mozumdar instead of fund-raising. One of the young women had previously been briefly involved with the Unification Church, so I set out to bring her back to the fold. I was briefly successful, and even got her friend to join the church for a while.

Around this time I was told that former Seminarians were being called to Washington, D.C. to be considered as potential employees for a newspaper that Father was starting in that city. (This later became the *Washington Times* newspaper, which commenced publication in 1981). I probably would have done well in that line of work, but I didn't heed the call to go to Washington because I was still intent on going to Primal Therapy; in any case, I knew the legal problems caused by my Canadian citizenship would likely be a stumbling-block.

Soon afterwards, I met a Chinese man in the neighborhood 24-hour donut shop (naturally, while writing in my journal), and I set to work to recruit him and his Chinese roommate into the church. I was able to get both of them up to Camp Mozumdar, but that was as far as that went. However, my being at Camp Mozumdar late in December presented a problem, because I had promised my parents in Calgary that I would visit them for Christmas (for the first time in four years), and they had offered to pay for the trip. I believed that it would be "selfish" for me to go home to my family while I was in the middle of recruiting a new member, so I called to tell them I was now planning to stay at Camp Mozumdar through Christmas, which caused them much disappointment. But just when I thought the whole matter was settled, new directions came from New York that changed my plans again.

Father announced that he intended to hold a "Matching" for eligible members around the end of the month. Having been a member for more than four years, I was eligible, so I looked forward to it eagerly, though this meant I would have to spend much of the money I had been saving for therapy. This was the most significant ceremony of all for church members: Father would be matching me up to my "eternity mate"—the woman whom God had selected as my wife forever. By becoming engaged to her, I would partake of the Holy Wine, thus supposedly removing my Original Sin and opening the way to perfection of the soul.

***

Upon arriving in New York, I was greeted by a scene of high excitement at the New Yorker Hotel, and I certainly shared in that feeling. Church members were arriving from many distant places, including a large contingent from Europe. French, Swiss, Italians, Germans, English, Japanese and other nationalities were all streaming through JFK airport on their way to the Matching.

Within days, the partially refurbished hotel was packed, and members who lived there year-round were expected to let others of the same gender stay in their rooms. I was assigned to such a shared room, and I unpacked my best pants and jacket to wear to Father's speech, which was scheduled for midnight in the Grand Ballroom of the former hotel. A rumor went around that this might be more than just a speech, and that Father might start matching us right away.

In my prayers, I reminded myself of all the things that members usually tell themselves at this juncture: that it didn't matter what race she was, nor even whether she spoke my language; all that mattered was that she must be loyal to Father, first and foremost. I reminded myself that the most significant aspect of the Matching was not the obtaining of a spouse, but rather the forgiveness of Original Sin. The Matching was not supposed to be about getting something: indeed, it was considered selfish for members to worry too much about what they "got" in the bargain.

In the days leading up to the event, I listened to much speculation about the Matching. One young brother said: "Father will probably match me up to a really old sister so I'll have to pay indemnity for the rest of my life!" Which prompted another brother to offer the obligatory response: "Yes, but that really old sister probably has a beautiful spirit that you can't see." In this way we all tried to convince ourselves that it didn't matter what the outcome of the Matching would be, so long as we were matched.

Yet even as I prayed that God's will would be done, I secretly dreaded the prospect of being matched to a Japanese sister, because Japanese church members were the most conformist of all, and the least likely to understand my intention to undertake psychological treatment. I told God to go ahead and give me whatever wife He thought best, but if it wasn't out of line for me to ask, how about that really nice American sister (I was thinking of Donna, the follower of Nancy) that I had befriended at the Seminary? (I couldn't ask for Fran because she had already been matched at a previous Matching ceremony).

If I'd had any connections with a top leader in the Unification Church, I might have been able to get him to pass along my preference to Father, and perhaps my wish would have even been granted. But as an ordinary member— and especially as an ordinary member whose status was doubtful, because of my plans to do therapy—I certainly had no right to put such a request to Father. My only recourse was to put it in prayer to God.

Pretending I was unconcerned about the outcome, then, but with my fingers mentally crossed, I entered the Grand Ballroom that night, sharing in the happiness and excitement of all the members. We divided ourselves into brothers and sisters, with the brothers sitting to the right of Father as he faced us from the front, and the sisters to the left, all seated on the floor as per our custom. After the warm-up songs and prayers, Father entered the room, interpreter in tow, and launched into one of his impromptu speeches in Korean. His wife, whom we called Mother, took a seat behind him as he began his spiel on a light-hearted note; he was feeling the excitement of the crowd. Suddenly, he took off his suit jacket, handed it to Mother, and rolled up his sleeves. We all knew what this meant, and roared out our pleasure. The Matching was on.

To make a match, Father would ask either a brother or sister to stand up and then would look around at the various candidates of the opposite sex. Suddenly his finger would thrust out in the direction of a person in the crowd. The stunned person would then stand up and move across the room to meet his or her future mate. The applause from everyone in the room was deafening after each match. The couple were then sent to an adjacent balcony to discuss whether or not to accept. The onus was definitely on the couples to accept Father's choice. After all, he was the Messiah, and could see your ancestry, and knew what was best for you. You wouldn't want to be faithless, would you? But in exceptional circumstances, a member really could refuse a match—for example, if the other person revealed something that was wholly unacceptable. I knew my interest in doing therapy might fall into this category, so I hoped to be matched to someone I could explain it to clearly.

I was selected after only two hours on the first night of the Matching, and excitedly left the room with my prospective spouse. The sister who had been chosen for me was a French-speaking Swiss woman who belonged to the Italian church. We sat at a table on the balcony overlooking the jam-packed ballroom to discuss, in English, this life-changing decision. Our words were frequently drowned out by loud applause. Under these conditions it was almost impossible for me to properly explain my bizarre, unheard-of "mission" to undergo Primal Therapy. She thought I was merely confessing ordinary doubts and struggles, and waved them off. Blonde, plump and pretty, with facial features that resembled my own, she seemed a very suitable choice, and certainly I saw no objections. We made our way down to a table in the corner of the Grand Ballroom where our names were recorded as having accepted the match. We then bowed to True Father and True Mother as the Matching carried on, and left the room. I was on a stupendous high.

During my first four years in the Unification Church, I had been expected to repress all my sexual feelings, and to think only of how I could be of service to Father and God. At first, this was not too difficult, since the culture of the San Francisco church encouraged members to regress to a child-like, pre-sexual state; and in any case I was always too busy to spend much time thinking about sex. If any such thoughts did occur, I prayed urgently to God, seeking forgiveness. But as the years went by, this constant repression became more difficult, and I again began to entertain thoughts of finding a love partner, just as I had longed for (without much success) before the church. Now at last I had been given my wish: I had a woman of my own! And I was free to love her! Of course I knew that we would not be allowed to live together for several more years—and sexual relations were forbidden during the entire time—yet I was elated anyway because she was mine. For once the irrational feelings of being undeserving, that had so completely blocked me from approaching women before the church, were absent. If Father said I was deserving, then I was—end of story.

My elation didn't last long. The next day I went with her and some other Italian members for a walk through the garment district—it was a Sunday, so the neighborhood was quiet—and because I was having trouble being understood in English, I decided to speak in French, though I am not fluent in that language. When she questioned me about what I did in Los Angeles, I began to explain in more detail, even admitting the suicidal feelings that trouble me occasionally. She stopped in the middle of the street, her eyes growing wide, as she backed away from me. She told me that she could not accept the Matching "under these conditions." "*Mais*," I said, aghast, "*nous avons déjà accepté!*" But her mind was made up. She went at once to the Italian Family leader, who arranged to break the match.

However, the Matching was still going on. Father had stopped in the middle of the night, only to resume the next day. I knew that if I presented myself again in the Grand Ballroom, there was a chance I would be given a new spouse to replace the Swiss sister. This time, I prayed desperately to God that I would be granted an English speaking person, to whom I could spill out in detail my controversial situation. Changing into my best clothes again, I returned to the Grand Ballroom.

More members from Europe had arrived overnight, replenishing the ranks of those already matched, so I re-entered a room scarcely less full than it had been the previous night. The atmosphere was more subdued, but applause still erupted for every match. I knew there was a chance that I might not get matched again. But after a couple of hours, I saw Father's finger stab in my direction. Could he really mean me? I stood uncertainly. Yes, he meant me. I went to meet my new match, already preparing what I would say to her. She was a thin, lively-looking sister with curly brown hair and a big smile. Lovely! But did she speak English?

As it turned out, I could have hardly done better—she *was* English. Her name was Eleanor. We climbed to the balcony where I selected a table that was as far away as possible from the noise of the Grand Ballroom. Once again, I laid out what I was doing, and why I was doing it, even mentioning the troubling feelings that had prompted me to seek a radical therapy. Eleanor listened to it all, and then declared herself ready to accept this. I replied rather formally that, in that case, "I should be happy to accept the match!" And with that, we went down to sign up at the Blessing table, and to bow to Father. Later, when encountering some church friends who had met my previous fiancée, I had to awkwardly introduce Eleanor as "the second one."

No matter: this time it really seemed to look promising. I took Eleanor to a small restaurant not far from the hotel and we had a long, deep conversation, which was further warmed when the restaurant owner's cat climbed onto her lap and she stroked him affectionately. I began to feel as much elation at the prospect of loving and marrying Eleanor as I had for the Swiss sister.

The next morning, all the matched couples assembled in the Grand Ballroom for the very serious, very formal Holy Wine Ceremony. Of all the ceremonies in the Unification Church, none meant more than this one; it was, for members, more important than the mass wedding ceremonies that are held in stadiums and arenas with much spectacle. The wedding ceremonies merely proclaim to the world that these church members are married before God; by contrast, the Holy Wine Ceremony proclaims that they are no longer of the blood lineage of Satan and must now be considered the descendants of the True Parents. Furthermore, it signifies that their Original Sin is removed—so long as they remain loyal to Father and follow him without question. The sharing of the Holy Wine, a kind of sacrament, marks the transfer of blood lineage from the Evil One to the Lord of the Second Advent.

I wanted the Holy Wine to be the first food or drink to pass my lips that day, so I ate nothing that morning. I knew that persistent rumors claimed that a drop or two of Father's blood was literally in the Holy Wine, though church officials denied it.

We lined up in rows of couples while a prayer was offered on our behalf by Father, and then after a representative couple received the Holy Wine, church elders brought it around in little glass cups carried on brass trays (such as are used in some Protestant churches to administer the sacrament). As instructed, Eleanor lifted up one of the cups and drank part of the wine, then passed it over to me to drink the rest. I raised the cup of sweet scented wine to my lips, and began to drink. That single act seemed filled with an inexpressible sanctity, as though my whole life had been a prelude for this culminating moment, when I was permitted to savor God's sweetest love.

After all the couples had partaken of the wine, we filed solemnly out of the Grand Ballroom. On the way out we were each given a handkerchief bearing a florid stain from the Holy Wine, wrapped in a plastic sandwich bag, which we were to retain until we were permitted to start our families (which was the euphemism favored by church members). What part the Holy Handkerchief played in that important moment was not explained; these instructions would only be given to us when we were permitted to live together—something that was more than three years away.

Eleanor and I had only one more day before she had to return to her mission in Scotland; soon afterwards, I would go back to Los Angeles. She told me that she was part of a small musical band made up of church members based in Edinburgh who gave free concerts in old folks' homes, prisons and hospitals. Eleanor had mainly a singing part in these performances; I was enchanted by this musical side of her. Indeed, in all that I saw of her, there seemed not a single thing to worry about. She was lively, cheerful, and creative, and I saw only happiness ahead for us, so long as we waited out the full number of years that Father demanded, and passed all the other conditions. In addition to waiting at least three years from the date of the mass wedding ceremony (whose timing was not even known at this point), we were also expected to each recruit three new members to the church. But this seemed perfectly possible, given that Eleanor had tentatively recruited her sister, and I had been getting people to go to church seminars in Los Angeles. So when I saw Eleanor off at the airport for her return trip to England, though I hardly knew her at all, the prospects for our future married life seemed unclouded by the slightest worries.

Eleanor may have had to leave after only a few days, but I was free to return to Los Angeles when I chose; so before I did, I went to the Seminary for a couple of days to visit my former classmates; and only then, *finally*, made it home to my family for a belated Christmas—my first visit home since 1978. While I was in Calgary one of my old high school friends, a prosperous lawyer, hinted that he would help me with my problem of being unable to afford Primal Therapy, and asked me to call him when the time came. I probably read more into his words than he intended, but this promise reinforced my conviction that God was helping me to undergo Primal Therapy. I had started to believe that in the future I might even be trained as a Primal therapist so I could help other church members with emotional problems, and thus I would pioneer an entirely new aspect of God's Providence: "psychological restoration". I honestly did not think there was any contradiction between Primal Therapy and the Divine Principle, and I believed that I was following the best "pioneering" traditions of the Unification Church by setting out to do these things.

***

By mid-January, 1981, I had returned to Los Angeles to resume working with the fund-raising team, and again began to save money for the therapy. I continued to write in my diary, but now most of my entries were about Eleanor; I loved to imagine her with delight, though I knew it would likely be a long time before I saw her again. I wrote letters to her frequently, and eagerly waited for her less frequent replies. I carried her picture around to remind me of how she looked, and would sometimes imagine kissing her. My letters were more effusive and less "mission-centered" than the letters typically exchanged between matched couples in the Unification Church. Normally such letters would contain little more than quotes from Father, small talk about each other's missions, and encouragements to "work hard!" Already, I was transferring my previous strong feelings for Fran to Eleanor, including my hope that she could magically, through her love, wrench free the knife inside me—this despite that fact that I hardly knew her.

Meanwhile, I felt it was high time to get started in Primal Therapy, though I still had far too little money to afford to start. I began calling my friend in Calgary to see if he would come through with his promised assistance, but I soon realized that the hoped-for help was not going to be forthcoming from that quarter. That meant I might have to continue fund-raising for as many as two more years before I could afford the treatment.

When I told my parents of this turn of events, they very generously stepped in to provide the considerable sum needed to start Primal Therapy. So early in April, 1981, I was able to pay for the first installment and I signed on to begin.

Primal Therapy is a radical treatment, which may explain why I was attracted to it. Primal Therapy claims that it can get to the source of emotional problems and relieve it. This is done by having the patient delve into the very same painful feelings that they are normally discouraged from (or medicated away from) feeling. Since people develop all kinds of "defense systems" to allow them to cope with their feelings—like drinking, smoking, or engaging in compulsive sex—patients beginning Primal Therapy are required to completely abstain from these behaviors. For a few days prior to the start of the treatment, they must check into a motel room and remain completely alone with their feelings, avoiding all compulsive habits. They are to intentionally allow themselves to fall into their pain and despair. These feelings are then aided by trained therapists who, during open-ended sessions in a small room with lightly-padded walls and carpeted floors, encourage their expression through crying or shouting or even pounding on the walls. For three weeks during the "intensive" portion of the treatment, a Primal Therapy patient sees the therapist every day, and the therapist is on call 24 hours a day in the event of an emergency.

I began my intensives, therefore, by checking into a small motel in West Los Angeles near Pico Boulevard and began to let myself drift down into my unhappiness. On the first day of the treatment, I was videotaped at a meeting with some other new patients; I was somber, nervous and fidgety. Later, I met the therapist who would assist me throughout the three-week intensive period: a thin, angular young woman who dressed in vivid reds or uncompromising blacks. We would begin each session with both of us sitting on the floor of the small room, talking mostly about my immediate thoughts and feelings; gradually, we would work towards deeper feelings. Ultimately, the goal was for me to recover a memory of some original trauma that lay behind my emotional trouble—usually a scene involving parents or family. This trauma could then be relived and released while I cried out the pain (hence the term "primal scream"). I don't recall having anything quite like that happen during my intensives. However, the whole process of spending three weeks entirely obsessed with my own feelings certainly led to being chronically troubled, as indeed I was expected to be, temporarily.

Since I had to go to the Primal Institute regularly, I could no longer conveniently work with the fund-raising team, so when the intensive portion of the therapy ended I began a new job working for a company owned by the Los Angeles Family known as "Bouquets Unlimited", which had wooden flower carts set up in key locations where dating couples might buy flowers. There was a cart in Westwood (a district densely packed with students and movie theaters), another cart that went to either downtown Los Angeles or to Santa Monica, and still another that set up daily on a resort pier well south of Los Angeles at Redondo Beach. It was to this latter location that I was assigned, so every day I would drive 50 miles to this beach town. This was a pleasant job: I had an attractive cart, beautiful scenery, and a variety of carnations, roses and other flowers to mix together into eye-catching bouquets. On the best nights the flower stand might turn $400 worth of business, of which I was allowed to keep a portion to pay for therapy.

After the intensives, I returned for weekly group sessions at the Primal Institute. The group sessions were held in a much larger room which, like the others, had no furniture except for lightly padded walls. Those who came for group sessions would lie down, clutching their pillows, in various places on the carpet and try to get into their feelings. Soon I would hear the sounds of crying or pounding on the floor or walls as their anger and pain emerged. Eventually one of the therapists would come around to talk to each person about his or her feelings. Finally, the group assembled to discuss the insights they may have gained through their feelings.

The issue that I recall bringing to my therapy sessions most often was unhappiness about not having a sexual companion, and I often spoke in glowing terms about Eleanor, though of course even if I could have visited her I was not supposed to even touch her. The therapists at the Primal Institute could scarcely believe that I—a 27-year-old man—had never had a sexual relationship. In general, they saw no purpose for the sexual prohibitions which I believed were an absolute requirement from God. In the Unification Church, to have sex outside of am officially approved marriage is regarded as the equivalent of murder, since the consequence is believed to be spiritual death. I took these prohibitions very seriously, but I knew that the therapists at the Primal Institute thought them absurd.

In fact, these therapists considered my affiliation to the Unification Church to be a mere "defense system", and indeed many of them placed adherence to *any* religious belief in the same category. I ignored their views, convinced that I knew better. For their part, they expected that in time the therapy would cause me to drop my defense system, and I would leave the church on my own. They might have been right in this prediction—had not something come up that forced me to quit therapy for a while.

***

In late spring I had noticed that Eleanor's eagerly-awaited letters were tapering off. I had to cajole her to write, even using unfair tactics such as implying she was planning to reject me. She denied this, but finally gave me an explanation. She had become depressed and withdrawn from her work, often refusing to go to performances with her musical band. She gave strong hints that she was thinking of leaving the church (which would have ended our relationship): "I am walking on the knife-edge, and playing dangerous games on that knife edge," she warned me. She then pleaded for me to come to England as soon as possible. It was clear that she was going through a spiritual crisis. I took her letters to the wife of the Los Angeles Family leader, and she agreed that I must go to Eleanor as soon as possible. Since leaving the church was considered spiritual death, I must do whatever I could to save Eleanor.

I was in a bind. I had just started Primal Therapy and it would be a set-back to stop so early. At the same time, I was desperate to "save" Eleanor, and my going to help her fit in with my overall aim to justify my existence through love. If I wanted to show empathy and support to other members, who better than to my future wife? I really felt I had no choice. I would have to divert some of the money my parents had given me for therapy, and fly to England at once. My father was very displeased by this but so far as I could see, I had no choice but to fly to Eleanor's side. Remembering my previous flight on Laker Airways, I bought a Laker ticket to Gatwick. I still had my Canadian passport from my 1978 trip. I was excited at the prospect of seeing Eleanor, who said she would travel down from Scotland to meet me. I fell asleep on the plane dreaming happily about the prospect of seeing her.

Upon arriving at Gatwick, I naively told the customs official I was coming to England "to see my fiancée". He questioned me closely, but eventually allowed me to visit and I soon met up with Eleanor, whom I scarcely recognized. She had put on weight because of her recent unhappiness, but that didn't displease me—in fact, I thought it made her even prettier. But then again, it would have taken a lot for her to displease me; I was simply delighted with the prospect of having a woman to love, and Eleanor was certainly attractive, with an infectious laugh and a lively manner, and a nimbus of brown curly hair framing her apple-cheeked face. We took the Tube to Victoria Station, and from there got on the train for Weymouth in the West Country, which was near the place where her parents lived, on an island known as Portland.

During the trip to Weymouth I had my first chance to speak to Eleanor seriously about what was troubling her. I had to approach the matter carefully, having no real idea what I could do to help her, apart from trying to be an understanding listener—the very quality I had been practicing ever since I was so emotionally touched by Fran. Eleanor had obliquely threatened to quit the church, but I knew it would not help if I went around officiously quoting Divine Principle to her, so I resolved to just listen to her.

The usual solution when a Unification Church member becomes troubled or threatens to leave is to send him or her back to the Divine Principle workshops. That would not have helped Eleanor, who had been through plenty of workshops and was impatient with the whole idea. Nor was I about to urge this idea on her, since I didn't believe in that approach either. Fresh from Primal Therapy, I viewed all emotional problems as artifacts of unresolved childhood trauma, so of course I speculated that Primal Therapy might be what Eleanor needed, too.

However, there was no practical way for her to get into that treatment, so I had to focus on how I was going to get her to go back to simply accepting her "mission" in Edinburgh without overt rebellion. All I could think of was to show her my loving support. On the train to Weymouth I made a daring move: with the nervousness of a teenager on a first date in a movie theater, I stretched out my arm along the back of the seat behind her.

Even this small gesture would have been controversial to many members of the Unification Church. We were supposed to encourage each other in our missions with "inspiring" words, not get caught up in base physical attraction. But Eleanor was not interested in inspiring words. So I let my arm rest there, and when she let this pass I eventually began to touch her shoulder lightly. That didn't bother her a bit. I was onto something!

At length we arrived in Weymouth, a small resort town with a beach on the south coast of Dorset. From there we took the bus over to Portland, a hamlet on a wind-whipped rocky outcropping that would have made an excellent setting for a Gothic novel. (Indeed, Eleanor told me that Weymouth was the setting for one of Thomas Hardy's novels, so I promptly started reading *The Mayor of Casterbridge*). On this tiny island, in the shadow of one of Her Majesty's aging prisons, there was a small town. Some of the townsfolk probably noticed with mild curiosity the arrival of an American-looking chap who went around wearing blue jeans and baseball caps.

Eleanor's parents were gracious people who put me up in the guest room. Her mother was known in the Unification Church to be a willing hostess to church members, but she soon found me to be a rather odd Unificationist indeed—not the relentlessly cheerful type who usually visited. For example, I continued my habit of writing in my journal every day, which meant that I stayed in my room every morning writing while everyone else was shuffling around downstairs. When at last I made my appearance, she would say (with an edge of disapproval), "Well, you had another lie-in, I see!" She was accustomed to members who thought it sinful to sleep past six o'clock in the morning.

My odd habits didn't bother Eleanor, who was impatient anyway with the stilted mannerisms of church members. As we explored the cliffs around Portland, and later went on day trips to the beaches of Weymouth, we soon found that we were getting along famously—rather too famously by church standards.

One scene that stands out with freeze-frame clarity in my mind is a blustery summer afternoon when Eleanor and I sat by the ocean, near the top of a craggy bluff. It was sunny and warm, but windy. I had my arm around her shoulder, and the breeze was toying with her curly brown hair, and some of it tickled my cheek. Below us, at beach level, a young man pointed at the choppy waves pounding on the sand, and shouted over to a woman seated on the rocks. I had my arm around Eleanor and she leaned her head against my shoulder. At that moment I simply could not refrain from kissing her.

Eleanor was the first woman I had kissed in many years, and I made a rather poor job of it. "I'm afraid I'm not a good kisser," I told Eleanor apologetically, but she didn't seem to mind. After a few more tries, I soon got the knack of it.

Kissing was just the beginning. I soon began to touch her even more daringly. She never protested, though we refrained from the one thing that was expressly forbidden. We both feared the consequences of the "Fall"—that is, of going through with the complete sexual act; but apart from that, I mapped out her entire body with my fingers, and caressed her luscious beauty with my hands. I felt as though I could never kiss her or touch her enough. That week in Portland remains for me a precious memory of a time when I loved a woman with untold delight, a memory which is not spoiled by later events. I had fallen for Eleanor, hard.

It seemed as though, for that short period of time, we lived in a world apart from the disapproval of the church; but it was only a brief interlude, and we knew that we would soon have to return to the church and its plodding, earnest ways. I suppose we could have impulsively left the church together to marry, but there was no practical way to make this work. I lived in Los Angeles, and still hoped to complete Primal Therapy; Eleanor lived in Edinburgh, where she dragged herself through the mundane routines of church life. Besides, I was not at all ready to abandon Father and his messianic vision; the idea of quitting remained an unthinkable prospect for me. So no matter how much we enjoyed our interlude together, the time soon came for us to go back.

Eleanor and I got on the bus to Edinburgh, and initially, we kissed as before. It was a night bus, so we were not the only passengers nuzzling each other. But as the bus traveled north, a cool north wind also swept over my heart—a wind of phobic anxiety. We were going back to the church, where kissing Eleanor was not allowed. I drew away from her, and she watched me, puzzled. It was like I was changing identities as the bus drew closer to the place where Eleanor carried out her mission with the other Unification Church members. My church identity was reasserting control, and now I felt I must no longer kiss her. I began to fear my own actions in touching her so passionately; perhaps I had sinned—perhaps indeed, I had betrayed Father and God.

I came to Edinburgh in this conflicted state of mind, but I concealed it as we made our way to the large house where the brothers and sisters in Eleanor's musical band stayed. The band was a very international group: it consisted of two Japanese brothers, two Austrian brothers, two German brothers, a Finnish sister, and a Norwegian band manager. A manic Englishman with a puckish sense of humor was the band's leader on stage; but behind the scenes, the serious, straight-as-an-arrow Norwegian arranged their gigs. From a spiritual standpoint, however, neither of these were in charge: that duty fell to one of the Austrians. Both Eleanor and the Finnish sister performed mainly vocals, though they also contributed flute parts or accompanied on cymbals. Meanwhile, as the band toured around playing free concerts in old folks' homes, prisons and hospitals, two other women maintained their house for them: the French wife of the band manager, and a Canadian sister, Jane, who befriended me at once because of our shared prairie background.

The band's instruments ranged from electric guitars to trombones, French horns and sousaphones, and the band played any musical style they could manage, from Dixieland jazz to pop. The band went by the awkward name "GWBB2" (an acronym for "Go World Brass Band 2"). At the Washington Monument Rally in 1976, the Go World Brass Band had been showcased as an international band that played patriotic numbers for an American crowd. Now, like the New Hope Singers International that I had met in New York, the band had been relegated to less prominent work, and was now divided into three sections to perform charity concerts in the wake of the Home Church campaign. One section was based in London and another in Bristol; GWBB2, meanwhile, was based in Edinburgh, with all of Scotland as its territory.

Normally Eleanor would have been expected to go back to work at once, but her central figure gave her permission to spend a few extra days with me. We took advantage of this opportunity to stroll through the Pentland Hills south of Edinburgh—a lovely rolling landscape. Away from prying eyes as we were, I could have easily gone back to touching and kissing Eleanor passionately, but I now felt it would be wrong to do so, so I contented myself with just holding her chastely. I still have a photograph from that day of Eleanor standing beside a field of tall purple flowers. The wind is blowing her hair and tugging at the modest hem of her dark blue dress, and Eleanor is wearing a glowing smile—a lovely woman among beautiful flowers.

Yet on the way back to the band house, I tried to encourage Eleanor to be more accepting of her situation in the church. Perhaps I used some church jargon or a standard Divine Principle phrase. Whatever I said, it triggered quite a reaction. Eleanor mysteriously disappeared soon after we returned to the house. Apparently this was not the first time she'd done this; the band members told me she could disappear for hours when she didn't want to go out with the band. It seemed that there was really nothing I could say to her that would reconcile her to her situation; my only role was to love her. But was that going to be enough, considering that I would soon have to return to Los Angeles?

At length her central figure asked her to go back to work, and the band began playing concerts near Edinburgh. I took the opportunity to go out sight-seeing, including visiting Edinburgh Castle and seeing the military "tattoo" which is staged there every evening during summer. But when GWBB2 set out to perform in Glasgow and Dundee, I went with them, and watched adoringly whenever Eleanor performed. She and the Finnish sister gave the band a lively stage presence that would have been lacking if only the brothers had performed.

I didn't get another opportunity to be physically close to Eleanor until the end of my stay, when Eleanor and I went down to the historic English town of Lincoln to meet my sister, who had become a Mormon missionary and had been assigned to that town. I was neutral toward the Mormons, so I certainly was not setting out to try to convert my sister (not then, at least). It was just a coincidence that seemed too good to pass up: she happened to be in Britain at the same time I was. We took a few photographs, but basically Eleanor and I were in our own mental space, and my sister was in hers. We were polite, though preoccupied. However, now that I was once again away from the other brothers and sisters, my physical passion for Eleanor was rekindled, and as soon as we were alone I again kissed her and touched her fondly.

But now it was time for me to return to Los Angeles. I had done my best: I had loved her all I could; I could only hope it was enough. As I got on the bus from Lincoln to London, and Eleanor waited for her own bus back to Scotland, she handed me a parting note that I treasured for years: "Thank you for coming to my aid," she told me, adding: "I can't imagine life without you."

After reading those words, I could have flown back to Los Angeles without the benefit of an airplane. I was on a cloud of euphoria, imagining Eleanor's soft lips, her broad smile and lovely curves, and I thought of nothing else for the entire trip back. I continued in this love stupor as I stood for a very long wait at the customs and immigration desk in Los Angeles. For some reason, though I had plenty of time to plan for it, I did not, even once, stop to think that the American authorities might question why a Canadian citizen was arriving at a U.S. airport with almost no money and a dazed smile on his face.

You would think, in view of my experience in 1978, that the possibility of a problem might have occurred to me. If I had obtained a one-way ticket to Vancouver, that would likely have been enough. But as I had made no such preparations, they detained me, searched through my luggage, and concluded I was at risk of becoming a "public charge." I became the responsibility of Laker Airways. The airline put me up at a nearby hotel, guarded by a Laker official and her husband, until my case could be heard the following Monday. At the hearing, I was given the same choice as in 1978: leave voluntarily, or be deported. Fortunately, the Los Angeles church accountant was a friend of mine, so he loaned me the money for a one-way trip to Vancouver. After two days at the Jericho Beach youth hostel in that city, I approached a young man with American license plates on his car and asked if he was heading south. He was, so I joined him and shared gas expenses to Bellingham in Washington state, and then made my separate way to Seattle. The church accountant then got me a ticket from Seattle to Los Angeles, and I returned to my life there, intent on resuming Primal Therapy.

Which was all very well, except now I had virtually wiped out my savings. I also experienced another guilt attack for my physical closeness to Eleanor, and felt compelled to confess to a church leader. My ambivalence was profound, with my church identity alternating with my normal identity, depending upon whether I was around other church members or on my own. Eleanor was understandably furious about this vacillation; she wanted to keep the love that had passed between us private.

Since I had been a month away from my flower-selling job on Redondo Beach Pier, I had been replaced in that job by another member, so I started a new practice of taking single wrapped roses out to office districts to sell them. I would pay for the roses at the wholesale rate and then resell them for the usual mark-up. This did not pay very well, but at least it was something, and it had the advantage of being flexible, allowing me to take days off whenever I needed to attend Primal Therapy group sessions. Often I would stand on a long open concourse in Century City (a part of Los Angeles that consists almost solely of office towers) soliciting office workers during breaks. I had to ride long hours on the Wilshire Boulevard bus to get to these rose-selling spots.

I could not have resumed Primal Therapy if I hadn't received more financial help from my parents, yet even with this help I couldn't go as often as I wanted to. Just as I was beginning to get back into the treatments, Eleanor again began sending distressing letters to me implying that she was thinking of leaving the church. It was as though she subconsciously wanted to pull me away from finishing the therapy. But now that I was so completely in love with her, it would have been unthinkable to let her slip away, even for the sake of Primal Therapy. It was clear that I would again be forced to divert my limited means to arrange another trip to see Eleanor. But this time, since Christmas was approaching and my parents were willing to pay for me to visit anyway, I decided to use what money I had to bring Eleanor to Calgary for Christmas.

Eleanor told me a happy tale when she arrived at the Calgary airport; it seemed the young woman in the seat next to her on the plane was also flying to Canada to see her fiancé. Now that we were far away from other church members, we quickly resumed our relationship of passionate touching. I had told my parents that because of church beliefs we must stay in separate rooms, but even with these arrangements we often spent long moments behind closed doors engaged in frantic kissing.

It was a typical cold Canadian winter. My parents gave me permission to drive their car, which I explained I needed so I could "show Eleanor the sights". Instead we found quiet country lanes where we could grope each other with desperate joy. We still refrained from going all the way, but in Calgary I had the immense pleasure of seeing Eleanor nude—such a lovely sight. One evening I was cleaning the dinner dishes while Eleanor was bathing and washing her hair. After I had finished I went down the hall to Eleanor's room and softly opened the door. She was seated at the vanity table, naked, brushing her hair. In that moment she was breathtakingly beautiful.

Not even with Sandy many years ago had I experienced such pure passion. Those times of loving Eleanor were such a rarity for me, piercing as they did the loneliness I have mainly known. One fine, bright, cold winter day we took the bus to Banff, a famous mountain resort. It was just after Christmas, 1981, and bitterly cold, yet despite the temperature Eleanor insisted on hiking the long and twisting Tunnel Mountain trail. I remember warming her with many kisses—and much fondling—that day.

But once again the time came when I had to see Eleanor off on the plane to England. "Good-bye, honey," I told her, giving her a parting kiss at the airport, and hoping that this time my love would be enough to tide her over until we were finally able to live together. I stubbornly continued to hope that Eleanor could reconcile herself to her church mission, so I could return to mine. I was convinced that God wanted me to do Primal Therapy, even though many church members disapproved of it. Yet at the same time, my duty to Eleanor was greater, I felt. Though it was beginning to look impossible to have it both ways, I believed that God would somehow make it happen, perhaps even by allowing me to win a miraculous windfall.

Again, I returned to Los Angeles and to flower selling and to occasional Primal Therapy sessions. In the spring of 1982 the opportunity again arose for me to work the flower cart at Redondo Beach Pier, which was more lucrative than selling flowers from a bucket in Century City, though it tied me down more. Eleanor's distressed letters resumed soon afterwards, and I had to again decide how I was going to be able to afford another trip to visit her, or whether to risk losing her by telling her I simply could not do so. In any event, before I was forced to make this painful decision, word came down from church headquarters that eligible members must come to New York for the "Blessing"—meaning the public wedding ceremony, which would be held in Madison Square Garden on July 1. So although I still had to come up with the money for the trip, now I needed only get as far as New York—not as expensive a proposition. I began to look forward to seeing Eleanor again.

***

The massive public wedding ceremonies which have become Sun Myung Moon's trademark—with rows upon rows of couples marching into a open-air stadium or an indoor arena, the men all dressed in similar blue suits, the women clad in white bridal gowns sewn in an identical pattern—do not have the same meaning as a conventional wedding. In 1982 there was little prospect for those who participated in that Blessing to actually end up living with his or her spouse immediately afterwards. For most of us, a wait of several more years was in order, since each of the partners were required to recruit three new members, and in any case the normal minimum three-year waiting period for all couples started not from the date of the Matching, but from the date of the Blessing. I knew very well Eleanor was unlikely to be able to wait that long, but since I didn't want to leave the church, I hoped and prayed that God would help her to keep going until then.

As always, I returned to the World Mission Center, where members were assigned unfurnished rooms—brothers with brothers, sisters with sisters, three or four to a room, sleeping on the floor in sleeping bags. Eleanor arrived soon afterwards, and we had a few days together before the wedding rehearsal took place. On one of those days, we took the Staten Island Ferry and found a lonely stretch of beach, where among the reeds and grasses we hungrily kissed and petted each other.

On June 30, we arrived for our wedding rehearsal in Madison Square Garden in our street clothes. Altogether, some 2,075 couples were to take part in this Blessing, and this number was divided in half, with one half of the couples in the circular rotunda that surrounded the arena coming from one direction, and one half coming from the other. The couples were to march four abreast, alternating men and women, and when they reached the doors of the arena, the two columns were to merge, enter the main doors and march over the raised dais, where they were to pass between Father and Mother who would splash them with Holy Water, after which they would file into the main part of the arena, taking their places on the floor or in the bleachers behind them. We were to remember the couple who had marched beside us and the place where we ended up in the arena, so that this could be repeated exactly the following day.

On July 1, the real ceremony was set to go. Everyone carefully unpacked their wedding clothes. While the grooms had all brought new navy blue suits, black shoes, white shirts, white gloves and maroon ties for the occasion, the brides wore gowns that they had made or that others had made for them using Simplicity Pattern #8392, with the neckline raised two inches. The men were told to wear a maroon tie that had been especially made for the occasion, which bore a label on the back embroidered with the words: "WORLD PEACE THROUGH IDEAL FAMILY, July 1, 1982." Dressed as required, I met Eleanor in the lobby of the World Mission Center as we waited for our turn to go over to the arena.

To avoid jamming the streets, couples were supposed to walk over to the Garden in small groups, so it took some time for everyone to assemble in the Felt Forum (a smaller hall in the Garden) in preparation for the actual ceremony. Finally, word came to assemble in the Rotunda for the procession. Eleanor and I found ourselves standing next to a different couple from the one we had been adjacent to at the rehearsal, but there was no time to worry; it would sort itself out somehow. The procession started late because there was a bottleneck due to members having to pass through metal detectors. Finally, the column of brides and grooms began moving towards the arena doors, and when we entered we were joined by the column moving from the other direction, forming a small but powerful phalanx that marched over the raised dais and then spilled onto the floor of the arena. Being the furthest to the right of all the grooms, I passed directly under Father, who was wearing white robes and a white crown. He anointed me with a liberal splash of Holy Water as we passed by. We moved into the back of the arena, into the bleachers as we had done during the rehearsal, although we didn't end up in the exact position we had been told to memorize. The procession carried on, as Mendelssohn's "Suite for a Midsummer Night's Dream" was played by a live orchestra, until all 2,075 couples had entered the arena and had been blessed with Holy Water. The entire floor of the arena—which had so often been the venue for hockey games and boxing matches—was now covered with deep-pile white carpet, through which the couples moved as in a dream. When the procession ended, and all 4,150 people stood looking toward the front, Father asked us four questions, all intended to reaffirm our loyalty and faith. The first was: "Do you pledge to keep the heavenly law as original men and women, and should you fail, pledge to take responsibility for that?" (The mention of "heavenly law" was a clear reference to the prohibition against adultery and pre-marital sex, and the reference to "taking responsibility" was a reference to the terrible spiritual consequences which awaited those who violated this rule.) "YES!" we all screamed, as we did whenever Moon asked for reassurances during his speeches.

After the four pledges, Father prayed at length in Korean, and then called for the ring exchange. The "Blessing" rings we had been given were gold bands engraved with the Twelve Gates symbol of the Unification Church, and I had both of ours in my possession. I fluffed this part; since I was afraid of losing them, I had placed the rings in the finger of my white satin glove. This resulted in a long awkward moment while I tried to retrieve them from the place I had put them, before we could proceed with the ring exchange, which we finally did well after everyone else was finished. The rings were placed on the middle finger of our right hands, rather than on the fourth finger of our left hands.

Following the ring exchange, Father declared us husbands and wives, and several short speeches followed from other dignitaries before Father gave the unmistakable signal that the ceremony was about to end, by calling for a cry of "Mansei!" (meaning "Victory for ten thousand years!"). He did this by shouting the Korean word for father: "Aboji!" We all crouched down to place our hands on our knees, and then lifted them above our heads while shouting: "Mansei!" We gave this cry three times, and then, as the orchestra struck up again and began to play various numbers, we filed out of the Garden into the harsh July sunshine of an ordinary New York day.

Eleanor was just glad it was over. Chronically impatient with ceremony, she was in a hurry to get back into her regular clothes and go back to being herself, away from her church identity which she increasingly endured like an ill-fitting costume. Not for her to remain for hours in her bridal gown, as some of the other sisters did, chatting with church friends; she found church jargon and ritual an irritant she would rather avoid.

Eleanor found me puzzling and frustrating, because I was equally capable of going into "church" mode—by speaking church jargon and attending Pledge and other church rituals—or of going into a rebellious mode, when I would doubt the value of these very things. Eleanor wanted me to be all the latter, but I was not ready to be exclusively rebellious, while only putting on a false front for the church. When I was around other church members, I would change and become very much like them—a real member with an earnest church identity. I was unable at that time to see any contradiction in this.

Two days after the vast public spectacle of the Blessing, a much stranger ceremony was privately held for the "Blessed couples". This was the Indemnity Ceremony, in which, using wooden sticks, the newlyweds were to symbolically beat the evil spirits out of each other. Because of the large numbers of couples involved, the ceremony was divided up into different locations depending on the mission of the bridegroom. Since I was attached to the Los Angeles Family, that meant that Eleanor and I were supposed to beat each other at the same center on 43rd Street where I had lived in 1977. Eleanor went along reluctantly, saying, "Let's just get this over with!", though as usual I was ambivalent, with part of me hesitant, and part of me actually believing in the spiritual meaning of the ceremony.

For once, instead of the men and women sitting separately, the couples sat together on the floor of the main meeting room as we were instructed in the significance of the ceremony and the practical details of how to do it. The ceremony derives from a Korean custom where newly-married couples hit each other in a ritual fashion to drive out evil spirits. For Unification Church members, the spiritual meaning is less clear—something about paying indemnity from the position of Adam and Eve before we could begin our married lives (even though for most of us this was still a long way off).

The indemnity sticks used for the ceremony were small wooden bats with a paddle-like end, which was to be applied with vigor to the posterior of one's Blessed partner. We were instructed not to hold back, but to give our spouses good, solid blows, though we were to be careful to ensure that we struck only the gluteus maximus and not the lower spine, for fear of injury. First the wife would receive her due, and then she was to deal the like to her husband. So Eleanor, along with all the other Blessed wives present, kneeled down and presented her vulnerable bottom (fully clothed, of course) for me to hit.

Well, as much as I loved her, I was also still a believer, so I hit her three times as directed, though I would much rather have held her and kissed her. Then I kneeled down and Eleanor returned the favor. Fortunately Eleanor was not some weak delicate flower, but was healthy enough to give nearly as good as she got; indeed, tears momentarily sprang to the backs of my eyes.

Suddenly it was all over, and Eleanor and I wordlessly walked out into the hot humid night and found our way to a fast food restaurant. We didn't know what to say to each other. We had just spent our weirdest evening ever together.

There was about a week remaining before Eleanor had to leave. Making the most of it, we flew to visit my brother and his wife who lived in upstate

New York, and then returned to Manhattan for a few days. Now that Eleanor's roommates were gone and she was the only one occupying her room, we had a great opportunity to be together without being observed. One morning I went up to her floor and knocked. By coincidence Ken Sudo, a prominent church leader, was in the same corridor when I knocked, entering an adjacent room. I could almost feel his shock and disapproval when Eleanor opened her door, admitted me, and closed the door behind me. The look he gave burned into the back of my head as I walked into her room. (Sudo later recommended that the doors to rooms in the New Yorker be removed to prevent misbehavior). Immediately after the door was closed we began to kiss fervently, and soon we were in full necking mode, with clothes in disarray and hands groping everywhere. But I was guilt-stricken because Sudo had seen me, so I asked Eleanor if we could go somewhere else. I simply couldn't do this with Sudo in the very next room. So we found our way to the top of some tree-lined cliffs in New Jersey overlooking Manhattan, and again I felt free to touch Eleanor with my intense passion and desire.

Our situation was impossible. So long as we were together, we were enormously happy, but we could only see each other for brief visits, and my financial means were almost exhausted. Neither of us were citizens of the United States, so we couldn't legally stay there, yet I still wanted to finish my therapy in Los Angeles. Eleanor would never have considered emigrating to Canada, and though I would have been willing to move to England, I wanted to finish Primal Therapy first. In any case, I still was not prepared to quit the church completely, so I could not just run off with Eleanor—yet only this would have satisfied her. Nevertheless, I continued to ignore all these contradictions, trusting that God would help me to solve them.

When I saw Eleanor off at John F. Kennedy Airport in early July, 1982, my delusions were at their greatest height. I believed—contrary to all evidence—that I could prop up Eleanor's morale so that she would still remain a member of the Unification Church. I believed that I could still find a way to finish Primal Therapy; and not only that, that I could persuade others in the Unification Church to attempt the same treatment. I believed that I would find the means to do these things even though I was dependent on the limited tolerance of the church leaders. I believed that since God had appointed Eleanor to be my bride, while simultaneously asking me to do Primal Therapy, that somehow there must be a way to do both of these things, despite the fact that they conflicted with each other more and more as each day passed.

CHAPTER TWELVE

SUMMER'S END

Before returning to Los Angeles, I decided to take the 21-day Divine Principle training again, to see if it could do for me what many members believed it could; that is, heal emotional problems without all the trouble and expense of Primal Therapy. It may seem surprising that I would have even considered this, given my skepticism about repressing feelings. I suppose it was simply the other side of my dual personality kicking in, demanding that I at least give it a try before returning to my psychological therapy. Certainly once I was caught up in the 21-day workshop, I reverted to my full church identity: I dutifully took notes at all the lectures, even the tedious "Victory Over Communism" series, which discusses eye-glazing Marxist theory. I did my best to gain the alleged benefits of the workshop, which many church members believed was all the therapy I would ever need.

I also arranged to see an elderly Korean woman that church members called "Lady Doctor Kim", who claimed to be "spiritually open" and able to see a person's ancestors. Kim was famous for prescribing an "ancestral liberation ceremony" to church members, which supposedly exorcized problematic ancestors. According to Kim, the ancestral liberation ceremony allows these troubled spirits to quit bothering their descendants and go do something useful: they are sent to the 38th Parallel of Korea, where they become part of a spiritual barrier defending the South from invasion by the North. Though I was skeptical of these claims, I was still enough of a believer that I couldn't rule out the possibility that emotional problems might have a spiritual source; I just didn't think it was the complete explanation. So it seemed to me that the ancestral liberation ceremony was worth a try.

Kim had a room in the New Yorker where she would receive members and advise them on how to carry out the ancestral liberation ceremony. Most of the members she saw were English speakers, so she had a Korean translator, a young, cherubic-looking American man who clearly relished his role as the assistant of the great seer. Among other things, Kim briskly inquired if I was able to relieve my sexual feelings through masturbation. (This was an odd question since many church leaders considered masturbation a sin). I replied affirmatively. She also asked me about former girlfriends, and I told her about Sandy and mentioned that her death still troubled me. Kim asked if I was referring to a person whose hair came down over her forehead (she made a gesture as though she could see Sandy's appearance). I said yes. She advised me not to think about Sandy too much. She told me to make up a list of my immediate ancestors from both sides of my family, including the dates and manner of their deaths, which I was to burn in a ritual fashion while offering certain prayers. Simultaneously, I was to carry out a 21-day "cold shower condition" during which I would stand under cold water for a set number of minutes every day to pay indemnity for my ancestors.

I carried out these instructions when I returned to Los Angeles in September of 1982. The ceremony had no noticeable effect (though of course believers would attribute this failure to my lack of faith). When trying to decide where to carry out the ritual burning, I knew I had to find a place where I would be undisturbed for about an hour, and the busy church center on Huntington Drive was certainly not suitable. Instead I chose the patio of my friend Nina, who lived in a modest home in Alhambra, a city bordering on Los Angeles. Nina was a Unification Church member who lived on her own while she raised her young son from a marriage that predated her church involvement. Nina was an attractive woman who had little of the rigidity that hard-nosed church members were apt to have. She was also my boss, since she was in charge of Bouquets Unlimited, the flower company for which I worked. Nina loaned me the use of her barbecue and patio to carry out the burning ceremony during which I attempted to send all my troubles to the 38th Parallel.

Since I worked closely with Nina during the time I managed the flower cart at Redondo Beach Pier, I had become close friends with her. My attraction to her was considerable, but because I was a sincere believer in Divine Principle, I never did a thing about it. I laid my feelings for her away in my heart alongside my even greater passion for Eleanor, and just carried on with my work as a flower seller, driving to Redondo Beach every day, as I had always done. I began again trying to save enough money for a few group sessions at the Primal Institute (since by then I had given up on regular attendance and just went whenever I could).

As usual, the period of calm in my life was brief. Eleanor again began sending me troubling letters asking me to visit, along with threatening to quit the church. By now I had used up all my savings and had just barely enough money to get by from my flower cart earnings. I was forced to tell Eleanor that I couldn't do what she asked. Her fury was boundless; apparently, lack of money was no excuse. I became more and more distraught as she continued to press me to do what I simply didn't have the means to do. My distress was so great that one rainy night, returning from Redondo Beach, I momentarily fantasized crashing the truck into a concrete freeway underpass, because I felt so trapped by Eleanor's demands and by my inability to meet them. Finally, I decided to trust that somehow God would open a way to meet her request. I told her I would visit her, even though I could not see any way I could afford it.

Her next letter expressed relief: "I feel loved again." Eleanor, for her part, had now separated from any involvement with the church and was working as a live-in nanny for a family in London. Her only real connection to the Unification Church was now through her "Blessed" marriage to me. But how was I supposed to find the money to visit her? I dreamed of sudden windfalls, and started collecting game pieces in fast food restaurants, as well as following contests in the newspapers.

When Christmas of 1982 came, my parents again offered to pay for a trip for me to visit them, which I accepted, but this time I had no money to bring Eleanor over to join me, unlike the previous year. I went by myself, and even stayed a few extra weeks in order to get dental surgery, which my dentist insisted I needed, and which my parents also paid for. Eleanor was barely patient with my explanations for the delay in returning to my work in Los Angeles. I had now broken the pattern of seeing her every six months, which had begun with my first visit to England after our initial engagement. Could she endure a longer separation? She seemed to be in constant emotional pain, and was endlessly needy.

Around this time Arthur Janov opened a new branch of the Primal Institute in Paris, France. I mentioned this to Eleanor, suggesting that Primal Therapy might be the answer for her problems, too (though actually I hoped she would come to the original Primal Institute in Los Angeles, so I could be with her). Yet somehow it was always out of the question for her to move to North America, and instead she began making plans to go to the new Primal Institute in Paris. Within a year she had found a job as a nanny for a French family, and soon afterwards, began her own intensive therapy.

Meanwhile, upon my belated return to Los Angeles in January 1983, I found that I had lost my position with Bouquets Unlimited and that Nina was no longer the business manager of that company. Moon had appointed a new leader for Southern California, to replace the one who had tolerated my involvement with Primal Therapy. The new leader was much less experienced. He had been at the Seminary during the same years that I had, but this earned me no favors. He moved me from the center on Huntington Drive to the witnessing center near downtown Los Angeles. I was forced to find a new way to make money for therapy, since I was not permitted to go out with the fund-raising teams or to sell flowers; yet I was a Canadian without a work permit. I took a job selling sandwiches in offices, but this earned almost no money. Then I went to the all-night flower market where I had once picked out flowers for Bouquets Unlimited. I went around to all the wholesale flower vendors until I found one who was willing to take me on, no questions asked. He already had several Mexican men working for him who likely also had no permits. I stuck with this job until it became intolerable; the hours got longer and longer, until I was working 14 hours at a stretch. Finally, one day, I just didn't show up, much to the dismay of the new church leader. He regarded me as a problem member, and he had little patience for me.

My parents were still generously sending me money to get me through Primal Therapy, but I was being forced to use the money just to get by. I didn't feel this was fair to my parents, and one day I wrote them a letter telling them not to send me any more money. I knew I would now have to give up all hope of finishing Primal Therapy for the foreseeable future. It was the end of my dream of plucking out the knife inside me through therapeutic means, and I felt very sad.

***

In retrospect, I doubt this therapy was as beneficial as I believed it would be. Even so, I had staked my future on becoming a healthy, non-neurotic person through Primal Therapy. I had reasoned that after I got all fixed up mentally, I could go back to full-time commitment to the Unification Church, and be an even better member. But instead, despite my continued loyalty, my efforts to heal myself had merely ended up discrediting me in the eyes of the church leaders.

Not all Unification Church leaders are opposed to psychological therapy. Even Moon has made some ambiguous comments that appear to endorse therapy for some members, and because of this, a few members have tried various treatments. But overall, the church position has not changed since I joined: psychological problems are considered "spiritual" problems, and the best solution is to "pay indemnity" through working for the church. It was this attitude that the new regional leader, Reverend Cheung, brought with him when he arrived with much fanfare in Los Angeles in early 1983.

Cheung was one of several church leaders who had been brought over from Korea to keep the American leaders on a tight leash. He was chauffeured around in a gray station wagon, accompanied by a Japanese sister who acted as translator. He would give his speeches in Japanese, and she would translate them into English, and would also translate anything members said to him. She was a sharp and imperious woman, and her last name happened to be the same as that of a notorious Japanese crime family. I later came to think of that as rather appropriate. From the beginning, it was clear that she considered me to be a useless member. If I was ever going to get Reverend Cheung to understand my situation, I would have to use a different intermediary. I chose a much friendlier Japanese sister to act as my translator, but even with her help, my words were not persuasive. Reverend Cheung simply thought I was a very queer duck, and he likely considered sending me to another part of the church or away from the church altogether. All that kept him from doing this was my status as a former Seminarian and a Blessed member.

Since it was clear that Reverend Cheung was never going to understand my situation, I decided to avoid him. Whenever I saw his gray station wagon arriving in the driveway, I made a bee-line for the exit. On my own initiative, I moved back to the center on Huntington Drive, where I could make myself scarce more easily. This move was tolerated—barely—and I was not ordered out. But it was clear that I had to find a new situation as soon as possible.

First, there was the growing urgency of Eleanor's letters. She was impatient with me and couldn't understand why I had not yet come. She also asked the impossible: she asked me not just to visit, but to stay. Yet the church would not have tolerated us living together without official permission. I wrote to the Blessing Committee in New York explaining Eleanor's desperation. I asked them if an exception could be made so we could live together with full church approval. Of course they refused.

I knew I needed to get away from Los Angeles. Had I been an American, I might have taken a job on the staff of *The Washington Times*. Many of my Seminary friends had been hired by the *Times* during its early years. But my Canadian citizenship blocked that route. Instead I wrote to the Seminary and asked them if I could return to finish my Divinity Program; but they were uninterested in this idea.

Meanwhile, how was I to find the money to meet Eleanor's impossible request? There seemed no way left except to find an ordinary job. Nina, who was herself on the outs with Reverend Cheung, told me that she had found work through an office temporary service in Pasadena. I was able to get work from the same agency as well, based on my one marketable skill—my ability to type. (I gave them a Social Security Number taken from a card plainly marked "NOT VALID FOR EMPLOYMENT", but since I didn't show them the card, they never knew the difference). I soon had a temporary assignment as a clerk typist in Pasadena.

Yet even with my best efforts, I was not going to quickly find the money to fly to Eleanor's side. I had to hope and pray she could wait for me. Her letters became more and more infrequent. When she started Primal Therapy, she told me she didn't even tell her therapists about being a Unification Church member. I couldn't understand how she could leave out this important aspect of her life. She asked me in one letter, "Do you know what Janov thinks of religion?" Of course I knew; I just thought I knew better.

I started feeling guilty about working in the United States without a proper visa. I could have rationalized it as God's will if one of the church leaders had ordered me to do it, but here I was doing it on my own, while the church barely tolerated my existence. It occurred to me that I might as well go home to Calgary to live with my parents, since I knew that they would not challenge me on my religious beliefs—and if I returned to Canada, I could work legally. I was also motivated by the fact that the Huntington Drive center had just been taken over by a new version of the I.O.W.C., similar to the team I had been involved with in 1977. The place was now overrun by members vowing to win "victory for God!", some of whom were incensed that I didn't get with the program.

Finally, on August 1, 1983, I said goodbye to my dear friend Nina and took the plane to Calgary. I saw it as just an external move: in my heart, I believed, I was still loyal to True Father. But I knew very well what other church members would think about my move; they would believe I had left the church. I knew that if I lived in Calgary—given that the nearest Canadian Unification Church center was nearly 2,000 miles away in Toronto—I would become effectively a *persona non grata* in the Unification Church. Despite all this, I was not ready to give up thinking of myself as a member.

When I unpacked my few belongings at the house where I grew up, and my parents showed me to the basement room which had once been my brother's, I at once took out my pictures of True Father and True Mother and put them on display. I took out my hardbound copy of *Divine Principle* and read it every day. I even performed Pledge Service on Sunday mornings at 5:00 a.m. as before. As far as I was concerned—no matter what anybody else thought—I was still a believer in Father.

Eleanor, however, was angered by my move, even though I had done it for her sake. She still seemed to believe that I could somehow remain a respected member of the church, as if by doing so, her own failure to remain involved in the church would be redeemed. She seemed not to understand how completely lacking in credibility with the church leaders I was, even though I had explained it to her in many letters.

My next task was to find a job. I still had only one marketable skill, so I went to various office temporary agencies to find typing jobs. Calgary had just gone through a sharp economic downturn, and for several weeks I had nothing. I knew Eleanor would be impatient and angry, but there was nothing I could do about it. Hold on, Eleanor, hold on! I silently pleaded. I'm coming as fast as I can!

Finally, work began to trickle in, and I learned word processing as well, which paid off about a year later. I applied the diligence I had learned in the church to my office jobs, and this helped me get more work. Even so, I was only being paid at entry-level, so my savings were fairly modest. As gloomy winter came on in Alberta with still no prospect of being able to afford a trip to France, I was mindful that Eleanor had actually asked me to come "to stay." There was no way I could get a visa to do that. Still, I tried to placate Eleanor, and to keep her going with my letters.

Spring and then summer of 1984 passed as I watched my bank account growing slowly, and I kept hoping. Canada had just been through a diplomatic tiff with France, so visas to that country were now even harder to obtain. I waited longingly for Eleanor's letters, still tenderly remembering her the way she had been two years before. But she rarely wrote, and when she did she dropped broad hints: "I can scarcely write this letter, because whenever I sit down on a park bench to write, lonely men keep approaching me," she told me. Was she trying to arouse my jealousy? I still didn't have enough money for a round trip air fare to France, let alone for accommodations when I got there. I had to ignore Eleanor's pleas, praying that she could wait, and hoping she would be as steadfast in Divine Principle as I was myself.

It is hard now to believe that I could have ignored so many clear warnings. But even if I had been able to see them, I doubt that there was anything I could have done about it. The Unification Church would not have given me financial help to rescue this woman one more time, and I simply didn't have the means to do it on my own. In the summer of 1984, there was a long gap in Eleanor's letters, but I just continued writing to her as much as I could.

Meanwhile, Father had been in the news. He had lost his appeal of a conviction for tax fraud in the United States, and in July he began serving an 18-month sentence at a minimum security institution in Danbury, Connecticut. In those days I believed his conviction was unfair and he should have received,

at most, a fine for what I believed were mere reporting errors. But I decided to
tell Eleanor about the imprisonment (since I knew she was completely out of
touch with the church) so I began one of my letters to her saying: "My darling,
I am sorry to tell you that today Father began serving his jail sentence . . .".

On September 7, I returned home from work to find a letter from Eleanor
waiting for me. After such a long gap without a letter, I sensed at once what it
meant. Before I even opened the envelope, I knelt down and told God that I
would remain loyal to True Father no matter what the letter contained. Then I
fearfully opened it. Eleanor told me, "Dear Gordon, I have something to tell
you that is going to hurt. How much it is going to hurt I don't know and can't
bear to imagine." She went on to say that she had decided to leave the
Unification Church and that there was nothing I could do to prevent her. Our
marriage (which had never been legally binding) was now ended. To
discourage me from rushing off to France to try to save her, she added in firm,
bold letters at the end: "This decision is irreversible."

She underlined it three times.

End of Part Three.

PART FOUR:

JUSTIFICATION BY PERSEVERANCE

Chapter Thirteen

On the Fringe

For four years, the idea of earning "justification by love" had sustained me through mounting rejection by the Unification Church. I always believed that eventually I would pull through it all, and would begin my married life with Eleanor while remaining loyal to the church, and then it would all have been worth it. Now, however, it was clear this was not going to happen.

At this point, with such uncertain prospects ahead for me, it might have seemed only reasonable for me to sever all connections to the Unification Church; but I still believed that God expected me to remain loyal to Father. I also still believed that the only form of marriage that God could accept was the Matching and Blessing of the Unification Church. So to my mind, no matter how much I dreaded going back to being overruled by uncomprehending church leaders, I had no choice. Though I had lost all interest in the internal politics of the Unification Church and the things I would have to do in order to get on the good side of a church leader, there seemed no option but to go back. I had to have a church leader who would vouch for me to Father (and to the Blessing Committee in New York) before I could be included in the next Matching, whenever that might take place.

For the first time I dared to speculate on what grounds I might feel able to quit the church honorably. I concluded that the only way I could leave would be if I had reached the point where I was on the verge of killing myself. In other words, if I had the barrel of a shotgun pointed at my head, and was about to pull the trigger unless I quit the church, then—and only then—could I quit with God's permission.

On the other hand, my belief in Divine Principle did give me something to hold onto in the face of the crushing loss of Eleanor. I am not sure I could have borne such a devastating blow before I joined the Unification Church; but as a believer, my theology offered me a higher power to comfort me in this time of overwhelming heartache.

However, my options were few. If I wanted to continue living on my own and working at my own job, I would have to stay in Canada, which meant relocating to Toronto—even though the leader of the Canadian branch, a bombastic and high-strung German, had a reputation in the church for being narrow-minded. The only other alternative seemed even worse: going back to the United States to live and work illegally, where I would be completely at the mercy of the church leaders to decide whatever they wanted to do with me.

Toronto it would have to be, then. Perhaps once I got there the Canadian leader would relent and find a niche for me, even though I wasn't a full-time member. I began making plans for the move to Toronto, but I was in no great hurry. I wrote to some Unification Church friends who lived there— specifically a woman who had participated with me in the 21-day workshop in New York in 1982, along with her husband and daughter—and told them of my plans. Still, I remained in Calgary for the rest of the winter, slowly saving money from temporary office jobs.

So meager were my earnings from temporary work that it took me the entire winter to save enough money to move to Toronto. In any case, I was in no big hurry to present myself to the head of the Canadian Unification Church, knowing he would probably reject me. Indeed, as if to confirm my hesitation, in the early part of 1985 I spent some of my savings to visit a friend in Winnipeg.

That friend was Jane, who had been a housekeeper with Eleanor's musical band in Scotland. Like me, she had returned temporarily to stay with her family, and also like me, she wanted to remain a church member, but didn't want to continue living the nomadic lifestyle of a "full center" member. She had been Blessed to a Japanese man who was more ideologically committed than she was, and though she had not renounced her marriage to him, she was obviously wrestling with it. We had kept in touch since meeting in Edinburgh in 1982, and of course she knew all about Eleanor's departure from the church. Jane had invited me to visit, and it's possible she was pondering whether we should start a relationship together, but if so, she didn't let on in any obvious way. She was probably waiting to see if I would take the initiative. But as usual, I continued to repress all such feelings, as I have always done with any young women I meet. There was not only my natural shyness to contend with; but also my overwhelming fear of disobeying church teachings about sex. So my visit with Jane was a friendly visit, but nothing more.

Finally, in May of 1985, I was ready to face the Canadian Unification Church leader. I stayed with my friend from the 21-day workshop and her family in Toronto until I could find my own place. She knew that I was going to have problems dealing with the Canadian church leader, because she and her husband were also on the outs with him. Despite their long years of loyalty to Father, he couldn't accept their decision to live independently, though this was necessary because of her own and her daughter's health problems. I arrived late in the evening, and happily camped out in a sleeping bag in their living room. The next morning their young daughter was the first to wake up. It was still too dark in the room for her to see me, so while she lay in her bed, she asked me where I was from, and what color I was (since she had met people of all races in the Unification Church). I told her I was purple and came from the Planet Jupiter.

I began both a job search and an apartment search the next day. I again went to temporary agencies, but I needed a steady address and a phone number before I could get much work. I finally found an address in a rooming house in a working class neighborhood—namely, Queen and Bathurst. I would have preferred an apartment, but couldn't afford one, so I took a clean room that had an oddly slanting floor in a house not far from the Unification Church center. Along with the room, I received a loquacious Jamaican landlord whose accent was so thick it took me several weeks before I could even understand him; and another roomer, an Afghan who regaled me with tales (probably invented) of escaping from Russian troops, and who later got into a loud argument with the landlord when he tried to bring a prostitute into his room.

I soon found temporary office assignments, but I needed to establish a relationship with the Unification Church and its notoriously prickly leader. Their center was an aging mansion in a well-heeled area close to the University of Toronto. I only had to walk for ten minutes to get from my humble neighborhood to the genteel one where the center was located.

The use of venerable mansions as Unification Church centers was familiar to me. Such houses had to be grand because they were "Father's houses", but they also had to be large so that many members could live there. Whenever I visited the one in Toronto, I was allowed to wait in one of the outer rooms while a member who had been designated to deal with me grudgingly passed whatever time was necessary to endure my presence until I left. I had been hoping they would have ideas as to what volunteer work I could do for them whenever I was free from my office work. I pictured myself working enthusiastically and gaining stature and respect in the Unification Church in Toronto, because I was perfectly willing to work very hard, so long as I could still have my own place and my own job, too. But they had no concept that a person in my position could be useful to them; as far as they were concerned, the only acceptable option was for me to move in with them full-time.

For my part, I was sure that Father supported my wish to live independently. Many American members already had this situation. So I refused to live with the Canadian Unification Church leader and to be at his total mercy, and consequently he didn't take any interest in my situation or show any desire for my help. When I told one of the Canadian members (an Austrian who happened to be the same man who had brought Eleanor into the Unification Church) that I hoped to be a candidate for the next Matching, he told me coldly that the Canadian leader would laugh at the very idea. I later learned that he blamed me for Eleanor's departure from the church. I made several visits to the church headquarters, yet never once met with their august leader, who was always too busy to take time for a mere fringe member. It was beginning to dawn on me that I was never going to get any further than the downstairs parlor in my association with the Canadian Unification Church.

Around the same time as my own move to Toronto, Jane also moved there, and stayed with her sister and brother-in-law. We became firm friends, and often went out to movies and museums and other points of interest. I could no longer ignore my feelings for Jane; I was very drawn to her, and could not completely repress the sexual fantasies that sprang to my mind when I saw her. Jane did not overtly encourage these feelings; they just seemed to emerge naturally from our friendship and from the amount of time we were spending together. Yet I became very fearful about the spiritual consequences of the Fall, so Jane and I never exchanged even one kiss, though I often imagined doing it. At one point I became so depressed by having to constantly push away my feelings that I told her I was in a "blue funk" and didn't want to see her until I emerged from it.

Though Jane, like me, would have been conscience-stricken if we had become lovers, I suspect she would have gone along with it had I taken the initiative—but I never did. I was still much too committed to Divine Principle to risk doing something that was regarded as such a grave sin.

Instead I told her one day that I was going down to New York to see if I could find a situation where I could be accepted as a "real" Unification Church member while still maintaining some degree of independence. In 1985 my brother was living in upstate New York, so I took a train to the border town of Cornwall, Ontario, and he met me there. I stayed with him for a day or two and then made my way to New York City, basically going on impulse, hoping to find someone who could assist me. I went to the former New Yorker Hotel and after proving to the security guard that I was indeed a church member, I was allowed to rent an inexpensive room there. I went around looking for people I knew who might help me, especially other former Seminarians. I even met up again with Nancy, the woman who had been sent away from the Seminary to become a missionary in Africa and who had now returned from her sojourn in the Gambia. She and Donna had become friends again, and I spent time with them and saw Nancy's charming baby daughter —the product of a rare (and brief) opportunity for Nancy and her husband to actually live together. But I found little that would help my own situation. My best bet was the struggling newspaper, the *New York City Tribune*—formerly the *News World*—which was still publishing in obscurity despite the more visible success of its cousin, *The Washington Times*. I met with some editors at the *Tribune* who felt I had the skills to be a copy editor. They would have hired me, except I was a Canadian without a work visa. I knew the Unification Church would never deign to spend its precious money on a lawyer to help me with this problem, and I certainly could not afford to hire a lawyer on my own. There was nothing to do but to return to Toronto, admitting to myself that my trip to New York had always been a long shot, but it was a long shot that I felt I had to try anyway.

Unsure of what to do next, I returned to accepting temporary office assignments in Toronto, and to spending time with Jane occasionally. One day, after Jane and I had spent a hot humid day walking around Toronto Island and then found our way to a Chinese restaurant, I asked her if she knew what had become of Eleanor. I admitted that I still cared about Eleanor and missed her, even though I knew it was definitely over between us. Did she have any idea what had become of Eleanor? Jane took on a thoughtful look.

"Eleanor? Oh . . . She must be married by now," she answered, and then immediately stopped when she saw how mortified I was by this news. I should have known, of course. Eleanor had even hinted at it in some of her letters, when she spoke of the "lonely men" who kept approaching her whenever she tried to sit down on a park bench to write. But still I had blocked out the possibility in my mind. I had tried to believe that her departure was only because she wanted to quit the church, and not because of another man. I was crushed.

Jane went on to explain that Eleanor had married a man from the Ivory Coast in Africa, and that she had sponsored her husband's immigration into England. But I was so obviously devastated by the news that when we parted Jane told me gently this would be a good night to "go home and cry."

Once again, I couldn't sleep, as had been the case a year before when I had received Eleanor's letter. I went through my photo albums and destroyed every picture I had of Eleanor. To my later regret, I even destroyed a large picture of Eleanor and myself in our wedding clothes, that had been taken by a photographer in the New Yorker Hotel a day or two after the Blessing. I was later able to recover copies of all the other photographs, but not of that one.

I had given up my odd room with the slanting floor when I went to New York, so upon my return to Toronto I stayed with an elderly aunt for a couple of weeks before taking a room in an aging hotel on Queen Street. After three weeks there, I again moved to a small basement room in Scarborough, on the northeastern fringe of Toronto, at the suggestion of a church friend who had recently arrived in Toronto with his wife and young son.

John was another long-time member of the Unification Church who had been left to his own devices when it came time to raise his family, and who received scant respect for living independently. Building on the fund-raising skills all church members acquire, he went into sales of cleaning products, which he sold from booths at small fairs, flea markets and home shows. His charming Japanese wife often assisted him as he did demonstrations, especially of a Dutch-made "shammy", orange in color and shot through with tiny holes, that was very effective for cleaning glass.

Abandoning office work, I began assisting John with his "shammy" sales, along with his other sidelines, such as a brass cleaning products. John had been given franchise rights by a friend in Vancouver for these European products, and he traveled across the country in his small van, encouraging other Unification Church members who were in a situation like his to earn a living by selling these products.

I soon learned the knack of selling the "Super Shammy" at flea markets in Southern Ontario. I would take a small square mirror and smear it with Nivea Creme (which is an oil-based facial cream). I would then demonstrate how the Super Shammy could remove the Nivea Creme without leaving streaks. I would dip the "shammy" in moderately hot water, then wipe in a smooth stroke. If I did it right, there wasn't a trace left of oil, and the glass looked better than ever. I worked on straight commission, and though I did acceptably well, it was clear after about two months that the "Super Shammy" was not going to be my financial salvation, either. What is more, John would not have been able to vouch for me in the event that Father had announced another Matching.

I now saw that I had few options left, if I wanted to remain a Unificationist. I suppose I could have simply surrendered to the Canadian Unification Church leader and agreed to become a full-time member in Toronto after all, but by this time I detested that leader because of his haughtiness, and I suspect he would have humiliated me for not coming to him immediately. So my only other recourse was to look for a more tolerable situation in the United States, where I could work as a full-time member until I was again allowed to participate in the Matching.

I began contacting leaders of state churches in the United States whose names were familiar to me from my Seminary years. I discovered that the state leader for Montana was a laid-back guy who seemed unlikely to act autocratically the way the Canadian Unification Church leader had, so he looked like my best bet. Montana was also a good choice because it borders on Alberta; I could, therefore, winter with my family in Calgary and then would only have to travel a modest distance in order to attempt my last-ditch strategy in the spring.

In October of 1985, I packed all my bags and boxes and put them back on the plane to Calgary. It was time to play the end game. It looked like there was only one last thing I could try if I wanted to remain a follower of Father— but I believed that God would never forgive me unless I at least tried.

CHAPTER FOURTEEN

LETTING GO

While I passed another winter in Calgary, saving money by working at temporary office assignments, I began to write articles for *The Round Table*, a free publication put out by unhappy members of the Unification Church. The group that put together *The Round Table* consisted mainly of former Seminarians living in the New York area whose Seminary background emboldened them to believe their own views might be worthwhile even if church leaders were against them.

The newsletter created an outlet for church members who wanted to talk about problems in the church, without being immediately silenced by a church leader. Published monthly (later bi-monthly), *The Round Table* was assembled entirely by volunteers and mailed out to anyone who requested it. It was a labor of love by sincere believers who wanted to reform the church so it could achieve its noble goals. Most of all, *The Round Table* stood for taking a realistic look at the church instead of just accepting the views of the church leadership. This was seen as an outrageous rebellion by the church's top leaders, and although the publication continued for nearly two years, it received many angry letters from influential members.

I knew that once I went to Montana to live at a church center, I might no longer have either the time or permission to continue to write these articles. But as it turned out, I was not prevented from writing for *The Round Table* while I was in Montana, and I even wrote satirical pieces for another similar church members' "zine" named *Our Network* which was mailed from California.

My parents agreed to drive me down to Montana one spring weekend in March, when I finally decided I was ready to go. They took me through the Crow's Nest Pass to a British Columbia road that turns into a Montana road and eventually wends its way to the town of Missoula. We stayed one night at a motel. The next morning I knew that even though I was quite apprehensive and really didn't want to do it, I could put it off no longer. I would have to surrender to the Unification Church in Montana, and I would have to accept whatever assignment or situation they put me into. I privately speculated that it might prove so unbearable that I would be compelled to leave again within a few days. Still, my parents did what I asked, withholding their own opinions as usual. They took me over to the church center and drove away. I greeted Tim, the church leader for the state of Montana, and met the other members.

The church lifestyle in Montana was nowhere near as oppressive as I had feared. Tim was casual and laid-back, just as I had remembered him to be: he was the same man who had haunted the T.V. room at the Seminary, while I had been too busy to even poke my head into that room. He welcomed me and introduced me to the usual disparate group of young people that often wind up in remote Unification Church centers: among others, there was a Finnish sister, an English brother, a Japanese sister, and an American who ran the Montana chapter of Moon's anti-Communist group, CAUSA. A few other members came and went from other smaller church outposts in Helena, Great Falls, Bozeman and Miles City.

Tim was a small, slight man who did not lay on the heavy judgment in his morning sermons. Though not a Montanan, he reflected the state in many ways: independent, tolerant, and open to diversity. Montana has room for all kinds of strange people, perhaps because it has so much room and so few people. A few Moonies, therefore, were of little concern to most Missoulians.

Missoula is a university town, and therefore more liberal than Great Falls or Helena. It was probably because of the university that the Unification Church decided to establish its state headquarters there. The part of Montana that contains Missoula is mountainous, but a mere hour's drive to the east lie the plains which typify much of the state. Missoula is a picturesque town nestled in a mountain valley that during winter is often shrouded with smoke from wood stoves. When I arrived in March, the winter season was just ending, and the trees were blooming. It was a promising beginning; the members welcomed me, and I actually felt happy there.

I was especially welcomed because I had some training on computers, mostly with word processing programs, and the church had just acquired a computer for CAUSA activities. I seemed to be the only one who knew how to operate the machine, so my arrival was viewed as a Godsend. The computer was rudimentary even by 1986 standards—a small Radio Shack machine—but it was certainly equal to my own limited knowledge. I quickly became the resident computer expert by creating a CAUSA mailing list using the word processing program.

"CAUSA" was not an acronym in those days (though it was later turned into one). It was simply a word that stood for a new Unification Church front organization that focused on criticizing Marxism while proposing a Taoist view of God (based on the first chapter of the Divine Principle). CAUSA dispensed with overtly Christian or Biblical teachings. The CAUSA doctrine was called "Godism" and was viewed by church members as the only real antidote to Communism. On the national level, CAUSA held conferences in which prominent senators and congressmen were courted and were taught its ideas, and at least a few legislators became enthusiastic supporters of CAUSA. In Missoula, local conservatives who supported CAUSA were placed on the mailing list I drew up.

The most prominent of these local supporters was a woman named Beryl who owned two small grocery stores and a number of rental houses throughout Missoula. Though not fabulously wealthy, her holdings were enough to make her influential. Montana Unification Church members devoted a large part of their time trying to keep this woman friendly to the church and to CAUSA. Early in my time there, I went with the members to cut grass on her rental properties, and later I began to work full-time at one of her grocery stores—the one she was least concerned about—without compensation. Meanwhile, the Finnish sister spent her days looking after the woman's aging mother. In return, this miniature plutocrat rounded up her conservative friends for CAUSA events, which were held from time to time on the university campus.

Besides my CAUSA work, which initially was only a small part of my activities, I assisted around the Unification Church center. The church center occupied an old-fashioned two-storey house near the campus with a prominent peaked roof and a front veranda. Behind it was a smaller infill house which served as the "C.A.R.P." center. Two students from the university lived there, enjoying what was, by church standards, a rather casual lifestyle. One of them, a man named Bob, turned out to be a regular contributor to *Our Network* and could often be found studying while seated on a lawn chair in the back yard. Bob worked as a dishwasher in a restaurant and even owned (but never wore) a baseball cap from a nearby tavern that sported the slogan, "Liquor up front. Poker in the rear!" If Tim had been a more traditional Unification Church leader, he would have put a stop to Bob's unconventional behavior, but he was not inclined to confrontation and seemed to know that it would have had little effect anyway. Instead, Tim concentrated on his own empire; which, for some reason, he decided should be an agricultural one.

Though the house rented by the church was well within town limits, Tim bought a large plump duck which wandered all over the yard and all over the neighbor's yards as well. The duck was relatively sedate and even laid an egg or two which could be enjoyed for breakfast. But Tim's farming ambitions were not satisfied. His next acquisition was a young goat which—unsurprisingly—decided that he didn't want to be penned up in the back yard all day. On several occasions he took off, and had to be rounded up blocks away by Tim with the help of other church members. Tim finally sold the kid but, still not finished with his farming experiment, purchased a calf instead. Of course the calf could no more be contained in an ordinary back yard than the kid, and after one embarrassing incident involving animal control officers and a rampant calf on the other side of town, Tim was forced to rent some land from a farmer outside of Missoula. The Finnish sister and I used to go to the farm to feed the calf whenever the farmer was away. Bob explained Tim's dotty behavior to me this way: "Tim doesn't want to be a church leader. He just wants to retire and run a farm!"

Meanwhile, CAUSA was getting busier, since Father was placing more and more emphasis on this group. Only a few weeks after my arrival in Montana, we put together an event featuring Russell Means, one of the former leaders of the American Indian Movement. Means had traveled to Nicaragua and observed that there was a group of native Indians called MISURASATA operating within Nicaragua that fought with the Sandinistas. Means quite reasonably asked why so much American money and resources were being given to the Contra armies when a more effective fighting group was already operating *inside* Nicaragua. Although Means' activities with the American Indian Movement had once made him a darling of the left, his support for MISURASATA cost him their support but garnered instead the support of right-wing groups like CAUSA. Means' own viewpoint was neither right-wing nor left; he was merely concerned about the welfare of native people, whom he felt were being harmed by the Sandinistas. Means later wrote in his autobiography, *Where White Men Fear to Tread*, that he felt at the time that even if he was being "used by the Moonies", he was equally using them in return.

Means' talks for CAUSA always followed the same pattern. After showing a film which had been shot by a Unification Church member who infiltrated Nicaragua, depicting the devastation caused by the Sandinista army on the Miskito, Sumo and Rama Indian people, Means gave his talk, which was coolly received by the mainly liberal crowd, but resoundingly applauded by the CAUSA contingent.

I knew little about Means or his background with the American Indian Movement; I was mostly just glad to be able to fight Communism in Montana. About a month later, CAUSA brought in another speaker, a former KGB operative who had defected to the United States. This man suffered from advanced alcoholism, and would scarcely have been able to make it through his speech had not Tim, in the middle of the talk, discreetly brought him a beer in an opaque tumbler disguised as a glass of water.

Soon afterwards, my involvement with CAUSA meant that I was sent to stay full-time at the CAUSA center, which was a very small house owned by the CAUSA godmother, abutting the Burlington Northern railroad tracks. The house consisted of two small bedrooms and a main room plus kitchen and bathroom. I stayed in one of the bedrooms along with the computer, and Hank, the leader of the CAUSA chapter, stayed in the other. My move to this smaller house brought with it a more independent lifestyle.

Now that I was working as a full-time CAUSA member, my immediate central figure was Hank, not Tim, though I still went back to the church house for Sunday pledge services. Hank was a student at the University of Montana, though he had only one class, which was perhaps just an excuse so he could register CAUSA as a student organization. Hank was Montanan, born and raised, and had been in the church on and off for as long as I had. He had quit the church after some four years as a member, and had even subsequently married, but later returned to the church after his marriage soured. Hank was the opposite of me in many ways: not as intellectual or complex but certainly more confidant. He was tall and handsome and just the sort of person who would be given a leadership role in the church simply because of his manner. But Hank's real love was country music, and he put together a cassette tape, produced by a local studio, containing some covers and some original songs that featured his dulcet vocals and mellifluous guitar stylings. All in all, it was not a bad beginning for an amateur musician. Hank's idea was to sell the cassette tapes to raise funds for CAUSA. The most blatantly ideological song on the tape was a melancholy ditty titled "God Bless the Little Children With No Hands" (about Afghan children maimed by Soviet land mines). I helped Hank put together a mail-out publicizing the cassettes, but they received few takers.

As a CAUSA member, my focus was now almost entirely on fighting Communism, and for the most part I gave only passing thought to the religious aspects of Unification life. This was, in many ways, a reflection of where the church itself was headed; by the summer of 1986, its focus had become almost entirely political. Most of the news coming out of church headquarters pertained to either CAUSA or to *The Washington Times*, which was offering one million dollars of its own money to support the Contra fighters, who had been temporarily cut off from funding by Congress. But the *Times* was losing money in 1986 (and continues to do so), so the money could only have come from the newspaper's corporate owner, Sun Myung Moon. Though I had come to Montana in order to remain a Unification Church member, my entire focus was now on working for CAUSA.

I might have gone on for some time in my role as CAUSA's computer expert, assisting Hank in his plodding, country-music approach to his work, if another church member had not jumped into the anti-Communist fray, using a much more confrontational approach. Paul was a scrappy Englishman from the northern part of his country, and he was impatient with both Tim and Hank and insisted on doing things his own way, even if it got everyone in trouble. Tim had given up trying to control Paul, and Hank and I spent most of our time looking for some place to hide whenever Paul became active.

One night while I was asleep next to the CAUSA computer, Paul came into my room and woke me to announce that he had just been chased by the police after spray-painting a hammer and sickle on the outer wall of the town's only newspaper, the *Missoulian*. Apparently Paul felt that this paper was too liberal. He was positively chuckling and gloating about his experience, as if he had struck a great blow for freedom. On another occasion, falsely claiming to be a student of the university, Paul borrowed a bullhorn from the student union and harassed some demonstrators because he deemed their cause too liberal. This in turn made CAUSA look bad and might have threatened that organization's status on campus.

Paul might have been reigned in more sternly if it were not that he was favored by the CAUSA godmother, Beryl, who preferred his confrontational approach over Hank's mild-mannered leadership. Whatever Beryl wanted, the church leader leaned over backwards to provide, so if she liked Paul, he stayed, no matter how much trouble he caused. I was certainly of two minds about Paul, because he could also be a charming friend who was more fun to be around than the strait-laced Hank. One evening Paul and I went with Bob in a car to a small park. Sitting in the car, sipping beer (which church members were normally not allowed to have), we listened to David Bowie's "Heroes" on the tape deck. These were really nothing more than high school antics, but since we were Unification Church members, we felt we were doing something radical and daring.

Having discovered that, like him, I was fond of beer, Paul and I soon began haunting some of the taverns in Missoula. Paul always insisted that the best brand was Coors, because the founder of that brand "supports the Contras." This allowed us to feel we were striking a blow against Communism while spending our meager funds on drink. Paul also introduced me to an old-fashioned western saloon which featured a dish of hash-brown potatoes and gravy he regarded as heaven itself. Paul, Bob and I would pass evenings talking over beers and hash browns. Of course we knew the church would never approve of what we are doing, but we had all reached the point where we no longer felt we had to conform to the church's "standards". Like many Unification Church members—such as those writing for *The Round Table*—we were disillusioned by the church's perpetual campaigns which never seemed to bring it any closer to the goals it claimed it was aiming for. Yet even though we were disillusioned, we were not prepared—yet—to quit the church entirely. We still hoped that it could be reformed, or that we could each find some independent role inside the church that would still be meaningful. We feared leaving the church entirely, with the spiritual void that we believed we would then enter; and so, hesitating from taking this final step, but not knowing what else to do, we ended up spending many evenings merely laughing and joking, drinking beer and forgetting.

Paul might have been more fun to have a beer with, but as a fellow fighter against Communism, he was obnoxious and unmanageable. I was more than a little relieved when he suddenly decided it was time to light out for the territories—Minnesota, to be exact. His presence had been making it more and more difficult for me to have any hope that we were accomplishing anything in Missoula, since he kept undermining everything the local CAUSA chapter was trying to build. With his departure I felt like a weight had been lifted off me, and now I could get back to work. That summer, I helped Hank in his more patient, less confrontational plans for CAUSA, and also assisted him with his musical career, by going to some competitions where he sang and played guitar, such as the "True Value Country Showdown." I have never been a big fan of country music, but at least with Hank's influence, I developed some appreciation.

Then suddenly, Paul was back again. He had hitch-hiked to Minnesota to work with a particular Unification Church leader there that he favored, only to decide that he didn't want to work with him after all, and so had returned to Montana the same way he had left—by slipping away suddenly without leaving a word. His unpredictability was getting worse, and he was certainly no less obnoxious during his second coming. I did a slow burn as I watched CAUSA's plans slide back into chaos again. Tim, as usual, did nothing to prevent it, though in theory he could have sent Paul away on his own authority. That just wasn't his way. Besides, Beryl was happy to have Paul back.

I had some sympathy for Paul, because he had endured a loss like my own. He, too, had been matched and Blessed to a woman he had fallen in love with, and who had then quit the church to marry someone else. Like me, he was having a hard time getting over this loss. So I understood his pain and frustration, and yet I was finding that his way of dealing with it—constant rebellion and obnoxious behavior—was making it impossible for me to continue. A summer of having a relatively independent lifestyle, with lots of time to think about the deal I had struck with myself, had brought me to the point where I was now seriously thinking of quitting the church entirely. But I still didn't want to; I wanted to hold on somehow, to make some last-ditch effort, or try some final desperate strategy to keep going. Yet Paul was becoming so unbearable that he was making it impossible to keep going.

During that summer I had become less active in writing for *The Round Table*, and instead I began to write comic pieces for *Our Network*. This quirky "zine" welcomed poems, cartoons, and gag lists along with the more ponderous discussions about Unificationism favored by its East Coast counterpart. For one issue I submitted a story, "Twenty Eighty-Four", in which I parodied Orwell's *Nineteen Eighty-Four* by imagining the world in a hundred years if the Unification Church really succeeded in converting everyone. I imagined people still waiting years and years to be allowed to live with their Blessed partners, and people being sent on M.F.T. missions to other planets. At the end of the piece, I tried to make amends with an afterword suggesting that this was not a prediction, but merely a warning of what might happen if the church didn't mend its ways.

Clearly, I no longer believed that the church leaders were capable of bringing the Kingdom of Heaven on Earth. In still another piece for *Our Network*, I imagined Divine Principle as if it were a battered car that I was planning to trade in at a used theology lot. The used theology salesman took one look at it and offered me fifty bucks. He then tried to sell me a Methodist, a Mormon, a Catholic, and a Buddhist, but finally I told him I would stick with my current theology and if it ever broke down, I would take its spare parts to build my own. That was how I felt about the Unification Church teachings: they were worn out and no longer satisfactory, but nothing else appealed to me either.

I had despaired that the church was ever really going to achieve its goals, but I still didn't want to give up entirely. I didn't want to rethink an entire decade of my life, and conclude that it had all been misspent. More importantly, the knife inside me was still there, driving me to justify my existence. After giving up on justification by works and after losing the object of my love, I had finally settled on a sort of justification through perseverance alone. My right to exist was now based on the mere fact that, despite everything, I still followed Father. But was that enough? I pondered the example of two other members who seemed determined to stay in the Unification Church, yet who were heartily sick of the way it operated. First, there was Tim, who was just going through the motions as the Montana state leader, without much enthusiasm. Second, there was Paul, who dealt with his frustration by being in a state of constant rebellion. I doubted that God would want me to follow either example.

I cast about for some way to go on. The Finnish sister recommended a friend of hers who was a spiritualist. This woman told me some strange things, including that I had a very intense aura; but she also gave me one piece of advice that was very helpful. She told me to write down 10 reasons why I should stay in the church, and 10 reasons why I should leave, and then compare them.

I also went to another woman (recommended by a different church member) who was training to be a conventional counselor, and her consultations were free. She did help me to rethink my situation; yet even so, neither of these women really understood how completely I was stuck.

I knew that I actually wanted to leave the church, but since I had not yet reached the point where I was ready to kill myself unless I quit, I felt that God still expected me to remain. I imagined what life might be like without the church, and two things seemed particularly fearful about this prospect.

First, I imagined that I would be plunging into a spiritual void, since Divine Principle had made me too skeptical to accept conventional Christianity, and other religions didn't interest me either. If I left the Unification Church, I would be left with a bare belief in God but would have no structure through which to relate to Him. I would not know what to believe about Jesus, or faith, or any other theological issue, so I imagined myself leading a shallow, materialistic life without any spiritual component, and the prospect made me shudder.

Secondly, I feared that if I quit the church, I would never know the love of a woman. Before the church, I had connected with very few women, apart from Sandy; and even with her, it had been incomplete. I never felt that I was entitled to love or be loved by a woman, and it always felt as though I needed the permission of some external authority. In the Unification Church, that permission flowed from Father, who told me I was permitted to love only the woman he matched me to. If I returned to the outside world, I would again need permission to love someone, and I could not easily find that permission within myself. So as hopeless as Father's cause now looked to me, and as frustrated as I was with the way his church had treated me, I still felt that I had to go on, so I could be given a woman I could feel entitled to love.

Finally I made a decision: I would pray for 21 days to know if I should leave the Unification Church or not. Twenty-one-day prayer conditions are often used by Unification Church members when they need to ask a question of God—but never this sort of question. I knew that I could not offer this prayer condition through my central figure, Tim, even though the doctrine stated that if I didn't go to Tim, God would be unable to hear my prayer. I still felt that I could only ask it directly to God. Every night, then, for 40 minutes for 21 days, I prayed urgently to my God to know whether I should quit the Unification Church.

There were no visions or revelations. The answer came instead in an unexpected way: I saw notices on shop windows that a writer I admired, Dr. M. Scott Peck—author of *The Road Less Traveled*—would be visiting Missoula to speak near the end of August. His talks would coincide with the last two days of my prayer condition. I had been sustaining myself with pocket money in Missoula by drawing on a savings account in Calgary (another unusual practice that Tim tolerated), so I had just enough money left to go to the lectures of Dr. Peck, whose books had so much moved and inspired me.

Dr. Peck gave a number of talks, some of which would have been considered controversial to Unificationists, such as his examination of the parallels between sexuality and spirituality. I took long-winded notes as I had once done in the Seminary, trying to paraphrase everything he said. One of his talks particularly struck me, when he spoke of the four stages of spiritual growth. According to Peck, people start out in an entirely self-centered stage, but many progress to a kind of rigid faith or fundamentalist belief. After that, some of these people rise above their rigid beliefs, and go into a stage he calls "emptiness" or "not knowing", where they have no clear beliefs about God—a kind of agnosticism. Finally, from this stage a few are able to return to a new kind of inclusive, mystical faith, which he saw as the highest stage of spiritual growth.

At first I thought that Unificationism was surely at the highest stage of spiritual growth, since it was destined to unite the world's beliefs. But suddenly it occurred to me: what if Unificationism is nothing more than a rigid, fundamentalist kind of faith, merely the second level of spiritual growth? That means it would actually be *progress*, not failure, for me to step into "emptiness" or "not knowing." I suddenly felt I had the answer to my 21 days of prayer.

But even with the seeming answer in hand, I was still afraid. Peck's talk addressed the first of my fears, but not the second. I hesitated for another two full months, dithering, even after I had already told other church members that I wanted to go. I still wanted to see if there was some last-ditch solution that could keep me going, and keep me in the church, and therefore able to receive the Blessing. I heard about a Christian congregation on an island near Seattle that had been helping some Unification Church members with emotional healing, and thought perhaps I could go stay with them.

By late October Tim had been replaced by a new state leader, a young woman fresh out of the Seminary who had been allowed to live with her Blessed husband temporarily. She was now well into her first pregnancy, yet the couple had been split up again for the usual reasons—"urgent" Providential work. She had been instructed to bring the Montana members to Seattle for a regional meeting. I figured I could go with the Montana members, then remain behind in Seattle to visit the Christian community on the island.

It was the last day of October. The next day I was to go with Paul—the very man who had been driving me crazy for months—to Seattle in a small car. The other church members were to go in a station wagon. An argument with Paul broke out over a trivial matter. My frustration flared up. "I'll kill you, you bastard!" I snarled at him, after he launched into his own tirade. He pursued me next door to another house that had been rented by the church (also from the CAUSA godmother). There I met the very pregnant Unification Church state leader for Montana and admitted to her that we had been fighting and threatening to kill each other. It was clear to me that there was no point going on. I was finally going to have to leave.

I gathered my few belongings and went to a church friend who was living "on the fringe", and she loaned me the money I needed to take the bus back to Calgary (around $100). The bus would not leave until late at night, so I stayed well away from the church center while I waited. When the time came to catch the bus, I was given a wonderful surprise. Many of the church members I had known during my time in Montana were there—even Paul, who had been so infuriating, but who had now returned to his more affable self. They gave me a cheerful send-off, even though they knew I was leaving the Unification Church, probably forever. I climbed on the bus and began my journey, a circuitous route that took me through Helena and Great Falls before it finally reached a border town bearing the lovely, evocative name of Sweetgrass.

I was finally going home. I had done it many times before, but this time it was different; and I could feel the difference. I was no longer going back to Calgary as a representative of Father. I was not going back as a stubborn stalwart, the one who would not give up. This time I was going back as myself, though I hardly knew who I was. The only certainty was that Father could no longer tell me what to do.

A sudden weariness came over me as I pondered ten years of trying to serve Father, and I was hardly able to stay awake during the entire bus trip. I thought of nothing in particular, just felt a sense of great loss and emptiness. And, as the bus rumbled on its long journey into the night, I lay my head against the window and allowed myself to drift down into that emptiness. Closing my eyes and drifting into sleep, I gave myself permission to just let go.

Epilogue to the First Edition:

Caught Between Two Worlds

Once again, I returned to temporary office assignments in Calgary and to living in the basement of my parent's house. But now that I was no longer planning to go anywhere in the near future, I decided to choose an apartment in the downtown area and a full-time job as a word processing operator for a law firm. The biggest psychological change for me was that I finally felt I was free to look for a girlfriend on my own. But I was as inhibited as I had ever been. At one point I resorted to a dating service; I chose one that served people who were round of figure (as I was) called "Plump Partners", and with their help met a woman who began dropping by my apartment unpredictably and behaving oddly. After that experience, I went back to my old method of only occasionally approaching women very hesitantly, and then giving up almost immediately when they failed to show any interest.

I also began to try attending Christian churches, to see if I wanted to attend one regularly. I tried a small Lutheran church that was close to where I lived; later, on a whim, I went to an Evangelical French church just so I could practice my French. Yet I never fit into the conventional Christian mold. For the most part, I continued to believe in Moon's Divine Principle, including his teaching that it was not God's original plan for Jesus to be crucified.

In many ways, though I wanted to return to the "outside world", I remained enmeshed in Unificationism. I was caught between two worlds, yet at home in neither. I was still not angry with either Moon or the church for the callous way I had been treated; instead I blamed individual church leaders, but not the organization or its founder. Like many former cult members, I felt that perhaps I had been simply "too weak" to sustain the demands the group had made on me, but I continued to believe that those demands had been for a good purpose.

It was fortunate that my home was a city where no other Unification Church members lived, because if there had been other members around I might have been drawn back eventually. I did continue to correspond with some members and occasionally received some of their publications. One day I peered into the back of my closet and found the navy-colored sports jacket I had worn to the Holy Wine Ceremony—which I had preserved—with the wine-stained "Holy Handkerchief" still tucked inside its inside breast pocket. I destroyed the jacket, but feared to discard the handkerchief, believing it held some sacred significance, so instead I mailed it back to the Blessing Committee in New York.

Now that I no longer spent my days trying to save the world, I turned to simpler concerns, such as decorating my apartment or watching sports events. Not long afterwards, as often happens to former cult members, I became caught up in another enthusiasm that resembled the cult environment I had left behind. I enrolled with a multi-level marketing scheme which sold health products, believing that this would allow me to make a lot of money quickly. The health products did indeed help me to slim down nicely, but the sudden wealth never materialized. Multi-level marketing schemes operate similarly to cults because they are often deceptive—they don't reveal up front the extraordinary amount of work it takes to succeed in such a business—and they always insist that if you aren't succeeding, it must be your own fault. After about a year, and two visits to sales conventions in Los Angeles that I couldn't really afford, I concluded that I was simply not going to make it in that business.

Feeling adrift, and unhappy about my failure to find a girlfriend, I began going to a psychological counselor. He was very helpful. In the process of treatment, I recalled my former ambition to study Creative Writing at the University of British Columbia. Why not go back there and do just that? At first I worried I was "too old" to go to school, but I soon realized that 36 years old is not really all that old; furthermore, I had no obligations that would prevent me from trying it. I became fired with enthusiasm at the prospect of returning to my original dream, which has always been to become a novelist and short story writer. I saved money for the course and applied to begin the Master of Fine Arts program in Creative Writing in the fall of 1990.

That same year, Eleanor came back into my life briefly. In a rather strange turn of events, I had recontacted her in an attempt to draw her into my multi-level marketing scheme. She responded to my query without revealing her own entirely different plans. Eleanor, I learned, had rejoined the Unification Church following the failure of her 1984 marriage, and now hoped to draw me back into the church also, though she did not say so explicitly. I was still quite angry with her because of her decision to leave me for someone else, so I told her that if she wanted to see me she must visit me at her own expense. Eleanor replied that she preferred for me to come to visit her in England, and I finally relented, saying I would only do so if she paid for the whole trip.

By this time, some four years after leaving the Unification Church, I was quite skeptical about any suggestion that I should return to that group. Not long before, I had received an unexpected phone call from Nancy. She told me she was willing to spend some money she had set aside for her daughter's education to bring me to Washington, D.C. so I could attend a public meeting with a prominent church member from Zimbabwe. Sun Myung Moon had proclaimed that this man was channeling the spirit of his dead son (who died in a car crash in 1984). Many members hoped that the putative resurrection of Heung-Jin Moon would finally bring in the reforms the church so desperately needed. Nancy, for her part, hoped I could be drawn back into the church through this reform movement.

Fortunately, I didn't take Nancy's offer. As I began making inquiries with other members about these miraculous events, I learned that the African man had been given sweeping authority in the church, and had abused it by administering heavy beatings to many members, including senior church officials (such as Bo Hi Pak, who was savagely assaulted, according to a report in *Time* magazine). Such a report should have been enough to cause me to completely reject the church, but because I had never been formally treated for the effects of mind control, I remained suggestible, and was still capable of thinking that there might be some "heavenly" reason behind these terrible events. Even so, this gave me strong doubts about the church, and I expressed these in my letters to Eleanor.

Instead of calling them doubts, however, Eleanor called them "questions", and assured me that the explanations to these questions would be forthcoming if I visited her. More importantly, Eleanor met my chief demand; she came up with the money for the return fare to England. In April of 1990, therefore, I decided to go.

I went primarily because of the fond memories I had of Eleanor personally. I even foolishly hoped I could persuade her to come to Canada to join me in my student life. I did not really intend to return to the Unification Church. However, I had never completely closed the door on that idea, either. There was still an opening in my mind that Eleanor hoped to walk through. She very nearly succeeded.

When I arrived in London, where Eleanor now lived and worked as a nanny, I found that she maintained her connection to the church by occasionally visiting a member who was considered her "central figure". She lived in a modest flat, but set me up in a bed-and-breakfast down the road. This time, I was determined to see the sights of London, which I had been too conscientious to visit during the Home Church campaign of 1978. Eleanor was annoyed that I would place such a high priority on visiting tourist traps like the Tower of London or Madame Tussaud's, but she tolerated it because she hoped that I could be persuaded to return to the church. From Eleanor's point of view, her desire to draw me back to the fold was a personal act of repentance, whereby her own sin in leaving the church could be redeemed.

For my part, I had a secret plan that if Eleanor and the other church members became too overbearing, I would hop on the train for Cardiff in Wales. At one point I was set to do this, but changed my mind. When I was around church members, I would have needed to make a scene and become rude or accusatory in order to convince them to leave me alone, and I never wanted to go to that extreme. I hoped I could persuade them through calm reasoning that it was not in my best interest to move to England to rejoin the church.

This merely played right into their hands; as in Boonville in 1976, anything other than a flat rejection is taken as conditional support. Gradually, the more I stayed around them and associated with them, the more I began to see myself as one of them again, and to think that my views had not actually altered very much since leaving the church four years before. After all, they were offering me exactly what I had been hoping to obtain in Toronto in 1985: the opportunity to live in my own home and work at my own job, and yet still be considered a "real" church member. Furthermore, this time I would be able to do it legally, since one set of my grandparents had been born in Scotland; so under the rules that were then in force, I could have emigrated to the United Kingdom. On the personal level, I still liked Eleanor, and could imagine enjoying being with her again. Even so, Eleanor dismayed me by admitting that she had still not gotten around to legally divorcing the other man. Yet even this, she ultimately persuaded me to overlook.

By the end of my two week stay, I had forgotten most of my doubts about Moon and the church. Everything now boiled down to my willingness to accept a drastic change of plans. Instead of going to university to study Creative Writing, I was now to emigrate to England to rejoin the church and marry Eleanor—that is, whenever the Unification Church leaders decided to permit this marriage, which would likely have taken several more years.

Internally, I began to feel like a church member again, and again the key issue became my personal salvation, which depended on being a member of the Unification Church, lest disastrous consequences follow. By the end of my two-week stay in London, I had come all the way back to this view; and therefore, with great hesitation, I told them I would do what they asked. I would go back to Canada, wind up my affairs, and return to England to rejoin the Unification Church as soon as possible.

Almost as soon as I got back to Calgary, I found myself full of doubts about this extraordinary new plan, though I told my parents I intended to do it. However, after only a couple of days, I felt so distinctly uncomfortable with the new plans that I resolved to hold another prayer condition to settle the question.

This time I gave myself just three days to pray and reflect. I had an evening job, so my mornings were wide open, and I used those mornings to go up and sit on a large boulder on Calgary's Nose Hill (what geologists would call a "glacial erratic") to offer a lengthy prayer and to just talk over my new plans with God. At the end of three days, I felt I had an answer: I must *not* do what Eleanor asked. When she next called me, I broke the news, which I knew would be very upsetting. She hung up in tears, and at that moment I felt myself moving more firmly away from the Unification Church and more irrevocably into the "outside world". I began to feel that I could no longer remain neutral toward the church, but must now firmly oppose it, though I still didn't understand why it was necessary to oppose it.

Spiritually, I felt as fearful as I had been in 1986, when I made my original decision to leave. I again felt that I was risking spiritual destruction by my choice. However, I more quickly got past these struggles and eventually returned to my hopeful outlook about my university plans. Eleanor, however, was not finished with me yet.

In September, 1990, I began my classes at the University of British Columbia. I studied poetry writing and short story writing, all the while feeling a certain giddy exhilaration at being back in school again. Meanwhile, Eleanor was still writing to me, saying that she was planning to visit me around Christmas time. Initially, I was prepared to accept this, though it meant I would be staying in Vancouver at Christmas instead of returning to Calgary as my family expected; but I soon realized that if I was going to be able to afford my university work, I would have to go back to Calgary in December to take a temporary job at a Calgary law firm, because I had not had much luck finding employment in Vancouver. Since Eleanor's plans would stand in the way of such a solution, I had no choice but to give her the bad news by telephone. This time, I spoke to her with great forcefulness and abruptness, so that she would truly get the message. It worked. I never heard from her again.

Even after sending Eleanor away, I still had not completely separated from the world of Unificationism. There were a few church members living in the Vancouver area, and I visited them occasionally. I would still defend the Unification Church to any critics I met, saying it was just another church, not a cult. I insisted that there was no such thing as mind control or "brainwashing", at least not as far as Unificationism was concerned. Even so, because I had been forced to send Eleanor away so firmly, I felt I was being called upon to take an even stronger position opposing the Unification Church, though I still didn't know why.

My early poems and stories at the university did not address my cult involvement. Now, however, I was studying under the same Creative Writing professor who had once taught me in 1975, before I joined the Unification Church. He knew my whole history and began to ask me to write stories about my experiences in the church. At first, I approached the subject matter very tentatively, then began to come to grips with it.

By 1992, during my second year at university, I was planning a novel in which a Unification Church member would be forced to endure a deprogramming. I was strongly opposed to this practice, but I wanted my novel to condemn both the church and the deprogrammers equally. Yet since I had never experienced a deprogramming, it seemed logical that I should read something by someone who had been through it or assisted it, in order to understand the rationale behind it. One day while browsing in a book store I came across a book that made me cringe: *Combatting Cult Mind Control* by Steven Hassan.

I had never met Hassan, who had been deprogrammed out of the Unification Church before I was a member, but I had heard many negative things about him. I almost hated him for writing this book. But shouldn't I at least read it so I could understand his viewpoint? I had to admit that I probably should read it, even though I expected to disagree with everything he said— and so I finally bought it, and sat down to read it, with great trepidation.

The book completely overthrew me. By the end I was astonished to realize that mind control, which I had always dismissed out of hand as false, was a real phenomenon. I recognized the process by which I had been indoctrinated, and how it resembled the process described by Robert J. Lifton in his book, *Thought Reform and the Psychology of Totalism.*

Hassan's book rejects deprogramming. Instead, he advocates a non-coercive approach to helping cult members escape from their groups; however he does state that cult members such as Unificationists are under mind control, and he makes this case with great persuasiveness. After finishing Hassan, I felt an insatiable desire to read other books I had been too afraid to read previously, such as accounts by former Unificationists who had quit the group. Reading Hassan and these other works gave me the one thing had been missing during my previous quest to reclaim myself: they showed me why it was only sensible to be enraged by my experiences. With that, I felt the final door slam between me and True Father, the Reverend Sun Myung Moon. I knew then that I was finished with him forever. I was no longer caught between two worlds.

And as for the knife inside me? It is still there, though I have benefited from psychological treatments which have made the pain less desperate and the need for a solution less urgent. During the time when I believed in Primal Therapy, and later when I was committed to Sun Myung Moon, the thought of settling for a mere acceptance of the knife inside me was intolerable. Back then, I wanted nothing more than to wrench it wholly from my breast and to send it sailing away in elegant spirals—blade over handle, handle over blade, blade over handle into space. But I now believe that such a perfect solution to emotional pain is ultimately illusory, and that in order to sustain a belief in such an emotional Paradise, one must delude one's self on a constant basis. How much better, then, to set the delusion aside, and to pursue straight-forwardly one's own truest dreams and fondest hopes. When I finally set out in pursuit of my dream to be a writer, I began also to feel—never wholly, but in a way that grows stronger the more I persist in the pursuit of my dream—that my existence has always been justified, whether I knew it or not.

Epilogue to the Second Edition:

Home

My decision to publish the first edition of this book in 2002 was mainly driven by my need to get my story out. I wanted people to know the real story of what it was (and often still is) like to be a member of Moon's Unification Church. Also, I wanted to move on to my next project, a collection of short stories about people caught up in cults or in cult-like situations.

I did not expect, in 2002, that this publication would ultimately lead me to move to the United States to marry the woman I had always longed for, but that's what happened. In 2005, I received an email from my publisher saying that a researcher in upstate New York wanted to ask me some questions. I began corresponding with this researcher, who turned out to be a former member of the Unification Church whose doctoral thesis had been about accounts written by former members of non-mainstream religions. Our correspondence became warmer in tone as we became more acquainted, and in 2006, I travelled to upstate New York to meet her.

I soon found that Mary Jo and I shared many common interests, including a strong interest in the writings and life of Henry David Thoreau. On July 12, 2009 (Thoreau's birthday), we were married in a beautiful ceremony near the shores of Walden Pond.

Later, I had the opportunity to visit the small town of New Sarepta, in Alberta, and to look for the place my family once called "Camp." Camp is the place where my earliest memories were formed, and though the Camp buildings are long gone, it remains the place that first comes to mind when I think of "home."

All during the ten years that I followed Sun Myung Moon, moving from city to city, I was, in a sense, looking for my true home. But what does it mean, really, for a person to be "home?"

To try to answer this question, I wrote the following brief memoir, inspired both by my visit to New Sarepta and by my appreciation for Mary Jo's beautiful and redeeming love. The style of this piece is different from the rest of this book, because I wrote it, in part, from the perspective of the small child who once lived at Camp. Nevertheless, I felt it would be a sweet and fitting conclusion to this second edition.

All That Remains

The sun's following me. When I move, it moves. When I stop, it stops. What's going on?

I'm three years old, and I'm walking down a gravel road carrying a jar with holes punched in the lid. I'm going to catch grasshoppers. My brother Mike will be there. So will Jerry and Beverly and some other kids. But first I have to figure out what to do about this pesky sun.

I stare up, puzzled. It doesn't move. Finally, I set out again.

When I reach the farmer's field, the other kids are already there. My first step into the tall grass makes lots of grasshoppers jump. We shout and laugh as we try to catch them. If I see a grasshopper sitting on a long blade of grass, I might try to pick the whole blade and shove it into my jar. I grab for one, but close my hand too quickly. "Oh, no," I groan. "I squished 'im!" The other kids laugh. We keep going until we all have grasshoppers. We put grass into the jars so they'll have something to eat. Then we walk back to Camp to show our mothers.

* * *

This morning it's very cold, and I'm curled up in my bed with my arms around my wife. The woods and yard outside our house are blanketed in snow. While I savor Mary Jo's soft exhalations on my cheek, I'm remembering a place I once called home. It was a place we knew as "Camp."

Camp was a clutch of temporary buildings that an Alberta oil company put together for its workers. The small house at the end of the gravel road where my mother and father lived had no bathroom – that was in a building down the road. My father worked in a nearby office trailer, keeping track of oil production figures, while my mother raised three small children in that house before we moved away in 1958. In the pictures I have of the little house, I see cheery window boxes that my mother filled with flowers.

Even after all these years, Camp still calls out to me. Should I try to find it, though the buildings are long gone? There wouldn't be much to see. Yet I have to go. The next time I'm in Alberta, I'll take a hotel in Edmonton, rent a car, and look for Camp.

My wife stirs beside me. Softly I kiss the top of her head while she sleeps. Outside our window, chickadees are pecking at the bird feeder. It's a perfect morning to sleep in: cold, quiet, and peaceful. My eyes close and I snooze, with my breath ruffling Mary Jo's hair.

* * *

Camp is somewhere near the village of New Sarepta, southeast of Edmonton. When I get there, I drive down the main road until I see the village office. There's only one person in the building, a bank teller for Alberta Treasury Branch. She tells me the village unincorporated several years ago, and now no one occupies the front office. Then I explain why I came, confessing my vague and inexplicable quest. She asks if I remember any names. I give her the family name of my childhood friends, Jerry and Beverly. That's all she needs. She phones their mother, who still lives near Camp. Then she gives me directions, and tells me that if I go quickly, I might find her at home. But the whole place is laid out differently from the way I remember, and I get lost. By the time I find Camp, my friends' mother has gone out.

All that remains of the place I remember so fondly is a worksite trailer and a bobbing pumpjack. The land where Camp stood is now surrounded by a fence with a locked gate. As the pumpjack's horsehead rises and dips, the whole machine groans and creaks. I stand uncertainly outside the gate, next to the road where I once stared up in puzzlement at the sun.

* * *

I don't remember the pumpjacks, if there even were any in 1956. Instead, I remember the farmers' fields where the Camp kids picked strawberries and caught grasshoppers. I remember the ditches that in the dankness of late autumn were choked with tall, reedy cat-tails. I remember the swing set we played on, and the simple toy gun my father carved from wood so I could pretend to hunt. And I remember a small white house dressed for Christmas, and the stockings – we used real socks – that my brother and I set out on Christmas Eve. The next morning, we found them filled with Japanese oranges, chocolate bars and tiny puzzles.

* * *

My youngest sister – the family historian – recently sent me snapshots of Camp. There's a picture of my father awkwardly holding me, framed by the doorway of our home. The photo was probably taken soon after I arrived in 1953. He has the slightly pained look of a man not quite sure about holding babies and just wanting to get it over with. I don't look very happy, either.

In another picture, Mike and I are sitting in a galvanized steel tub that our mother bathed us in. Two small wet boys peer shyly over the edge of the tub. I'm pointing at the camera, as if to say, "What's that thing in daddy's hand?"

There's also a photo or me standing on the gravel road, staring solemnly at the camera. It must be early spring, because I'm wearing boots and a jacket with a hood. Behind me is a small building – could that be the bathroom trailer? Camp is home, but I'm still trying to figure it all out.

* * *

Dad's gone down the hill to the work trailer and Mom's busy, so Mike and I are playing Snakes & Ladders. We set out the pieces and roll the die. The game has pictures to teach us lessons.

I'm hoping I get to go on the tallest ladder. It goes from 41 all the way up to 85. At 41, there's a picture of a girl putting money in a purse. Next to her is the word "Thrift." At 85, she's standing beside a tricycle with the word "Fulfillment."

The snakes are more interesting – I just hope I don't land on them. If you land on 75 – "Mischief" – you're on a tree limb, dangling down a string, trying to trick somebody. But then you slide down the back of a reddish purple snake and land on 47 – "Woe" – where you fall in a pond. And if you get to 88 – "Indulgence" – you get to eat a lot of apples, but then you slide down the back of an enormous snake and land in bed at 36 – "Illness".

I don't have much luck. I keep getting snakes. Today Mike beat me twice.

I hate this game. As soon as Mom and Mike aren't looking, I'm going to take the Snakes and Ladders game and throw it in the ditch.

* * *

There's nobody at the Camp work site, so I drive down the road to Joseph Lake Centennial Park. Near the shore of the lake, a large array of pumpjacks bob up and down.

I walk to the shore, listening to the creaking and groaning of the tireless machines. There's not much else I need to do here. I don't know anyone. I might as well take one last look at Camp, then return to Edmonton.

But when I get back to the work site, I see a pickup truck next to the trailer. The gate's unlocked. I start walking toward the trailer, but then stop. What would I say? How would I explain myself? I go back to the car and wait. Eventually a man gets into the truck and drives out. He stops at the entrance, rolls down his window, and looks at me inquiringly. I explain my connection to the site, and he confirms that, yes, there once were houses on the property. But that was long ago, when the site was owned by a different company. Then he drives away.

* * *

Sixty years have passed since the day I arrived at Camp in my mother's arms. My hair is gray now, and I live near a small creek that empties into the Mohawk River, thousands of miles from Camp. Yet part of me is still back there, squinting up at the sun. Probably that little boy will always be there, waiting for me. Last summer I went back to try to find him, but he was nowhere to be seen. Thomas Wolfe had it right: you can't go home again.

A cold wind rattles the bedroom window. No birds peck at the feeder now. I turn over, and take Mary Jo once more into my arms.

Home is wherever there is love.

BIBLIOGRAPHY

Hassan, Steven. *Combatting Cult Mind Control*. Rochester, VT: Park Street Press, 1988, 1990.

Releasing the Bonds: Empowering People to Think for Themselves. Somerville, MA: Freedom of Mind Press, 2000.

Janov, Arthur. *The Primal Scream, Primal Therapy: The Cure for Neurosis*. New York, NY: G.P. Putnam's Sons, 1970.

Lifton, Robert J. *Thought Reform and the Psychology of Totalism*. New York, NY: W.W. Norton & Company, Inc., 1961.

Neufeld, Gordon. "Parker's Elect". In *Canadian Short Fiction Anthology*, ed. Cathy Ford. Vancouver, BC: Intermedia Press, 1976, pp. 137-149.

Peck, Dr. M. Scott. *The Road Less Traveled: A New Psychology of Love, Traditional Values and Spiritual Growth*. New York, NY: Simon & Schuster, 1997.

Acknowledgments to the First Edition

I would like to give grateful thanks to a number of people who provided help or encouragement during the arduous five-year process of writing this book. My greatest debt is undoubtedly to the Creative Writing Department of the University of British Columbia (now known as the Theatre, Film and Creative Writing Department). This memoir could not even have been written if I had not attended the Master of Fine Arts program in Creative Writing at that university. In particular, I would like to express thanks to professors Andreas Schroeder, Keith Maillard and George McWhirter who guided me through the early stages of the creative process. Special thanks are also owed to professor Jerry Newman, who was delighted when I returned to the Creative Writing Department after a fourteen-year absence, and encouraged me throughout my time studying there. Thanks should go as well to the Alexandra Writers Centre Society (AWCS) of Calgary, Alberta, which is currently helping me as I build a new career in writing. Faye Holt and her students in the Non-Fiction course from AWCS provided editorial advice on a few of the chapters in this book.

Also offering encouragement and moral support (in no particular order) were Jane Scott, Deb Brandt, Craig Maxim, Mike Kropveld, Dr. Stephen Kent, Benjamin Wittes and Naomi Wittes Reichstein. Special thanks to Max Wyman of the *Vancouver Sun*, who took particular interest in my experiences, and kindly agreed to publish several of my articles in the *Sun*. Special thanks also to Janet McConnell, who preserved my old letters and thus gave me important insights into my past. Likewise, I thank my parents and family for preserving other pieces of my old correspondence—as well as, of course, for their general support and their forbearing attitude throughout my lengthy sojourn in the cult.

Thanks to Perry Snow for assisting me, not once, but *twice*, when I needed a change of direction in my life. Thanks to Dr. Dana McDougall for greatly easing the pain of the "knife inside me."

Finally, thanks are owed to the many patient waiters and waitresses who plied me with pints of dark ale while I wrote down my thoughts at length in notebooks while sitting in numerous pubs and restaurants in Calgary and throughout B.C.'s Lower Mainland. For whatever reason, much of my best writing gets done in precisely this manner. (Special thanks to Culpepper's in Vancouver and Bottlescrew Bill's in Calgary for being my host on many occasions during the writing of this book. Hey, Greg, here's mud in your eye!)

ACKNOWLEDGMENTS TO THE SECOND EDITION

In addition to all those who were mentioned in the Acknowledgements to the First Edition, I should give grateful thanks to my mother, and to my friend, Janet McConnell, who both separately preserved a few of the letters and postcards I wrote when I was first a member of the Unification Church. Rereading these letters gave me great insights into my mindset at that crucial turning point in my life, and as well, it helped me locate events in time. As well, I would like to thank Bobby Bernshausen and the staff of Virtualbookworm.com, who formatted and prepared the First Edition for publication in 2002; and Kim Staflund of Polished Publishing Group in Calgary, who encouraged me to try publishing a second edition.

Finally, and most of all, I thank my dear wife, Mary Jo Downey, for agreeing to be part of my life, and for letting me be part of hers. I'm so grateful.

CPSIA information can be obtained
at www.ICGtesting.com
Printed in the USA
BVHW071308111221
623816BV00004B/145